T0385029

text + FIELD

text

Edited by
Sara L. McKinnon, Robert Asen, Karma R. Chávez,
and Robert Glenn Howard

text + FIELD

Innovations in Rhetorical Method

The Pennsylvania State University Press | University Park, Pennsylvania

Library of Congress Cataloging-in-Publication Data
Names: McKinnon, Sara L. (Sara Lynn), 1979– , editor. | Asen, Robert, 1968– ,
    editor. | Chávez, Karma R., editor. | Howard, Robert Glenn, editor.
Title: Text + field : innovations in rhetorical method / edited by Sara L. McKinnon,
    Robert Asen, Karma R. Chávez, and Robert Glenn Howard.
Other titles: Text and field
Description: University Park, Pennsylvania : The Pennsylvania State University
    Press, [2016] | Includes bibliographical references and index.
Summary: "Explores the benefits of utilizing field methods for studying rhetoric as
    a complement to text-based approaches in order to address questions about text,
    context, audience, judgment and ethics"—Provided by publisher.
Identifiers: LCCN 2016002017 | ISBN 9780271072104 (pbk. : alk. paper)
Subjects: LCSH: Rhetoric—Methodology. | Rhetoric—Fieldwork.
Classification: LCC P301 .T44 2016 | DDC 808—dc23
LC record available at http://lccn.loc.gov/2016002017

The Pennsylvania State University Press is a member of the Association of American
University Presses.

It is the policy of The Pennsylvania State University Press to use acid-free paper.
Publications on uncoated stock satisfy the minimum requirements of American
National Standard for Information Sciences—Permanence of Paper for Printed
Library Material, ANSI Z39.48–1992.

CONTENTS

ACKNOWLEDGMENTS

This project has emerged from periodic conversations over the past few years that occurred in the department hallways, at colloquia and other events, and in social settings. Purposefully and serendipitously, each of us has found ourselves engaged in fieldwork as a complement to the methods of textual analysis that we employ as rhetorical scholars. Recognizing this confluence, we had entertained the possibility of working on a book project together—and we finally decided to make this possibility into a reality.

First and foremost, then, we want to acknowledge one another, as friends, colleagues, collaborators, sounding boards, allies, debate partners, counselors, and more. Before we started this project, our mutual connections were strong. Our work together on this project has only deepened our mutual connections and regard for one another.

We have been fortunate to work in an intellectually diverse and exceptional department with colleagues who study various aspects of rhetoric and communication. Our department colleagues—all of them—have fostered an environment in which faculty and graduate students are encouraged to push the boundaries of our respective subfields. Over the years, the Department of Communication Arts at the University of Wisconsin–Madison has been an intellectual leader in the discipline, and we hope that this project will continue in this tradition.

Our work with Penn State University Press has been productive and enjoyable. Kendra Boileau has been a terrific supporter of this project. Her vision for this project and for Penn State's books in rhetoric and communication have produced innovative scholarship and brought together scholars across the discipline. Hannah Hebert was a great source of information and a responsive communicator during the development of this project at the Press.

Jennifer Norton steered us ably through the production process, and Regina Starace designed a great cover. We are grateful to Liz Barr and Hana Masri for their proofreading and indexing skills, and Nicholas Taylor was a careful copyeditor.

Chuck Morris and Jeff Bennett reviewed the manuscript for the Press. Their feedback was crucial for bolstering the volume. We have the utmost personal and professional regard for Chuck and Jeff, and their insights provided yet another example of their trenchant critical perspectives and their commitment to the discipline.

Our development of this project benefited from a National Communication Association preconference seminar we organized and a department colloquium. We wish to thank all the attendees at the seminar, titled "Text + Field," which occurred in conjunction with the 2013 NCA annual convention in Washington DC. The daylong seminar enabled us to discuss themes from this project with a wonderful group of attendees. Further, some of the chapters in this volume started out as position papers submitted by participants in our seminar. We also had an opportunity to present a draft of the introduction to this volume at a Rhetoric, Politics, and Culture colloquium in the Department of Communication Arts at UW–Madison. We want to thank our super-smart colleagues and graduate students for their insightful feedback.

At the 2014 NCA convention in Chicago we organized a panel in which we presented the introduction and asked a few esteemed colleagues to respond. As respondents, Dan Brouwer, Robin Claire, and Jim Jasinski offered helpful feedback. Their insightful remarks enabled us to rethink and reconceptualize some key issues.

Innumerable conversations with colleagues and friends have allowed us to develop and bolster our ideas and aims for this project and our understanding of the relationships among text and field, including Sarah Amira de la Garza, Kelly Jakes, Jenell Johnson, Steve Lucas, Christa Olson, Phaedra Pezzullo, Jerry Rosiek, Sarah Tracy, and Mike Xenos.

We wish to thank Sue Robinson and Megan Zuelsdorff for their support, feedback, and inspiration. And we have been inspired, too, by people we have met and engaged with in our fieldwork.

Introduction

Articulating Text and Field in the
Nodes of Rhetorical Scholarship

Sara L. McKinnon,
Robert Asen,
Karma R. Chávez, and
Robert Glenn Howard

In his 1965 book *Rhetorical Criticism*, Edwin Black set in motion a methodological shift in rhetorical studies that would forever change what it meant to analyze rhetorical discourse. Black excoriated the reigning critical method of his day—an approach that took its name from a classical figure yet, in Black's view, stifled the quality of judgment that Aristotle associated with rhetoric. The limits of neo-Aristotelianism seemingly indicated to Black the limits of methods altogether, as he expressed a desire to refocus criticism on the judgment of the critic. In clarifying this move in his preface to the 1978 reprint of *Rhetorical Criticism*, Black asserted that "a specific person—the critic—is the sole instrument of observation" for rhetorical criticism.[1] Whereas some methods, like geometric equations, appeared to function similarly regardless of who performed them, rhetorical criticism occupied the end of a methodological continuum where the performer left a unique and indelible imprint on the subject. Rhetorical criticism belonged to a group of methods "that require personal choices at every step, methods that are pervaded by contingencies."[2] As a subjective method, rhetorical criticism resisted systematization, which meant, as a consequence, that the critic resisted giving an account of his or her procedures. Positing a rhetorician's critique as "an extension of the writer—an autonomous surrogate for a human voice,"[3] Black believed that good criticism would compel the same judgment in other readers. Personal writing style, he believed, must "acquire probative force."[4]

Even as he dissociated rhetoric and method, Black contributed to a methodological upheaval in rhetorical studies. In a 1957 special issue of *Western Speech*, scholars expressed an emergent interest in Burkeian criticism while also resisting the "mechanistic, formulaic, scientific application of an apparatus."[5] As Charles E. Morris observes, repudiations of neo-Aristotelian criticism and inquiries into alternative approaches developed into a full-blown "methods craze" in the 1970s and 1980s.[6] As scholars articulated approaches such as feminist criticism and ideological analysis, they expanded the processes available for rhetorical criticism. While rhetoricians, with a few notable exceptions,[7] focused the bulk of this work on textual analysis, the introduction of new methods did much to diversify the objects analyzed, the questions asked, and the means employed to answer these questions. Such openings gave way to further innovation as scholars developed approaches centering the rhetorics of historically marginalized groups.[8] Shifting issues of importance and consequence, this turn enabled a direct critique of the power structures that shape how rhetors and their words enter the public. Politically engaged scholarship grew even more prominent with the critical turn in the field; interpretive methods expanded scholarly goals from description, explanation, and cultural interpretation to include critiques of power.

In the period of experimentation of the 1970s and 1980s, some rhetoric and communication scholars drew from related fields to consider ethnographic approaches to speech and communication. This scholarship was influenced by anthropologists like Clifford Geertz, who called for a "semiotic" approach to study culture involving "thick" documentation and "interpretation" of how the "small facts" recorded in fieldwork "speak to large issues" about social action and culture.[9] More directly, Dell Hymes's ethnography of speaking/communication approach was taken up to account for the ways "communities differ significantly in patterns of code-repertoire, code-switching, and, generally, in the roles assigned to language."[10]

Pioneering essays published in the *Quarterly Journal of Speech* emerged from the engagement with disciplines where ethnographic sensibilities were already deeply embedded. In works like "Speaking 'Like a Man' in Teamsterville" and "Places for Speaking in Teamsterville," Gerry Philipsen evidenced the necessity of culturally grounded, interpretation-based methods, while Joseph Hayes analyzed "gay" speech patterns, Jack Daniel and Geneva Smitherman detailed cultural dynamics of communication in a black church, and Marsha Houston Stanback and W. Barnett Pearce identified strategies of communication that marginalized groups use to address those in positions of power. All of these scholars demonstrated early moves to approach communication and rhetoric research with an interpretive, emergent design.[11] Importantly, these essays also reflected a history of analyzing embodied speech as a central focal point of rhetoric and communication studies. Theorizing of bodies and embodiment exploded among performance scholars as they made their own move from text to field in the 1990s, paving the way for rhetoricians to reconsider the role of bodies/embodiment in the rhetorical encounter.

In more recent years, a wider turn to the field has emerged in the work of prominent rhetoric, communication, and performance studies scholars like Bryant Keith Alexander, Jeffrey Bennett, Carole Blair, Barbara Browning, Bernadette Calafell, Robin Clair, Dwight Conquergood, Danielle Endres, Aaron Hess, D. Soyini Madison, Michael K. Middleton, Shane Moreman, Omi/Joni Osun Olomo, Phaedra Pezzullo, Della Pollock, Samantha Senda-Cook, and John T. Warren, among many others. As these scholars demonstrate, cultural processes and meaning systems, dynamics of space/place, body knowledge, embodiment, and the rhetorics of marginalized and excluded groups are often difficult to access through texts. They instead necessitate a prior first step—collection and documentation.[12]

This volume seeks to build on these efforts to draw greater attention to field methods as tools for rhetorical scholarship. In particular, we believe that a renewed focus on field methods may help rhetorical scholars arrive at new or complementary answers to methodological questions about text, context, audience, judgment, and ethics. These five methodological topoi, around which we have structured our introduction, have engendered debates about various modes of scholarship and may serve as points of access for integrating text and field. We believe that topoi of text, context, audience, judgment, and ethics not only allow rhetoricians to ask and answer different research questions but also offer opportunities to rethink our objects of study, our role in the research process, and ultimately what it means to do rhetorical criticism.

We posit that field methods resonate with an expansive sense of method as how we do what we do as rhetorical scholars. From this expansive perspective, all rhetorical scholars, regardless of what they analyze, approach texts in distinctive ways that comport with their critical inclinations. Field methods allow us greater opportunities for talking about and articulating these unique methodological processes, to make them discernible to our reading audiences. Our move is one of opening doors: an effort to look for ways that field methods may enhance, clarify, or widen our understanding of rhetorical criticism. In what follows we outline definitional parameters for the concepts that we contribute to these conversations about method in the field, and then elaborate on the potential that field methods offer to address consistent methodological concerns with text, context, audience, judgment, and ethics in the field.

As a humanities discipline or an interpretive social science, rhetorical studies best fits with research methods that work to interpret people's cultural, political, and social systems of meaning—what is most often viewed as a qualitative approach. In recognizing that rhetorical criticism itself is a qualitative mode of research, we describe the methodological option we advocate here by invoking "the field" and field methods. We do this not only to demarcate rhetorical scholarship that engages texts with projects that move beyond texts, but also because we believe the field and field methods offer exciting options for rhetorical scholars in attending to discursive practices.

"The field," as a concept representing a site of investigation, certainly carries baggage with it. Norman K. Denzin and Yvonna S. Lincoln explain that the concept often conjures the tradition of ethnography where "the observer went to a foreign setting to study the customs and habits of another society and culture."[13] The ethnographer functioned as the expert, while the people who lived in the field appeared as subjects, perhaps even objects of study. The ethnographer's job was to investigate and examine the nuances of this foreign culture—to read it and ultimately write it—unlocking its secrets for audiences to consume and "know." Criticism of this version of the field, commenced by George E. Marcus and James Clifford in concert with feminist, postcolonial, decolonial, and women of color theorists,[14] has dramatically shifted how researchers approach the "location" of the field,[15] and the research process itself.[16] These critics have not abandoned the field; rather, they have reconceptualized what it means to be in the field and to do fieldwork. We see these critiques as instructive for putting rhetorical criticism in conversation with field methods. Rather than trying to minimize the legacy that the field conjures, we believe that keeping "the field" in the fore helps attune researchers' focus to the power relations that are always part and parcel of doing research.

With this in mind, we define the *field* as the nexus where rhetoric is produced, where it is enacted, where it circulates, and, consequently, where it is audienced. This definition situates people, places, events, material culture, and the digital milieu as potential fields that may be relevant to our investigations. It allows rhetoricians to engage with "live" and "*in situ*" rhetorics through methods of observation, ethnographic interviews, and performance.[17] And it enables reflection about rhetoric's emergence, meaning, and influence through methods like interviewing and focus groups. Conceptualized in this way, the field invites rhetoricians to attend to the way discourse moves, articulates, and shapes the material realities of people's lives in the everyday, in the public, and in their communities. It also allows scholars to attend to the often-unseen ways that individuals and groups respond, resist, and try to revise these instantiations. We believe that field methods offer rhetorical scholars more tools to illuminate the complexities of these rhetorical maneuvers.

Method provides the means for rhetoricians to move to the field. We conceptualize methods as the tools that researchers may use in order to collect data (e.g., field notes, personal reflections, transcripts, ephemera, and other documents), analyze data, and ultimately answer their research questions. *Field methods* may include interviews, focus groups, observation, personal narrative, ethnography, autoethnography, oral history interviews, performance, thematic analysis, iterative analysis, grounded theory, and many other forms of data collection and analysis. The researcher's choice of method should be guided by reflection on one's research questions and goals. For example, a rhetorical scholar seeking to understand how targets of sexual assault are represented in popular mediated discourse may appropriately pursue this research goal through textual analysis or discourse analysis, since this goal remains focused on representations and the implications of those representations. If, however, the scholar's goal includes understanding people's interpretations and their meaning-making of popular representations, then focus groups or interview methods may be appropriate. In bridging rhetorical studies with field methods, we must first ask whether our research goals and questions necessitate a move to the field.

As editors of this volume, we have each been drawn to field methods through individual work on online community-building, refugee and asylum contexts, activism, and local instantiations of public deliberation. Moreover, our conversations with one another have motivated us to consider the larger challenges and benefits of field methods for rhetorical scholarship. Thus we offer the introduction to this collection as just that, an introduction to our unique orientation to the encounters between and among text and field, to the possibilities and opportunities we see, and to the risks present therein. In the following sections we outline this vision for accessing the field and field methods, introducing each section with a narrative vignette from our individual fieldwork to illustrate the various possibilities that collaborations between rhetoric and field methods engender.

Text

A single mother of two girls—and a breast-cancer survivor—testified before the Elmbrook, Wisconsin, school board, expressing gratitude for the educational opportunities afforded her daughters. Yet she also expressed sorrow that future children would not have the same opportunities. The woman was African American and a Milwaukee resident, while the school district served the prosperous, mostly white suburbs west of the city. Her daughters attended school in Elmbrook because of a voluntary integration program that the district had decided to end. Powerful testimony by this woman and other parents could not overcome numbers portraying the integration program as a financial loser for the district's budget. Elmbrook relied heavily on numbers in their decision-making. Their local district culture was, as one board member put it in an interview, "data-driven."

By exploring rhetoric's engagement with field methods, we do not wish to displace scholarly interest in texts. We recognize that, since the establishment of the modern discipline, rhetorical scholars have defined text in many ways, including definitions that resist a notion of text as a static and/or discrete object. Early twentieth-century scholars like Herbert Wichelns contrasted the persuasive function of the rhetorical text to the aesthetic qualities of the literary text, yet Wichelns and others deferred discussions of the text as such.[18] Arising in the 1980s, close textual analysis challenged the persuasive-aesthetic dichotomy and others, recognizing instead the "dynamic character of the rhetorical text." Against static notions of a text, as James Jasinski explains, proponents of close textual analysis foregrounded terms like "process" and "action" when conceptualizing the rhetorical text.[19] Other scholars challenged the presumed unity of the text and autonomy of the rhetor in close textual analysis, but Jasinski holds that these challenges have advanced the complexity and diversity of conceptions of the text by suggesting that "the text exists in different modalities."[20] In this spirit, Leah Ceccarelli identifies various agents and forces that may multiply textual meanings: rhetor, audience, and critic.[21] Ceccarelli's work (and that of others) places the text in a larger process of meaning-making.[22]

Through field methods, rhetorical scholars can engage otherwise inaccessible texts, like local, marginal, and/or vernacular discourses that have not been collected and catalogued in archives and databases. In this way, Pezzullo explains that field methods offer scholars an opportunity to "study public discourse that is not yet recorded, a situation in which textual analysis is impossible."[23] An illustration of this opportunity appears in Robert Asen's analysis of school board deliberations as local sites of democratic engagement and policymaking.[24] While rhetorical scholars have long studied public policy, this scholarship has tended to focus on national and international cases—in part because these materials often are collected and transcribed by government and nongovernment agencies. For example, the U.S. Government Printing Office publishes transcripts of the hearings held by every committee of Congress. No such service exists for local governing and policymaking bodies. A rhetorical scholar interested in studying public policy at the local level must venture out in the field to collect materials for analysis.

Field methods also may expand the kinds of texts studied by rhetorical scholars. For Black, the object of rhetorical criticism was "persuasive discourse," which he discovered primarily in oral and written forms of expression.[25] In 1965 he could not have foreseen how a ubiquitous, contemporary digital communication network might complicate a focus on written and oral communication. Nor may Black have foreseen the explosion of interest in non-oratorical forms of rhetoric. For rhetorical critics who take their scholarship into the field, the opportunities for what constitutes a "text" seem more diverse than what Black had imagined. At least since Kenneth Burke described "the necessarily *suasive* nature of even the most unemotional scientific nomenclatures," rhetorical critics have approached increasingly diverse forms of discourse as rhetorical, albeit not in the overtly persuasive sense of Black's invocation of the term.[26] Considering such diverse cases as the folk songs of World War II resistance,[27] online responses to hate speech,[28] photographs,[29] monuments and memorials,[30] performances of tour guides,[31] and more, rhetorical critics have moved beyond the dichotomy between oral or written formal political discourse, exploring, in turn, discourses that manifest everyday, aesthetic, playful, and informative qualities. In the field, new kinds of communication become available to the rhetorical critic willing to explore the contexts where such texts emerge. Moving into the field may reward the critic with new perspectives on what constitutes rhetorical discourse.

Discourse located in the field may resist the unambiguous extraction of linguistic practices from their embodied and contextualized performance. Researchers may transcribe discourse discovered in the field, but beginning with the discourse rather than a completed transcript raises questions about how to represent multiple sources of meaning. In the analysis of school board deliberations referenced above, "texts" could be created by recording and transcribing the statements of school board members, but appreciating the multiple meanings of these transcripts depends on the knowledge of local district culture gleaned through fieldwork.[32] A critic studying non-deliberative modes of communication, for example, may enter the field to engage a public monument like the Vietnam Veterans Memorial. By traveling to the site and documenting the varied performances that occur, this critic may encounter and appreciate people's interactions with the memorial. Moreover, the personal commemorations that visitors add to the site may become part of what the rhetorical critic regards as a text. In their groundbreaking essay, Blair, Jeppeson, and Pucci observe that "the text of the Memorial changes materially over time," as visitors regularly leave items behind, especially at the wall bearing the names of dead soldiers.[33] These items include photographs, flowers, flags, medals, letters, and more. Carlson and Hocking add that many of the letters left at the memorial "are addressed to the dead, to a specific name or two found on the black wall."[34] As the items left at the wall are collected daily, new visitors place different items at the site. Blair, Jeppeson, and Pucci hold that "each addition alters the text, for it focuses on a different individual, a different aspect of the war or a different meaning" that visitors have associated with their experiences of the site.[35] Rhetorical critics may study reproductions of the memorial, such as photographs or models, but without traveling to the site such critics will find the "text" elusive.

Understanding texts as discursive practices allows the critic to examine bodies, embodied performances, and feeling/affect as material worthy of rhetorical analysis. Toward the end of his life, Conquergood criticized the discipline for a text-centrism that privileged verbal and visual modalities of knowing: "Only middle-class academics could blithely assume that all the world is a text because reading and writing are central to their everyday lives and occupational security. For many people throughout the world, however, particularly subaltern groups, texts are often inaccessible, or threatening, charged with the regulatory powers of the state. More often than not, subordinate people experience texts and the bureaucracy of literacy as instruments of control and displacement, e.g., green cards, passports, arrest warrants, deportation orders."[36] Situating performance and practice alongside the textual, Conquergood advocated, enables an analytic purview that attends to "intonation, silence, body tension, arched eyebrows, blank stares, and other protective arts of disguise and secrecy," among other bodily, affective, and sensorial elements as important types of information.[37]

Using field methods, the critic typically creates a set of diverse but complexly interrelated "texts." These documents may take the forms of video or photographs of observed objects and actions, the recordings of informal oral performances, the transcripts of formal interviews or focus groups, and the like. In some cases they provide contextual material to better understand other documents. In other cases these documents are the "texts." In both cases the bright lines between texts and between text and context become blurred. If a fieldworker documents a communication event or performance, analyzes it, and then turns to document a new event to aid in the analysis of the first, the new "text" becomes the contextualizing discourse the critic has provoked from rhetors by asking them about some other "text." Here the critic directly participates in the construction of a specific text-object from the constitutive bits of other imagined text objects that could themselves be wholly different objects of criticism.

Context

During the April 10, 2006, immigration march in Tucson, Roy Warden, a notorious anti-immigrant activist, infamous for burning the Mexican flag at pro-immigrant events, performed his signature act. Tucson police allowed him to perform his protest amid the otherwise peaceful marchers instead of off to the side or in a noncontact location. All the major newspapers reported that the marchers' response to Warden was violent and attacking, requiring police intervention. Activists I (Chávez) worked with scoffed at the charge of violence. Their version of the events differed significantly from what was reported in the papers. In their story, a young high school student threw a water bottle at the burning flag that was lit in the middle of the march, in order to put out the fire. She was immediately ambushed by police officers, who tackled her and other marching students. The only violent act according to activists was by police who let Warden in the middle of the protest, and then attacked students for trying to put out the fire. This point of view was not reflected in any newspaper story that documented the day's events.

Another key methodological concern in rhetorical studies circulates around the proper relationship between rhetoric, rhetorical criticism, and context.[38] Most rhetorical critics agree with Leff that rhetorical criticism must "hinge on the particulars of the case—the local circumstances that frame and motivate" the rhetorical performance.[39] Yet the extent and qualities of an appropriate "local circumstance" framing the analysis of a text have been the source of considerable discussion. John Murphy, for example, calls on scholars not just to analyze the immediate surroundings, but also to position rhetoric "within its 'universe of discourse,'" including the history of discourse that precipitates a text's emergence, such that texts constitute context.[40] Complicating things further, John Lucaites argues that a text's relationship to context will change over time. The task of the critic is to "examine the ways in which it [the text] functions in the larger context(s) in which it is made to do work," but we must always recognize that "both the function and the context are subject to variation throughout the life of the text, such that its significance (and perhaps even its internal action) change as it functions differently in different contexts."[41] Acknowledging this fluidity, others draw attention to the lines drawn between text and context as always already a matter of a critic's interpretation and judgment. Robert Branham and W. Barnett Pearce, for example, demonstrate a co-constitutive reflexivity between text and context that makes it hard to parse where text ends and context begins.[42] Critics, in their view, make choices in punctuating these beginnings and endings. These punctuations irrevocably alter the direction of critics' interpretations.

In line with this theorizing, we see field methods expanding the options that critics have before them in contextualizing the texts they analyze. Traditional studies of rhetoric often have relied on secondary sources, such as scholarly histories and news accounts, as invaluable resources in accessing the "particulars of the case," as Leff put it, and constructing a sense of the relevant contextual backdrop.[43] Field methods can add to and expand the insights gained from those secondary sources. Specifically, the "particulars" of the context can be made more richly available using even the most basic of field methods. Consider a well-established text for rhetorical criticism, the presidential speech. When a contemporary president delivers a speech, a critic may establish a context for this speech by re-creating a rhetorical situation that identifies relevant political, economic, and social developments and offers some explanation of their salience for the president and various audiences. As Murphy and Lucaites suggest, this speech may participate in a larger discourse about, say, race relations or health care. It may invoke and reimagine a contested history, and may champion, among several possibilities, a shared future for the nation and its people. In analyzing this speech, a rhetorical critic often will rely on a representation of the original—a transcript, or an audio or video recording.

Urging reflection on both the re-creation of context as well as the materials employed in an analysis of text and context, Blair asks rhetorical scholars to weigh the potential consequences of a "metaphorical 'flattening' of experience," achieved in this case by using news accounts as a proxy for the situation and a transcript as a proxy for speech.[44] Blair notes that experienced rhetoric matters in terms of both substance and significance. Without experience, she asks, "how can we make it *matter* to our readers" and, ultimately, ourselves? Imagining the critic preparing to hear a president speak in person, Blair continues: "Does it make any difference that televised reproduction separates us from the bodily experience of going through security checkpoints to be present, from the din of the Secret Service sirens as the cavalcade of black SUVs arrives, or from the reactions of other audience members? Does it matter that there is an audience in attendance at all, given that people are standing and applauding in a driving rain?"[45] Not surprisingly, she answers that these considerations do matter, "both to readers of criticism and to those who write it."[46] Amplifying Blair's position, we hold that these aspects of context matter by underscoring the eventfulness of rhetoric, which appears through multiple modes. Field methods facilitate an embodied presence for experiencing text and context.

In addition to the immediate context surrounding specific performances, field methods allow critics to engage a social group systemically over an extended period of time. Prolonged engagement with a community provides the critic with opportunities to explore broader characteristics of a context that enable or disable specific kinds of rhetorical practices. Such engagement also sheds light on a group's local habits and perceptions of deliberation, activism, coalition-building, self-representation, and so on. For example, Karma R. Chávez's fieldwork with immigration and LGBT activists in Tucson, Arizona, gave her access to understand how activists, in building and sustaining social movements, engage and make sense of the rhetoric present in the local contexts in which they organize.[47] She found local media, law enforcement, and policymakers to be important actors within those contexts who produced messages about migrants and LGBT people in the city. Through her nearly year-long observations in the field and interviews with activists, she also found the context and these actors to be primary sources of inspiration for the activists in producing public messages. In the "internal rhetoric" of these activists as they planned for protests, wrote policy and vision statements, and constructed public campaigns and responses, the activists spoke directly to and against the predominant constructions of migrants and LGBT people that they witnessed and experienced in the broader context. As Chávez's work illustrates, field methods provide the possibility for rhetorical critics not just to ask questions of specific secondary materials, but also to engage and even criticize the rhetoric that emerges from the embedded social norms of specific cultures.

Even in the case of a purely historical study, scholars might usefully deploy the methods of oral history to gain insight into past events and to nuance contextual backdrops. In the work of Dickinson, Blair, and Ott, for example, "memory places" are realized as particularly powerful rhetorical devices because they physically locate individuals at sites and in moments that constitute publics otherwise only imagined and abstract.[48] Similarly, the work of Maegan Parker Brooks illuminates the powerful vernacular voice of civil rights rhetor Fannie Lou Hamer. Brooks calls this work a "rhetorical biography" because her interviews with the individuals who shared the places and moments with Hamer provided contextual richness to illuminate why Hamer was so powerfully suited to address and inspire a freedom movement.[49]

In historical research such as that done by Brooks, fieldwork offers the opportunity to expand on other secondary materials typically held in archives. Archival sources are clearly the bread and butter of historical work. As Brooks demonstrates, field methods, when paired with archival research, allow the critic to create contextual texture, to fill in the gaps not captured by the archive's contents, and sometimes to add new elements to the archive itself. In fieldwork, documents are constructed from the ongoing threads of practices and perspectives of social actors. As such, they offer both freedom and an intense responsibility to the fieldworker. The fieldworker is dramatically responsible for the documents generated in the field whether the critic is documenting primary speech texts never before analyzed or seeking an experiential nuancing of the micro-context of a presidential address. In either case, field methods offer us powerful tools to better understand the context of rhetorical practice.

Audience

An immigrant and refugee rights organization is the pro bono legal representation for an HIV-positive gay male asylum-seeker from Mexico who is being detained before trial in an Arizona immigration detention center. The group asks if I (McKinnon) will meet with their client and write an affidavit attesting to the country conditions for HIV-positive gay men in Mexico. I agree to do so. After an evaluation of my credentials and a pat down from the security officers, I meet with the client. He is rightfully nervous, anxious, and scared; not only does he not have access to the necessary medicine in detention, but he has heard that the only way to win a gay asylum case is for the judge to see clients as effeminate—which he is not. A few weeks later

I sit to write the affidavit and am confounded with how to navigate the culturally essentialist ways homophobia and gender in Mexico are framed in U.S. discourse, the near-zero percent acceptance rate of Mexican asylum-seekers in this particular Arizona immigration courtroom, and the specific experiences that this asylum-seeker will talk about in testimony, with the judge's corporeal and narrative expectations for an eligible HIV-positive gay asylum-seeker. The writing process feels like I am navigating a field of rhetorical bombs—all waiting to blow up as the judge decides that the claimant is not worthy or eligible for refuge.

Encouraging engagement with audiences, field methods may bolster rhetorical understandings of audiences as active participants in processes of meaning-making. Existing approaches to audience in rhetorical scholarship tend to follow two paths, distinguishing audiences from texts as objects of persuasion or folding audiences into texts as aspects of their dynamics.[50] Field methods may present rhetorical scholars with opportunities to bridge audiences conceived as internal and external to texts. A prominent example of an external approach to audience is Lloyd Bitzer's account of the rhetorical situation, in which the audience figures as one element. For Bitzer, "a rhetorical audience consists only of those persons who are capable of being influenced by discourse and of being mediators of change."[51] As he elucidates situations, Bitzer underscores the separation of rhetoric from its audiences. "Rhetoric always requires an audience," but its audiences reside in situations that "are located in reality, are objective and publicly observable historical facts in the world we experience."[52] Rhetors may maximize the influence of rhetoric by articulating fitting responses to situations, but these situations take shape independently of an advocate's message. Situations—and with them audiences—come and go regardless of whether an advocate responds.[53]

The second approach has been to locate the audience internally as a textual dynamic, as Black suggests in his notion of a second persona. Black explains that the second persona refers to the implied auditor of a text. In this role it functions ideologically, betraying a textual worldview available for critical analysis: "The critic can see in the auditor implied by a discourse a model of what the rhetor would have [one's] real auditor become."[54] Yet, even as Black references a "real" auditor in this sentence, he distinguishes personae from actual audiences. Indeed, Black diagnoses a misguided focus on actual audience responses as a prime culprit in producing existing audience typologies that focus unhelpfully on demographic characteristics and predispositions toward a subject: "They are what has been yielded when theorists focused on the relationship between a discourse and some specific group responding to it." Black sees actual audiences identifying with texts rather than texts accommodating themselves to the values and interests of actual audiences. In this way, he asserts that "actual auditors look to the discourse they are attending for cues that tell them how they are to view the world."[55] Yet Black's unwillingness to engage actual audiences undermines the evidentiary basis for this claim, which stands less as a conclusion drawn from fieldwork and more as a theoretical stipulation that affirms the priority of textual personae.

Even so, Black's claim envisions a potentially provocative relationship between text and audience that field methods may substantiate. As Black suggests, beyond its propositional content, rhetoric exerts a constitutive force that helps shape people's understanding of their environments and identities.[56] As people form positions on public issues like environmentalism or education policy, for example, they develop individual and collective identities: thinking of oneself as an environmentalist invokes particular sets of values, beliefs, and commitments, and leads to particular lifestyles. Connecting texts and audiences may amplify the rhetorical dynamics of the text, revealing the ways that texts mean variously for various audiences, as some rhetorical scholars have suggested. For instance, Celeste Condit has combined textual analysis with studies of actual audiences to complicate our understanding of the opportunities for polysemous readings of media texts. Condit does not deny multiple readings, but she argues that audiences' readings of texts are constrained by such factors as "audience members' access to oppositional codes, the ratio between the work required and the pleasure produced in decoding a text, the repertoire of available texts, and the historical occasion."[57] Condit's work underscores important differences in position and privilege between scholarly readers and other audiences of media texts.

Acknowledging Condit's cautions, Ceccarelli observes that there are times when a resistive reading may occur as a "subordinate audience *does* develop a contrary understanding of the text's meaning." To elucidate these readings, she urges rhetorical scholars to seek out evidence of textual reception. Ceccarelli does not advocate field methods for this purpose—her example is Lincoln's Second Inaugural Address—but field methods may elucidate this possibility for contemporary cases. Ceccarelli encourages scholars to look for "texts that are experienced by both dominant and marginalized groups in a society and that are interpreted within the structure of intergroup conflict" in order to also gain critical insight into power relations and group conflicts that exist in a society.[58] Field-based explorations of audience, then, may contribute to rhetorical scholars' investigations of issues relating to power, inclusion and exclusion, multiple publics, and more.

Rhetorical studies of audience may consider connections with pioneering studies of media audiences. In Black, Condit, and Ceccarelli's projects we can discern resonances with Stuart Hall's famous encoding-decoding model of communication. In this model, Hall identified dominant, negotiated, and oppositional readings of media texts by audiences. Looking for textual cues for an implied auditor, the audience member seeking out Black's second persona manifests some similarities to the activities of Hall's audience member decoding a text from a dominant position, who "decodes the message in terms of the reference code in which it has been encoded."[59] For their part, Condit and Ceccarelli explore the capacities of audience members to negotiate and/or oppose the "preferred code" of a text.[60] Connecting audience with other aspects of context, media scholar David Morley holds that "the meaning of the text must be thought of in terms of which set of discourses it encounters in any particular set of circumstances, and how this encounter may restructure both the meaning of the text and the discourses which it meets."[61] To be sure, studies of audiences by media scholars have developed and diversified significantly in the decades since "active audience" theories arose, including considerations of new media and global audiences. Envisioning future research, Jonathan Gray and Amanda Lotz urge media scholars to "interrogate the borders of 'the audience.'"[62] Drawing on the resources of our own intellectual traditions and connecting with scholars in media and elsewhere, rhetorical scholars may benefit by engaging audiences in the field.

Field methods may elucidate meaning-making as a collaborative project of rhetor and audience. Sara L. McKinnon's research about asylum-seekers in U.S. immigration courtrooms demonstrates well the active nature of audiences in the process of meaning-making and points to the potential of field methods to illuminate these active processes. As potential refugees, asylum-seekers give testimony in U.S. courtrooms that speaks to their fear of returning to their home countries and eligibility for immigration relief in accordance with international human rights protocols. McKinnon finds that judges, as audiences to asylum-seekers' testimony, actively fill in the sense-making gaps by relying on essentialist discourses of race, gender, class, sexuality, nation, age, and linguistic ability in judging whether an asylum-seeker is credible and eligible for refuge.[63] Solely focusing on the rhetor's performance in this context would obscure the power relations between rhetor and audience that often shape the rhetorical practices we investigate. Field methods allow critics to witness and document that meaning-making as it happens. Depending on the rhetorical artifact one examines, opportunities for audience engagement may differ. A collaborative process of meaning-making may assume a different shape for the rhetorical scholar studying a public monument, for example, than the scholar studying speeches delivered at a political rally, yet field methods allow us to see these processes at work as rhetorical practices in action.

Judgment

In 1996 I (Howard) built a website at EndNear.com to engage in participant observation with the online community of fundamentalist Christians who believed in the rapidly approaching Second Coming of Christ. I received an e-mail announcing that the website had won "The Eagle Eye Award" from the "chairman" of the "Christian Intelligence Alliance." Hoping I would create a link to his website, the chairman stated, "With the utmost of praise! I have added a link to your webpage from mine." The Christian Intelligence Alliance was seeking to secede from the United States by whatever means necessary. Despite my commitment to open and reciprocal field methods, I did not link my site to the chairman's. Even in the most reciprocal moments of fieldwork, our actions limit and construct the representation of our subject. To deny that is to deny the power of judgment in our criticism.

Using field methods may also shift our understandings of the role of the critic and of critical judgment within the discipline of rhetorical studies. Many in the field have advocated a strong version of critical judgment, whereby the critic holds sovereignty over the text.[64] Even some of those who challenge the strong version of critical judgment continue to endow the critic with significant agency for evaluating and engaging with texts. Our position seeks to find a balance between the critic's agency in making judgments about texts and the critic's responsibility to the human beings making those texts. Black foregrounded the critic's aesthetic judgment, and other critics have emphasized locating injustice. These kinds of judgment remain central to the role of the critic. However, texts created from field-based documents confer an added responsibility. In the field, critical judgment must be balanced with an effort to understand the perspectives of the individuals who will continue to live in the worlds made by the texts we judge—and who may well suffer or gain from our judgments.

Critical rhetoricians Kent A. Ono and John M. Sloop advocate a materialist conception of judgment, through what they call "outlaw" judgments, or those that "disrupt dominant logics of judgment."[65] Although their framework potentially unloosens judgment from dominant approaches to criticism, these "outlaw-judgments" are ultimately in the service of the rhetorical critic. Therefore it is unclear how exactly the critic's sovereignty is challenged through their evocation. Similarly, feminist scholars who disrupt traditional understandings of what counts as a text worthy of criticism and who intervene in the implied subjectivity of the rhetorical critic (as individual, white, male, and professional) also maintain the primacy of the rhetorical critic's judgment. Such primacy may be sustained even when, in the case of scholars such as Sonja K. Foss, Karen A. Foss, and Cindy L. Griffin, among others, the rhetorical critic herself is not singular, but multiple.[66] The predominant mode of feminist rhetorical criticism, though, continues to be conducted by singular critics operating with the same assumptions about the critic's judgment as "traditional" modes of rhetorical criticism.

Some recent turns to the field attempt to dislodge these traditional assumptions. Aaron Hess's conceptualization of "critical rhetorical ethnography" uses field methods to theorize a different modality of judgment for the critic—one of the critic as advocate. Specifically, Hess turns the critic's judgment toward advocacy alongside an organization or group.[67] While the critic is framed as expert and primary actor in Hess's work, the critic's judgment is reduced to that of the people and groups he researches with and advocates for/alongside. We share parts of this impulse, but Hess's turn to advocacy as a normative prescription for what "rhetorical ethnographers" should do errs too far in taking all agency from the critic. In our view, field methods do not require such a strong turn from a critic-centered understanding of criticism, but any critic who utilizes field methods may experience a shift in their agency.

Take, for example, Robert Glenn Howard's fifteen-year ethnographic engagement with online Christian fundamentalist communities.[68] When confronted with the task of critically judging discourse that openly expresses anti-Semitism or actively encourages the systematic oppression of LGBTQ individuals, Howard could not "advocate."[69] He instead examined the hateful speech in order to denaturalize the logics undergirding it. While the dominant voices among the fundamentalist Christians he worked with furthered "prejudices," Howard kept an eye toward the inconsistencies and contradictions—in this instance the few rare examples of community members "demanding more tolerance." Such an approach allowed for judgment that was critical of the hateful messages espoused by this community with a critique that was still very much grounded in the community's words and worldviews. This work shows us that even while maintaining enough sovereignty to judge, the critic can step aside enough to allow the complicating, conflicting, and otherwise messy elements of a community to emerge from the community and the field.

Field methods challenge the assumed sovereignty of the critic because they necessitate reconciling with what Lincoln and Guba, in their foundational text *Naturalistic Inquiry*, named the "human instrument."[70] By this they mean that the researcher is the primary tool of qualitative field research because the researcher both collects and analyzes the data, a slightly different meaning than Black's endowment of the critic with complete agency. Rather, because the person or people conducting research in the field are the sole instrument of research, they bear great responsibility to those with whom they research and for the results they produce. Certainly, on this latter point about product, Black would agree. However, Lincoln and Guba maintain that the judgment exercised by the field researcher must, by definition, include the perspectives of those who are the participants represented in the research even when their beliefs or values are in conflict. Furthermore, even with analytic and stylistic choices, the field researcher cannot write only in a way that reflects his or her personality. Instead, those choices, too, should bear the imprint of the knowledge of participants, as their turns of phrase, their framings, and their voices may hold more agency in this type of work than we often allow texts to hold in traditional modes of rhetorical criticism.

Such an approach that disrupts assumptions about agency and judgment is in line with the interventions that Olga Idriss Davis's landmark essay on black women as rhetorical critics makes in explicating the racial and gender logics that undergird the project of rhetorical criticism, and challenging the assumptions about the subjectivity and agency of the critic.[71] Specifically, Davis's intervention places black women's intellectual and everyday ways of knowing and doing, their standpoint, at the center of the project of rhetorical criticism. In this respect, the center of analysis shifts in important ways. Articulating a perspective that emerges from the stories of black women's lives, Davis alters the basis for judgment and understanding as she seeks a merging of the intellectual and the everyday along with an attention to intersecting modes of power. Davis's work opens important space for the ways in which field methods might also complicate our understanding of both judgment and the role of the critic. A shift in the critic's agency necessarily creates the need for balancing the evaluative claims associated with Black against the responsibility of the people encountered and relationships developed in the field.

The shift in agency that field methods compel may also induce rhetorical critics to more actively engage in self-reflexivity, what Morris has called "critical self-portraiture" or "the silent dynamic between motive and method."[72] As a natural outgrowth of the ideological turn in rhetorical criticism, Morris suggests that the call for self-reflection was vibrant during the 1990s. He wonders what has happened to the articulation of self-reflection by rhetorical scholars, encouraging us to find inspiration in the fine work of our colleagues in performance studies, who regularly offer a "critical voicing of self."[73] For Morris and for us, this critical voicing plays a central part in locating critics' biases, positionality, and worldviews as central to the judgments critics offer. The return to reflexivity is also an ethical consideration, a point we elaborate below.

Ethics

Rhetorical studies has richly engaged in conceptualizing ethical frameworks to guide the practice of rhetoric.[74] As Christopher Johnstone explicates, "The morality of rhetoric is central to our conception of ourselves, our objectives, and our obligations as students, teachers, and practitioners of the art."[75] Taking this point to heart, a number of scholars have taken rhetorical criticism to be an important site for considering and conceptualizing ethical frameworks.[76] Most notably, Wayne Booth calls critics to recognize that our readings of texts always involve, *and should involve*, an ethical perspective from which we analyze and write, for "if ethical criticism is to be worth pursuing it will itself carry powerful ethical force and thus be subject to ethical criteria."[77] In terms of what this ethical stance should do, Booth highlights various ethical responsibilities that critics bear in the form of questions we must ask ourselves as critics or readers.

These include: *"What are the reader's responsibilities to the writer—the flesh-and-blood author or career author? . . . What are the reader's responsibilities to the work of art—which is to say the implied author? . . . What are the reader's responsibilities to his or her own self or soul—as flesh-and-blood reader? . . . What are the reader's responsibilities to other individual readers? . . . What are the reader's responsibilities to society, beyond the honest expression of critical judgment?"*[78]

The kinds of ethical questions that Booth poses can sometimes be ambiguous ones for rhetorical critics. Field methods help clarify what these ethical responsibilities might mean for our criticism. Qualitative field researchers both inside and outside the field of communication have done much to explicate what ethical considerations might best guide the research practice.[79] In part, this attention to ethics in research practice naturally grew out of the emergence of human subjects review boards on university campuses, which necessitated that researchers working with humans receive institutional approval for research protocols before delving into processes of data collection and analysis.[80] We find that the standards and questions developed by these qualitative methodologists help clarify the responsibilities of the reader which Booth called us to take seriously, and arguably make the imperative to do so even more urgent.

While Booth asked about the reader's responsibilities to the author, field methods necessitate that critics also consider their responsibility to the people and communities represented by our research. Thus we think of responsibility as a dialectical relationship that exists between the critic, those represented in the research, and the reader. This means that the shape this responsibility takes will necessarily differ depending on the context, and the structural power differentials between the researcher and those with whom the researcher works. For example, the critical ethnographer D. Soyini Madison urges that concern about responsibility is particularly necessary when researching with subaltern and marginalized communities. Our "primary responsibility is to those studied (people, places, materials, and those with whom you work)," she writes. "This responsibility supersedes the goal of knowledge, completion of a project, and obligation to funders or sponsors. If there ever is a conflict of interest, the people studied *must come first*."[81] This responsibility does not mean that the critic must kowtow to the opinions and wishes of those studied, especially when the critic encounters objectionable discourse and practices, but it does mean that critics take their needs and integrity into consideration in designing, conducting, analyzing, and writing up research. An ethic of responsibility encourages critics to ask the following questions of our work: How does this research design function for those studied? How are we relating to participants in the field? How does this relationality function for participants? How are we representing people and communities we talk with and about in this research? What do these representations do? What are the politics of the information and analysis we have constructed? These questions (and more) guide researchers to evaluate the motivations behind the research process and to question whether the research enhances and illuminates the way we think about and understand people's lives, or advances other, less responsible intentions and motivations. Such questions also give critics means to interrogate whether our own representations rely on discourses, beliefs, and stereotypes about groups that may objectify, exoticize, silence, or disempower the people we represent in our work.

Field methods encourage critics to be accountable for the research process as an ethic of research. Black's well-known adage to "be brilliant," or others' common advice to "say something interesting," may capture the creative dimension of criticism, but this approach offers little pedagogical value in demonstrating *how* research happens and what the process of gathering and analyzing data involves. Rhetorical critics, we believe, must be willing to account for the process—to account for what we do as rhetorical critics. Sarah Amira de la Garza explains that accountability reflects "our ability to explain how we came to know what we know."[82] Such a practice can be guided by questions like "What were the decisions and actions we made and took while engaging in our ethnographic research? While we discovered and opened awareness and cultural knowledge, what were we challenged with? To what did we close ourselves?"[83] Asking these questions calls critics to attend to the intricacies of the process itself and, as de la Garza explains, makes us *able* to *account*, or tell the story of our research. We need not divulge every detail, but our ability and willingness to explain makes research faithful to the accountability ethic. As a side benefit, the ethical practice of accountability serves communicative and pedagogical functions by allowing other critics to know how we have done what we have done. Our accountability instructs future scholars in the possibilities before them as they conceptualize collection and analysis processes in their own work. We do not use accountability to imply that criticism should be positivist or post-positivist and adapt the methods of science to rhetorical inquiry.[84] Accounting for the process, we believe, facilitates commitment to the community of scholars to which our ideas and analyses contribute.

As gestured to above, field methods also invite critics to an ethic of reflexivity. While responsibility and accountability call scholars to consider the communities that are connected to the research they produce, reflexivity flips the question and interrogates the researcher's connection, social location, and motivation in relation to the research. An ethic of reflexivity calls us to ask the following questions of ourselves: How am I connected to this research topic? What is my positionality, or social location, in relation to this research topic? What motivates me to do this research? These questions necessitate that critics remain *reflexive*, or mindful of our relationship to the research topic, so that we can be aware of the ways our own experiences, knowledge, identities, and worldviews shape not only what we choose to study and what we see as important, but also how we go about interpreting and analyzing the data. In examining the politics behind naming practices for Chinese women, Wen Shu Lee provides an example of how rhetorical critics might integrate reflexive practices into our work. She writes, "Who am I and who am I not? I was born into the Lee family in Taipei, Taiwan. My name, Wen Shu, was given by a paternal great great uncle, who was venerated as a scholar of high moral standards and as a patriarch who made major decisions for the extended family. I don't think my mother was consulted about my name."[85] Lee proceeds to address the politics involved not only in how she came to have her name, but also in what happens to her name when she moves from Taiwan to the United States. This reflexivity helps the reader understand Lee's social location as an analyst of the rhetorical dimensions of naming practices, and also why naming practices matter. As Lee's example reveals and as Morris also notes, reflexivity is not unheard of within rhetorical scholarship, but field methods create an even stronger ethical imperative.

Chapter Overview

The essays in this volume explore relationships between text and field in diverse and innovative ways. Chapter 1, "Interrogating the 'Field,'" engages conceptualizations of space and place through a case study of activists in Omaha, Nebraska, who transform public spaces to call attention to practices of consumerism. Authors Samantha Senda-Cook, Michael K. Middleton, and Danielle Endres explore the opportunities that field methods make available to scholars in studying peoples' behavior in space. In chapter 2 Joshua P. Ewalt, Jessy J. Ohl, and Damien Smith Pfister repurpose a rhetorical concept, taking up the classical tradition of *imitatio* as a resource to rethink the relationship between rhetorical texts and the field. Elucidating multiple meanings of *imitatio*, Ewalt, Ohl, and Pfister argue for a democratically inspired mode of writing that may capture the performative quality of rhetorical practice and suggest improvements to these practices.

Chapters 3 and 4 bring new theoretical frameworks to rhetoric in order to bridge the gap between text and field. Tiara R. Na'puti calls for a both/neither framework in chapter 3, "From Guåhan and Back." As she demonstrates, this framework is particularly compelling in assessments of places and subjectivities with ambiguous political positions (such as Guåhan/Guam as an unincorporated territory of the United States). Chapter 4 takes an affective turn, as in "Feeling Rhetorical Critics" Jamie Landau calls scholars to account for their affective and emotional responses when analyzing rhetoric. Through an analysis of a human bodies exhibit, Landau demonstrates that addressing these dimensions enriches scholarly accounts of rhetoric. Rounding out the conceptually driven approaches to rhetoric and field methods, in chapter 5,

"Embodied Judgment," Aaron Hess argues that the rhetorical concept of judgment may facilitate rhetoricians' ability to incorporate the different perspectives of scholar, activist, and audience in their criticisms.

The second half of the book demonstrates criticisms that begin with the rhetorical space as the inspiration for bridging text and field. In chapter 6, "Pa' que tú lo sepas," Kathleen de Onís explores the relationship of language and politics as Puerto Ricans situate themselves at the intersection of multiple lines of identity. De Onís addresses the complicated history of Puerto Rico and the United States, considering how Puerto Ricans maintain a distinct cultural identity and fight for social change. In chapter 7, "It's Like a Prairie Fire!," Valerie Thatcher considers successful and strained coalitional efforts to oppose coal plants in Texas, demonstrating how field methods bolster rhetorical scholars' understanding of social protest.

Chapter 8, "Being, Evoking, and Reflecting from the Field," makes a move toward accessing the rhetorical audience in new ways as Alina Haliliuc explores the rhetoric of Romanian public intellectual Dan Puric and her own engagement with his rhetoric as a Romanian teaching in the United States. Field methods enable Haliliuc to situate Puric's rhetoric in contemporary Romanian society and in transnational flows of employment and ideas. In chapter 9, "Holographic Rhetoric," Roberta Chevrette uses the metaphor of the hologram to urge public memory scholars to attend to what and who has been effectively eliminated, but which remains present, in public memory places. In chapter 10 Lisa Silvestri calls rhetoricians to think about how "Context Drives Method." Analyzing soldiers' use of social media during military deployment, Silvestri considers the complicated meanings of social messages. Through interviews with soldiers, Silvestri discovers that tools such as Facebook represent for soldiers both a connection with friends and family and a practice that fits uneasily with the rhythms of deployment. Rounding out the volume, in the afterword Phaedra C. Pezzullo reflects on the burgeoning moment for the encounter between text and field within rhetorical studies, and why this encounter is so necessary. While certainly not a definitive statement, each of these essays coheres into an introduction to cutting-edge thinking regarding many intersections among and between text and field within rhetorical studies in communication.

Interrogating the "Field"

Samantha Senda-Cook,
Michael K. Middleton, and
Danielle Endres

To emphasize the connection between food and transportation, Emerging Terrain, an organization in Omaha, Nebraska, closed a two-lane bridge and held a dinner party. The bridge they occupied is on 36th Street between Grover and D Streets and spans over Interstate 80, several sets of railroad tracks, and a small service road. With the permission of the city, Emerging Terrain invited chefs, designers, and diners to interrogate—albeit in a festive way—food systems and called the event Elevate. From the overpass, diners could see massive artwork (also commissioned by Emerging Terrain) oriented vertically on unused grain elevators. The art reinforced the event by commenting on the relationships between food and transportation. Local restaurants and organizations set up cooking and dining stations along the bridge. Attendees at the event circulated among these stations, choosing their meals and interacting with other participants and event planners. Hosting the event on a bridge highlighted a range of interesting rhetorical choices that the event organizers made. First, the use of transportation infrastructure as the location for the event functioned to draw attention to the distances food travels before it arrives on our plates. Diners were confronted with various modes of transportation—the highway and rail lines—that deliver food. Likewise, the temporary food stations reinforced the work done by local restaurants and organizations to transport materials to this location. Second, the event disrupted traffic and communication patterns in the neighborhood by blocking travel across the overpass, with reference to similar disruptions created by the original construction of I-80. The event organizers further emphasized these disruptions by displaying large posters with newspaper headlines about I-80 construction from 1957 that chronicled the thoroughfare's initial construction.[1] Emerging Terrain mobilized the event to critique contemporary society's approach to food. In doing so, the organizers hoped to encourage participants to elevate their expectations about food production and delivery. The bridge (and the surrounding environment) was the field where rhetoric was happening. In this respect, Elevate offers an opportunity to grapple with how the "field" brims with complicated and nuanced rhetorical forces, providing a case study through which to contemplate the "field" not only as rhetorical itself, but also as a space that encompasses shifting scenes of constraint and possibility for the rhetorical action it hosts.

Studying an event such as this (and the characteristics of field-based rhetoric more generally) necessitates doing fieldwork wherein the critic (1) inhabits the physical place of such rhetorical events; (2) takes field notes, photographs, and other records of the event; and then (3) analyzes them. Elsewhere we described this undertaking as rhetorical field methods and participatory critical rhetoric.[2] In this essay we problematize and add theoretical texture to the concept of the "field" by thinking of it not simply as a materially delimited area one enters to do research (i.e., field research), but instead as a rhetorical place[3] that contributes to and limits conditions of possibility for rhetorical practice, performance, and intervention. We aim to emphasize the rhetoricity of place that is activated by entering the field and to challenge conceptualizations of the field as simply a location, backdrop, or context in which rhetoric takes place. We argue that the "field" participates in and cocreates the rhetoric of its inhabitants. Recalling Endres and Senda-Cook's argument that places of rhetoric are often in the process of becoming insofar as "locations, bodies, words, visual symbols, memories, and dominant meanings all interact to make and remake place," field as place plays a crucial role in rhetorical dynamics.[4] Rhetorical practices create, activate, and challenge meaning differently depending on the specific field where they are enacted. For example, in her examination of the rhetorical practices of outdoor recreators, Senda-Cook explains that trail-running, while accepted and encouraged on some trails, is frustrating to some recreators on steep, slippery trails because of the danger it creates for themselves and others, and the perceived (dis)regard runners have for the environment.[5] Yet, in this example, meanings are not only interpreted differently depending on the field, or specific trail, but the trail/field itself is interpreted differently by walkers and runners who choose from the field's range of possible interactions. Similarly, several critics have explored how place itself is filled with potential meanings—that it enables the rhetorical actions of some identities and communities, while problematizing and constraining other bodies and practices.[6] Given this, the field itself needs to be examined as both a potential rhetorical artifact and a compelling factor in the creation, execution, and consequences of rhetoric.

Elevate emphasizes the field's role as both a site of rhetorical practice and a set of rhetorical fragments that create meaning for participants. Elevate, as a rhetorical "field," highlights the challenges faced by field-based rhetorical critics seeking to reconceptualize artifacts, recalibrate evaluations of "live(d)" rhetorical practice, and address the political nature of the field. These challenges generate questions that guide our essay as we interrogate how we might conceptualize the field within contemporary rhetorical inquiry. Elevate provides a heuristic opportunity to think about these questions because the field—in this case, a dinner party on a bridge—is part of the rhetorical performance of the event; its rhetorical force cannot be reduced to just the event's verbal messages. Examining Elevate as a rhetorical field adds depth to how we think about live(d) rhetorical practice by highlighting how such practices are embedded in a field that exceeds bodies and their words alone. It reveals the convergence of place, bodies, sounds, and ideas that are accessed experientially through co-participation. These critical insights challenge rhetorical theory to better account for the experiential, embodied, and emplaced nature of rhetoric.

We begin by defining the "field" and posing questions that this generates. Then we examine Elevate as a case study for addressing these critical questions, emphasizing how the field reveals political commitments and rhetorical possibilities that might otherwise be concealed by analyzing only the textual traces of an event. Finally, we discuss some implications of thinking about the "field" for ongoing discussions about material rhetoric.

Defining the Field

We contend that the field *acts*. It is a co-participant in the rhetorical activities that we go "there" to study. The field is not merely a site outside the critic's office for gathering rhetorical texts or only a context for rhetorical action. It does not simply constrain or enable the action of rhetors who engage in (extra)ordinary rhetorical practices, though the field does exert those influences. Rather, field-based rhetorical inquiry ought to be attentive not only to how the field names the combination of material and discursive constraints that imbue delimited places with meanings and power, but also to how the field is a rhetorical place that acts with, against, and alongside the rhetorical practices it hosts.

Our conception of the field participates in ongoing efforts to theorize the role of context in the practice of rhetoric.[7] Bitzer viewed context as a necessary condition for rhetorical action (text).[8] Critical rhetoric scholars have troubled neat distinctions between text and context, leading critics to analyze the rhetoric found in what has traditionally been seen as context. Similarly, critics have focused on place itself, seeing places as not merely contexts for rhetoric but as inherently possessing rhetorical force in excess of and prior to the rhetorical acts they host.[9] Further, critics have argued that the meaning, influence, and consequence of rhetoric are always differently felt and experienced when encountered in the places from which they emerge.[10] Building from these conversations, we conceptualize the field as a physical place that is both context and text, or from a Burkeian perspective both scene and agent. Defining the field as a place that acts, as opposed to context or setting, emphasizes that the field (as scene) is an agent that participates in a coequal manner with the other dimensions of the rhetorical phenomena encountered in the field.[11] Although Burke's theorization conceptualizes scene as a container for rhetorical action and an agent as someone who can "act in a scene," our conceptualization of the field reveals how scene can be a rhetorical agent in its own right.[12] Considering the field as rhetorical place recognizes its dynamic, polysemous relationship with rhetorical action. For instance, a public park is a polysemous rhetorical field. The rhetoricity of the park can vary by time of day and audience. The presence or absence of park benches, and the type of bench, can enable and constrain a variety of meanings, audiences, and interactions with the park. A park with circular metallic benches, which may be comfortable for a short break but not for sleeping, is not just a scene but also a rhetorical force. Urban parks are (re)made over the course of even a twenty-four-hour period as they shift between recreation spaces for professionals seeking respite from their offices to residential places for homeless populations who remap the city under the cover of night.

In this sense, the field is a socially constructed place imbued with meaning(s) that simultaneously enables, constrains, and constitutes rhetorical practices. However, the field can play a more or less dominant role in the practices of the rhetoricians who inhabit it. The subjective practices enabled, encouraged, and expected in that place reveal the normative role of places in policing the boundaries of rhetorical possibility. In doing so, places communicate meanings (e.g., decorum, propriety, belonging). Conversely, the improvisations made by rhetorical subjects in such places often refute these boundaries, challenge the rhetorical force of places, and begin to blur the "boundaries" of the rhetorical field.

This is especially apparent in civic places that often are the scene of rhetoric. As David Fleming writes, "Place remains a powerful basis for civic lives. . . . [It] reminds us of our embeddedness in, and dependence on, the natural and built worlds."[13] For example, the public square is defined by liberal democratic discourses as a place of public democracy, which enables and constrains what subjects do there: it both creates a place for political debate and creates limits like libel and defamation. It is further (re)defined by neoliberal discourse as a place of consumption, and it is put to such use by "good subjects." Finally, the public square is challenged by unruly subjects (e.g., LGBTQ activists, homeless, Occupy) and converted to a stage for insurgent discourse.[14] Such civic places enable "publicity" at the same time that they limit (but never fully) the rhetorical practices performed there.[15] Conceiving of the field as rhetorical place reveals that rhetoric does not operate in a vacuum; rather, it is created in places that "have a say" about what type of meanings can be created. In some instances, rhetoricians challenge the disciplinarity of (public) places by using their constraints as foils against which to talk back in efforts to create emergent, vernacular, and resistant uses and meanings. In short, the field itself is a dynamic player in the rhetorical action that field-based rhetorical critics analyze.

Field(ing) Questions

Engaging with rhetoric in the field offers enhanced access to the undocumented aspects of the (extra)ordinary practices of everyday life, as well as to the rhetorical force they exert. This access, however, challenges researchers to navigate a critical pathway that accounts for the complex interaction between rhetorical places and the rhetorical practices they host. These tensions should compel rhetorical theorists to ask questions about how rhetorical theory can be adapted to these challenges. First, the field gives an entry to recognize and analyze embodied and emplaced practices as they happen. When one enters a field of rhetoric, potential rhetorical artifacts proliferate and demand that critics grapple with, *How should critics define, delimit, and gather artifacts when in the field?* Second, having access to embodied and emplaced practices reveals the limits of textualization (including field notes). Although our means of evaluation may not change much, we must recalibrate the way we make sense of and report on lived experience. In the evaluation/analysis process, the rhetorical critic needs to ask, *How can the experiential nature of the field be represented?* Finally, as a complex live(d) rhetorical space, power circulates throughout the field. Critics' engagement in the field raises questions about the ethics and role of the critic seeking to capture, analyze, and publicize field-based rhetorics. Critics must sort out, *Whose needs are prioritized by publicizing the (often vernacular or hidden) rhetorical practices enacted in the field?*

Elevate

On June 3, 2012, people assembled on an overpass in Omaha to engage in a few hours of dinner, art, and conversation around the themes of food and transportation. Emerging Terrain, a nonprofit research and design collaborative,

FIG. 1.1 A food station "in honor of South Omaha," which demonstrates how some organizations transformed the bridge with decorations and themed menus. Photo by Samantha Senda-Cook.

hosted events like this aimed at challenging normative transportation options and rethinking the built environment.[16] This group had commissioned art to display on the unused grain elevators in Omaha (see fig. 1.4), and Elevate was the second dinner party to celebrate their unveiling. At both "art openings," guests had a clear view of the grain elevators and were encouraged to "focus on new possibilities for collaboration, reinterpret a place, and ultimately expand perceptions of our city."[17] Workers from restaurants and volunteers from non-profits constructed unique, visually arresting food stations, planned themed menus, and provided distinctive food to five hundred paying guests. In all, about twenty "Elevation Stations" served small-course dinners, drinks, and desserts that merged artistic presentation, locavore impulses, the politics of everyday life, and the practicalities of eating dinner on a bridge in the middle of the summer. For example, one food station towered above the others, but its height was not the only thing attracting participants. Organizers had created shade by swathing a scaffolding frame in bright blue plastic, mesh-like fabric. They enhanced the shade and created a cool environment by periodically spritzing the air with water. Although the visual effect of this station was whimsical from a distance because of the gentle folds of the fabric, up close the station offered a comfortable space for outdoor eating on a hot summer evening. For some participants, Elevate included other activities that started before the event. To foster a sense of collaboration and local production, Emerging Terrain gave burlap bags containing soil and edible plants to people in Omaha who agreed to act as caregivers prior to the event. The caregivers were responsible for returning the plants at the event to become part of a local food display that mapped food production onto sites all over the city and symbolically connected them to the overpass. This display occupied a central position at the event. Supported by thick, metal columns, a 15' × 15' map of Omaha made the ceiling of an awning-like structure. The map had holes drilled through it that represented the locations of the homes of the plants' caregivers. From the holes hung the burlap, soil-filled bags, suspended by steel cables.

On the whole, most workers, volunteers, and guests appeared to be white,[18] but judging from jewelry, clothes, and past interactions with individuals and organizations present at the event, people appeared to be from different socio-economic backgrounds. Cognizant of the economic privilege implicit in treating food as leisure, organizers attempted to include people in the event who might otherwise be deterred by economic or social barriers. For instance, different ticket prices were charged depending on the time of purchase. If attendees bought a ticket early, then they paid less than did those who bought late. Nonetheless, the event surely was influenced by the reality that its attendees were mostly those with adequate economic security to participate in "foodie culture" and/or to dedicate an afternoon to such an endeavor. An analysis of Elevate helps us answer the questions we posed about the field because it provides a limited instance to examine the interactions between place and rhetors in the field.

How Should Critics Define, Delimit, and Gather Artifacts When We Are in the Field?

Defining, delimiting, and gathering artifacts in the field relies both on conventional rhetorical criticism and on methods that are not part of typical textual analysis. As Middleton, Senda-Cook, and Endres state, "Rhetorical field methods avoid bracketing out insights that fail to gain the status of objectified texts and include more careful attention to the extradiscursive elements of rhetorical action."[19] This commitment means that the difference between context and artifact often is not as clear when using rhetorical field methods. Artifacts may include many aspects of rhetorical action that would formerly be considered part of the setting. As a location, the bridge on which Elevate took place easily qualifies as a context in which people might make speeches or hand out pamphlets. And yet, as Endres and Senda-Cook contend, the place itself can be rhetorical; the bridge enacts event organizers' goal to challenge common understandings of urban places and transportation systems.[20] As the event's name implies, the bridge literally elevates participants and their conversations about urban space. Further, by making the bridge a destination and closing off traffic for the duration of the event, Elevate enacts a variety of disruptions. Closing off traffic on the bridge interrupts modes of transportation that intersect with food distribution and positions the transport of food against locally produced food as part of the critical focus of the event. Moreover, Elevate temporarily changes the bridge from a place of transfer to one of destination; it disrupts typical flows of bodies, meanings, and capital. On its website, Emerging Terrain explains the significance of this location: "The . . . bridge over the Interstate 80 corridor . . . made two neighborhoods from one, and produced a massive flow of people and goods through the city—changing our movement, economy, and physical landscape."[21] These disruptions shift the bridge from a backdrop to part of the critical focus. In other words, seeing the bridge as a place recognizes the ways in which it not only acts rhetorically but also participates with, constrains, and enables the other forms of rhetoric performing at the event.

Responding to and critiquing how places perform in the moment, as well as in the long term, requires a different mode of thinking about artifacts and a different way of collecting and describing "textual evidence" for our critical claims. When in the field, evidence can take different forms to account for the feelings and experiences produced by the concurrent presence of (extra)verbal rhetorics, participants, and critics. Place, or field, as a rhetorical actor is one of these copresent factors, and it cannot be easily documented as a text as we traditionally imagine them. Commenting on the challenge of documenting an emplaced experience, Pezzullo explains, "Viewing this landscape provides me with no empirical evidence that this hill is full of waste or that it is a problem for the local community."[22] In other words, sometimes simply photographing what we, as researchers, see cannot capture meaningful fragments while in the field. For example, the conversations that happen at Elevate and the reactions of onlookers can be as important as the event itself. One conversation that captured the potential of such fragments took place between two people trying to make sense of this unusual experience by comparing it to a gallery opening. From where they stood, they could easily see the artwork on the grain elevators. The arrangement of the food stations on the bridge effectively created a front stage and a back stage because on one side of the bridge there was a sidewalk with a concrete barrier on one side and a chain-link fence on the other side. Stations were set up against the concrete barriers and workers used the sidewalk as a quick way to get around. Meanwhile, the fronts of all the food stations faced the road, the participants, and the artwork on the grain elevators, contributing to a feeling of all-encompassing art, like a gallery. This way of viewing the event spoke not only to the purpose of the event but also to the location of (and the discourses of class status present at) the event, emphasizing that it could not have happened just anywhere. It needed to be in view of the grain

FIG. 1.2 This organization combined serving methods with seating (*foreground*). Structures were made and transported specifically for the event (*background*), creating multiple individualized atmospheres that appealed to all the human senses. Photo by Samantha Senda-Cook.

elevator art. While an important implication of rhetorical field methods is that conversations such as these can be considered rhetorical artifacts, our focus in this essay on the "field" emphasizes that the field in which these conversations occur is significant. The conversation, though a nontraditional form of text, does not unfold in a vacuum. The conversation happens as people experience an event in a particular place. The conversation is informed by, responds to, and potentially challenges the rhetorical features of the place.

Temporary events, like Elevate, also point to the ephemerality of rhetoric, the power dynamics at play in what gets documented, and how places, though seemingly stable, are always in process.[23] Elevate happened for just one day and then disappeared except for its online presence. This highlights the distinction between what the rhetorical critic is able to access and make claims about at an event itself versus only using the documentation of it on websites and elsewhere. The latter acts more like a traditional text in that it selects some aspects of the event to report. Attending the event and using field methods accesses rhetorics that remained undocumented, as well as the interactions between the various rhetorics present in this material and experiential field and their differences from the documented versions of the event/site.

A critic in the field must view all these aspects of the field as potential artifacts. In addition to collecting typical rhetorical texts while in the field, rhetorical critics take field notes, photograph places and people, and record interviews to capture the intricate and interconnected rhetorical force constituted by the intertwined sensuous, temporal, embodied, and emplaced experiences present in the field. Elevate reveals how distinct artifacts expose conflicting messages manifested through *in situ* rhetorics. Although the event itself seemed complete and coherent, interviews revealed challenges faced by planners regarding what to make, how to transport it, and how to present it. For example, one participating food provider rode a bike with a basket full of miniature ice cream cups for guests to consume. She explained that the organizers initially proposed that she bring bikes to churn ice cream outside on the day of the event. Taking the June heat into consideration, the organizers scrapped that idea and said they would drive bikes to the event so that she could ride around and distribute ice cream. She protested that bikes are a form of transportation, meaning that having them delivered to the event as props ignores their utility. She suggested instead that she and some friends ride the bikes to the event. In the end, the event organizers agreed with her suggestion. Although the artifact seemed to be simply a person riding a bike, distributing ice cream, the interview uncovered tensions in the production of the artifact and, more significantly, the competing interpretive frameworks informing the event encountered by attendees. When we view the field as a place, we acknowledge the presence of multiple rhetorics in conversation and conflict with one another and attempt to make sense of their negotiations.

Additionally, some participants found the event too complicated, attempting to bring together too many disparate pieces of art and political sensibility. Despite an effort to promote the viability of growing food locally, some guests did not make that connection. One participant stated, "What this [event] means to me? I don't know how to answer that. I guess I'm not quite sure what else this organization does other than I know that they did this artwork. It's cool; I've enjoyed that since the first ones went up, three or four years ago, I suppose now. It's really nice, but I don't really think I've learned what this organization is. So, they probably need to do a better job of, maybe, informing people who are coming to these things, what it's about." These points of confusion that happened when participants experienced the event would likely be lost in our interpretation if we studied only the documented evidence provided by Emerging Terrain. Accessing these sentiments at the event troubled the "official" record and highlights the potential of the field as a focus for rhetorical inquiry. Although the bridge, the grain elevators, and I-80 performed a unifying function for Elevate, it also created space for and put in conversation the distinct rhetorics of the food stations, which ranged from celebrating the comfort foods of the immigrant populations in South Omaha (see fig. 1.1) to combining nostalgic agrarian aesthetics with contemporary foodie culture (see fig. 1.3). Mixing these food experiences (i.e., rustic, home-crafted food-stuffs intermingled with elite culinary practices, which further blended into the sights and smells of food trucks) represented them as coequal culinary practices. A station constructed to reproduce the feeling of a trendy bar scene with giant red cubes stood alongside one that used skateboards as a delivery method and another that appeared to be a greenhouse made of Bubble Wrap. For guests, the equal space given to each of these stations disrupted the class boundaries implied by each (even as it reproduced problematic racial and class distinctions between different sections of Omaha, as we discuss below). Engaging these rhetorical fragments materially makes accessible the view from the overpass, the competing discourses of the food stations, the negotiations between organizers and participants, and the enjoyment and confusion of guests. They expose the polysemy confronted by critics concerned with *in situ* rhetorical inquiry. By seeing the field as a place that performs, we can define, delimit, and gather artifacts in ways that record formerly unavailable rhetorics. While our argument builds on previous claims from rhetorical critics about accessing formerly suppressed artifacts, we extend this theorizing by emphasizing the rhetorical value to be found in the role that the field itself plays in the complex circulations of artifacts in the field.

How Can the Experiential Nature of the Field Be Represented?

Embodied, emplaced practices in the field that are recorded textually and digitally challenge rhetorical critics attempting to analyze the ephemeral and spontaneous meanings they represent. The rhetoricity of an embodied, emplaced, live event is always a gestalt that seems just out of the reach of the critic. For example, to analyze one piece of art or one food station falls short of the extra-discursive dimensions of the complete rhetorical experience (see figs. 1.1, 1.2, and 1.3). Two examples illuminate the troubling task of representing artifacts when we understand that the field does rhetorical work.

First, the physical place created at each food station performed much of the heavy lifting in terms of cultivating unique experiences for participants (see figs. 1.1, 1.2, and 1.3), but that was not easy to capture or represent. At the food station shown in figure 1.3, designers presented wooden pallets that contained jars of food for the event. Each lid said "elevATE 2012" on it (emphasizing the event's themes), and guests ate the pickled vegetables directly out of these jars. The group's canning efforts communicate the themes of small batches, slow preparation, and local-mindedness privileged by the event. Likewise, this food station linked its food with the nostalgia of homegrown, family-style cooking implied by the food canning process and the informal presentation of the food. In addition to photographing the station and taking notes about

FIG. 1.3 This organization served food in mason jars; the use of glass, metal, wood, and hay develops a nostalgic aesthetic. Photo by Samantha Senda-Cook.

the reactions of the guests, the mingling sounds of conversations and highway traffic, and the heat of the sun on the exposed bridge, Samantha—one of the co-authors who attended the event—interviewed people present. The designer of this station explained his collaboration with the chef to link the food with its presentation. They sought to evoke a

> memory association with having, like, this rustic foodstuffs that you have from your youth paired with, like, precision of craft. And so we took that idea and went with these bucolic, agrarian motifs of hay and wood pallets, and, um, juxtaposed them against finely crafted, finished wood that was painted white, um, to really contrast against the hay and steel and cables to facilitate the way that, um, you'd almost do this hunter gatherer, like, um, action of acquiring the food. So, we didn't want to plate anything traditionally, but go more towards the primitive, shared psyche.

Calling to mind imagery associated with a mythical (raced and classed) past, this group intermingled the tastes of food with the textures of wood and the smells of the hay. This earthy, somewhat sweet smell was misplaced both seasonally and proximally since it was summer in the city, not autumn on a farm. Coming close to this station piqued the interest of passersby because this distinct smell was incongruent with the rest of the event. Conceptualizing the field as a place necessitates recording the physical elements that contribute to the meaning of the experience. Likewise, it burdens the critic with attempting to relay to the reader the experiential dimensions of the event that informed the rhetorical experience encountered by the critic.

While the first example focuses on the sense of place created at the food stations, the second example addresses a more encompassing rhetorical place: the bridge itself. In choosing this location for Elevate, the organizers literally chose the high road, the overpass that goes over the highway, the means of delivering people and products across the country. The bridge functions literally and metaphorically as a way to connect and elevate. In this case, it joins both neighborhoods and abstract concepts such as food and transportation. It elevates diners, placing them literally above the highway, while it creates the opportunity to demonstrate a "higher" level of thinking. Organizers wanted diners to enjoy a better way of life, full of slow, delicious food, grown locally, prepared in small batches and served in a politically minded, artistic way. Coordinating these efforts to happen on an overpass emphasizes the opportunity to elevate our way of eating. In this basic, physical way, Elevate relied on the performance of the place itself to (temporarily) transform the normal practices of eating to an elevated, unique experience. The wind on the bridge was tempered by the food stations' structures, but the sounds of the highway constantly mixed with the sounds of dinnerware clinking and conversations happening. The concrete on which participants stood contributed a feeling of a street festival or block party while the view reminded participants they were above the traffic. Walking on the road of a bridge rather than driving on it or walking on the sidewalk of it shifted participants' experience of the bridge, skewing what the physical design of the bridge usually communicates (e.g., the fenced-off sidewalk that keeps pedestrians in their place and the road that keeps cars in their place). This field-based shift in experience does not easily translate to written words.

Attempting to capture and analyze the disparate parts of emplaced, temporally bound events makes defending claims and providing evidence difficult because the critic cannot reproduce the experience of touching a wooden pallet or of smelling hay while eating food. We depend on the reproducible—pictures of spatial relationships, quotes from speeches, tidbits from conversations—to support our arguments. When our descriptions of sensations and feelings become our evidence, we must reinvent representational practices. Gathering the threads of many kinds of material evidence around one abstract theme, pattern, or argument requires creative, generative thinking and careful documentation. In addition to these typical responsibilities, critics must consider the effect of the field and try to faithfully render the feelings, glances, and other un-documentable features of live rhetoric that make spaces overflow with potential layers of meaning.

Whose Needs Are Prioritized by Publicizing the (Often Vernacular or Hidden) Rhetorical Practices Enacted in the Field?

When we conceive of the field as a place, we acknowledge that it actualizes, oppresses, encourages, and undermines different groups of people. As Shome states, "Space is not merely a backdrop . . . against which the communication of cultural politics occurs. Rather, it needs to be recognized as a central component in that communication. It functions as a technology . . . of power that is socially constituted through material relations that enable . . . specific politics."[24] Rhetorical fields that confront dominant meanings of place, such as a bridge as a place for cars, challenge and remake place on a daily or hourly basis, as opposed to the comparative durability of institutionalized, normalized place meanings.[25] For example, Elevate temporarily disrupted normalized notions of transportation and urban space through ephemeral displays that can be experienced for only a limited amount of time. For most, Elevate was a one-day event to enjoy a unique dining experience and engage in some artistically minded advocacy. Yet the organizers of this event sought to make their message durable via their website and in the form of the more permanent grain elevator art that the event was designed to celebrate. The art covered twenty-five grain elevators and featured images of different forms of transportation, notably a space shuttle, a train, trucks, a horse and buggy, cars, boats, and planes. Some emphasized themes of nature with dandelions blowing in the wind or hexagonal patterns. A different local artist designed each sheet. As seen in figure 1.4, together the sheets of grain elevator art employ many artistic styles and represent many variations on the theme of food and transportation. By placing images of food next to images of transportation, these art pieces emphasize the connection that our society often overlooks. The grain elevator art remained visible from I-80 when traveling east and from the bridge on which Elevate took place for several months, but it was eventually removed because Emerging Terrain disbanded and no other group stepped forward to care for the public art. Those who attended the event or who read the news coverage interpreted the art as a reminder both of the event and of what it represented. For others, this trace of the event continued to provoke questions. The grain elevator art made a more permanent alteration to place than did the event.[26] This and other more durable alterations create new symbolic landscapes and potentially challenge the politics of the material structures they co-opt. What are essentially the decaying structures of industrial farming took on a new meaning when coated with large sheets of artwork that subtly

FIG. 1.4 The view of the grain elevators, highway, and rail lines from the overpass. Photo by Samantha Senda-Cook.

challenged relationships between food and transportation by depicting images of gasoline flooding a city, an ear of corn attached to a space shuttle, and fractal wing patterns next to an aerial view of farms across a landscape. The challenge is especially relevant in Nebraska, where swaths of land, devoted to farming, exist among countless rural food deserts.[27] The transformation of the grain elevators endeavored to provoke both diners at Elevate and drivers on I-80 to reconsider the relationships between food and transportation. Yet, as Shome contends, the field can simultaneously challenge and reinforce certain norms and assumptions. While temporarily challenging norms of transportation and food systems in place, Elevate also served to reinforce the economic privilege of its majority white participants.

The field encourages rhetoricians to conduct rhetorical criticism in ways that reflect the uncertainty of the field itself. Regardless of whether we focus on it, the field reflects the norms and processes of culture, creating both dominant and marginalized positions. The field is politically charged in ways that enable and constrain rhetorical possibility, and in ways that may not be perceivable in textual artifacts alone. For example, the sighs and sweat of those working this event contrasted sharply with the guests' laughter and freedom of movement, reinforcing conventional class distinctions between leisure and work. Organizations with more funding could create structures to protect them from the sun, but some workers, particularly volunteers from nonprofits that could not afford a large-scale structure (see fig. 1.1, for example), struggled with sunburn and thirst all day. One seasoned volunteer, talking to Samantha two years later, described this event as "the worst day of my life." Even those who were paid for their labor looked hassled and frazzled much of the time, serving and rushing "backstage" along the sidewalk to grab something from a vehicle or use a bathroom a few blocks away. Those who paid for the privilege to eat dinner on a bridge appeared to enjoy the day, but for those who did not or could not, the day effectively marginalized their existence. For some the event relied on both economic resources and leisure time they did not have; for others the closing of the bridge was simply another impediment to their efforts to conduct their daily lives. Conceiving of the field as place offers rhetoricians a chance to investigate the construction of the field as a rhetorical act, bringing the same critical advantages to what often goes ignored. For instance, Emerging Terrain created a place to critique dominant social practices and simultaneously enforced problematic hierarchies. The event revealed the double-edged sword of elevating—that is, someone else must always be "lower than." Being in the field expands critics' opportunities to articulate and critique the material enactment of these politics.

Conclusion

Entering the "field" challenges both conventional theories of rhetoric and rhetoricians themselves. In this essay we further theorized these challenges by thinking through the field as a rhetorical place in addition to a location to which a critic goes to collect rhetorical artifacts or observe the context for embodied (verbal and nonverbal) messages. In this sense, we argue that the field is a co-participant in rhetorical dynamics because of its own rhetoricity and its function in constraining and enabling the other rhetorical messages circulating in the field. We used one extended example to illustrate how entering the field prompts us to acknowledge and account for the messiness of the field, the circulating (extra)verbal rhetorical artifacts that constitute the experience of being there, the fluidity of rhetorical practices, and the politicization of live(d) rhetorics that are sometimes lost in their textualization.

Elevate joins a number of artifacts that continue to push rhetorical theory and criticism to expand our understanding of the role of materiality in rhetoric. As rhetorical criticism rounds the bend on the material turn,[28] we suggest that it is imperative for us to examine our assumptions, criticism, and fieldwork in light of an emphasis not just on the material consequentiality of rhetoric or the material conditions that intersect with rhetoric but also on the *material experience* of being a part of live(d) rhetoric. Rhetoric as it happens in the field is multi-modal, multi-sensual, emplaced, and temporally bound. While perspectives that examine the circulation and dissemination of rhetorical artifacts beyond their initial instantiation offer immense value, part of our goal in interrogating the field has been to better understand rhetoric in a physical, embodied, and emplaced sense. Fieldwork gives critics more access to the immediate material experience of situated rhetorical invention, audiences, and evaluation than do traditional rhetorical criticism approaches that draw primarily on textual representations, reconstructed context, and imagined audiences. Amid the current groundswell of critical investigation into the rhetoricity of bodies, places, affects, and sensations—topics that often intersect with materiality— we suggest that the field in which rhetoric happens is a significant factor in the material experience of rhetoric.

Attending to the rhetoricity of the field offers several implications for thinking through theories of the materiality of rhetoric. First, conceptualizing the field as a place offers an important reminder that the location of rhetoric matters for how we experience it and how it cocreates that experience.[29] Place functions as a social actor in a milieu of raced and classed bodies, physical structures, senses, and meanings that is always producing rhetorics to be reinforced or resisted. Thinking about the materiality of rhetoric, then, is not just a question of considering the preconditions for rhetoric or the consequences of rhetoric, but the spaces in between, the in-the-moment experiences. These experiences are inevitably messy, fluid, and polysemous not only because they are a swirl of intersecting artifacts in a particular field, but also because of the subjectivity of experience had by each participant in the field, as well as the multiple meanings and interpretations brought to the field by the participants in it.

Second, thinking about the material experience of rhetoric in relation to field as place brings in the concomitant consideration of temporality. Space and time are frequently seen as mutually constitutive phenomena. In this case, we see that the material experience of rhetoric influences and is influenced by a field that is time-bound. The material elements of Elevate existed together for just one day. Although it provided a material experience, the event was not durable in the sense of creating a permanent change in the meaning of the place; the bridge returned to its normal function once the event was cleaned up and cleared away. The durability of the highway, rail lines, and bridges emphasizes the cultural importance of speedy transportation for people and products. By contrast, the grain elevator art, one of the remnants of this challenge to dominant systems, has been removed in the face of a lack of funds to clean and maintain it.[30] In other words, those structures perceived as or made to be durable carry weight and indicate cultural importance. While traditional approaches to rhetorical criticism attend to durable texts, exemplars that stand the test of time, such a focus can shift attention away from the ephemeral and temporary material experience of embodied, emplaced rhetoric in the field. Interestingly, by documenting this event on its website, Emerging Terrain attempts to make its ephemeral event more powerful through durability. However, as we demonstrated in the analysis, this digital representation of the event neglects some rich details within the material event itself. Because they are an important part of how rhetoric works in the everyday world, those things that are left behind, that are difficult to express, that do not stand the test of time, should be included in our theories of material rhetoric. Fieldwork, and more specifically seeing the field as a rhetorical place, gives access to different forms of material rhetoric—those material experiences that come between preconditions and consequences.

In addition to its implications for material rhetoric, the field raises important considerations for rhetorical critics. Being in the field unceasingly confronts the critic with the reality that live(d) rhetorical practices produce unique types of data and that criticism's conceit is its effort to capture rhetoric in a stable, analyzable form. The description above illustrates some of the rhetorical forces revealed during data collection that are not accounted for when relying on textual traces after the fact, namely, the role of the field itself as a rhetorical actor. Artifacts in this case could be all or just some of the following: interviews, material structures made just for the day, durable material structures (e.g., the bridge), pieces of art that hang on grain elevators, and food presentation strategies. The experiential encounters with these textual fragments constitute the body of artifacts that then come to represent Elevate after the fact. Scholars choosing to venture into the field are confronted with the ongoing struggle between a desire to include the experiential insights and the constraints of representing communities in scholarly publications. Reflecting on his article about homelessness and citizenship, Middleton explains that returning from the field required choosing from those texts that often richly informed a critical understanding of the community a more limited set of artifacts that would effectively focus on the political interventions of the homeless activists.[31] We contend that by complicating our understanding of the rich rhetoricity of the "field," rhetorical critics can better position themselves to resolve these challenges in ways that illuminate the topics that attract their engagement.

Rhetorical Field Methods
in the Tradition of *Imitatio*

Joshua P. Ewalt,
Jessy J. Ohl, and
Damien Smith Pfister

[Scene] Occupy Lincoln Protest, Downtown
Lincoln, Nebraska, October 15, 2011.

OCCUPIER 2: [Approaches microphone set up on stairs of the Capitol.] Alright everyone, we are about to get started. First, thanks for coming today to join in solidarity with Occupy protesters across the country and across the entire world! Remember, the people, united, will never be defeated! We are going to march downtown throughout the business district and then turn back and regroup at the governor's mansion. This is a peaceful protest so please don't litter, block traffic, or engage counterprotestors at all. Be loud and be proud! Are you ready? LET'S GO!!!

ANDA: Alright, John. Get excited. This is where the real work begins.

[As they march, they pass Occupier 3, dressed
in black and wearing a devil mask.]

JOHN: Oh jeez . . .

ANDA: Hey. What's your costume about?

OCCUPIER 3: I'm supposed to be a corporate devil.

ANDA: Oh, that's cool.

OCCUPIER 3: Yeah . . . not many people get it.

ANDA: Well it makes for good discussion.[1] [Devil walks off.]

JOHN: You don't really think that do you?

ANDA: What do you mean?

JOHN: "Makes for good discussion"? That sort of stuff makes people think we should be laughed at, not listened to. You can't have a meaningful dialogue with someone wearing a costume.

ANDA: Come on, sure you can. Relax, John. It's fun. It's a conversation starter. Besides, he's expressing himself in a creative way. He's getting people to think about how they see things. He got our attention, didn't he?

JOHN: Yeah, but not in a good way. Drunken streakers get attention. Masked anarchists throwing bricks through Starbucks' windows get attention. But they don't get taken seriously. He has the right to dress and act how he wants, but let's be honest, that behavior only helps those who say this movement is just a bunch of crazy college kids with no message and nothing better to do. I mean what if a picture of that guy lands on the front page of the newspaper tomorrow?

ANDA: I dunno, no more Catholic supporters?

JOHN: My grandma already suspects that Satan is behind Occupy Wall Street.

ANDA: Well, think about it this way: having diverse personalities gives us strength. It means we are flexible and inviting and then we can attract more people to our cause. That's what made this thing global. If we are too controlling and restrictive then people will choose to do other stuff.

JOHN: Maybe . . .

ANDA: At the very least, it's important given our society's short attention span. Sometimes the only thing that gets the ball rolling is that spark that grabs the public's attention.

JOHN: Color me skeptical, but I don't think weird leads to real discussion.

ANDA: Well—

OCCUPIER 1: SHOW ME WHAT DEMOCRACY LOOKS LIKE!

OCCUPIER 2–12: THIS IS WHAT DEMOCRACY LOOKS LIKE!

OCCUPIER 1: SHOW ME WHAT DEMOCRACY LOOKS LIKE!

ANDA: Come on, John. It's ok.

OCCUPIER 2–12: THIS IS WHAT DEMOCRACY LOOKS LIKE![2]

This opening excerpt, a dialogical encounter between the composited characters of Anda and John over the Occupy movement's commitment to both direct action and consensus-based decision-making, is an example of "rhetorical scenes," or performative dramatizations of rhetoric-in-action. In 2013 we published an essay, "Activism, Deliberation, and Networked Public Screens: Rhetorical Scenes from the Occupy Moment in Lincoln, Nebraska," with five such scenes drawn from the protests, conversations, encampments, and digital social networking sites we observed during Occupy Lincoln in 2011. "Activism, Deliberation, and Networked Public Screens" is our effort to register overlaps and tensions between activism and deliberation as communicative performances in the context of a global social movement. One issue we grappled with while crafting these scenes was how the broader rhetorical tradition could animate encounters with, and scholarly reporting of, the symbolic activity encountered in the field.[3]

In this essay we contend that one way to retain a distinctively critical-rhetorical orientation to field methods is through the tradition of *imitatio*. *Imitatio* presumes that certain rhetorical exemplars—historically, public addresses by the privileged—are worthy of study and emulation in order to improve the civic habits of a citizenry. Rhetorical field methods, with their emphasis on studying the live rhetoric of vernacular communities, offer an opportunity to craft texts suitable for *imitatio* beyond the subjects and contexts historically authorized for emulation.[4] Drawing from our experience with Occupy Lincoln, we argue that crafting rhetorical scenes appropriates one of rhetoric's oldest and most dexterous traditions—the use of *imitatio* in rhetorical training and practice—toward more democratic ends. We will ultimately call this approach "vernacular *imitatio*" to distinguish it from what might be called the "institutional *imitatio*" of traditional rhetorical pedagogy.

To democratize *imitatio* by developing dramatizations of rhetoric-in-action invites scholars to think about inscription in two ways: composing rhetorical scenes *as imitatio* (distinguished from composing as representation) and composing rhetorical scenes *for imitatio* (encouraging textual, performative, and/or embodied citations of "rhetoric-in-action"). This essay unfolds in three parts: first, we recount our method of crafting scenes; second, we unpack this method in light of three relations between model and copy that inhere in the imitative encounter; third, we highlight the potential of developing a tradition of vernacular *imitatio*. Our argument is not only a call for more performative approaches to scholarly writing, but for rhetoricians to write in such a way as to embrace and encourage the ethic of improvement that accompanies the tradition of *imitatio*. In a modest imitation of Michael Calvin McGee, we assert that studying material rhetorical activity in the field offers an opportunity for critics to focus on inventing not only an "apparently finished discourse" that is "suitable for criticism," but also one that is suitable *as* and *for* imitation.[5]

Crafting Rhetorical Scenes

In October 2011, at the beginning of Occupy's encampment in Lincoln, Nebraska, we entered the field as participant observers to both record and contribute to live rhetorical activity. Our attunement to the rich symbolic ecology of Occupy resulted in a vast array of detailed field notes concerning chants, speeches, public conversations, our own reflections, photographs of signs and marches, casual conversations, and other rhetorical performances. We followed the flow of rhetorical exchange as it moved through layered iterations of embodied, mass-mediated, and digitally mediated sites of communication. We also conducted informal interviews with selected participants and accessed a video recording of the first Occupy General Assembly meeting.

After attending formal and informal events throughout the first two weeks of Occupy Lincoln and reflecting on our collected field notes, we identified a series of notable moments where activism and deliberation intertwined in this branch of Occupy. The challenge was to synthesize and textualize our observations in a way that did justice to the richness and dynamism of the event, while also bringing clarity to looming theoretical questions about this particular instantiation of protest. We felt this challenge acutely, as we had recently read Iris Marion Young's "Activist Challenges to Deliberative Democracy" together.[6] For all the strengths of Young's essay, which adheres to conventional norms of expository, argument-driven scholarship, we found ourselves wanting to witness how an actual dialogue would unfold between the two subject positions of activist and deliberative democrat that Young thematizes. We thought that Occupy's post-bureaucratic organizational form, created and sustained by a range of rhetorical actions, was especially amenable to an imitation of Young's piece in a more performative, dialogical mode.

Moreover, we came to realize that rhetorical field methods' embrace of "post-textual" objects of analysis invited scholarly experimentation. If rhetorical field methods move beyond textual hermeneutics to accommodate the turn to embodiment and embeddedness—to affect and ecology—then how might scholarly inscriptions of our research in the field similarly push against and beyond the exegetical frame?[7] It seemed to us that crafting scenes through performative writing, grounded in field observations but artistically refigured, was one way to account for the complicated dynamism of Occupy Lincoln's rhetorical ecology.[8] That we might *craft* rhetorical scenes nods to the legacy of creative nonfiction, as our process involved taking fragments of experience encountered in the field and weaving them into a composite whole that inventively reimagines and synthesizes actual rhetorical activity.[9] As we reinscribed rhetorical displays within our dialogue, we sometimes repeated the communicative activity of the field without modification. At other times we synthesized multiple observations into invented dialogue between characters that captured rhetorical dynamics—and tensions—unfolding in Occupy Lincoln.

By employing the phrase "rhetorical scenes," originally used in Peter Simonson's ethnographic account of the 2008 Democratic primaries in South Texas, we aim to access the double meaning inherent in the term "scene."[10] The first sense of "scene" can be understood in Burkeian terms as a type of container that "*realistically reflects* the course of action and *symbolizes* it."[11] When writing about the material scenes of rhetorical activity, we translated our observations into a written text. Each scene was grounded in a particular issue of relevance that emerged during Occupy Lincoln, such as the relative value of spectacle, the tension between activism and consensus, and embodied versus digitally mediated activism. In this regard, our collaboratively written scenes functioned as an imitation of the vernacular rhetorical activity in the field. The second sense of scene refers more explicitly to our efforts in crafting a text that invites performance. For Della Pollock, the incorporation of performance sensibilities into ethnography has "moved the *writing* in the 'writing of culture' into a performance frame such that performance ethnography . . . not only allows for but requires various sensuous retellings and ongoing re-creations, in word and body."[12] In the same way, rhetorical scenes provide the means for embodied and sensuous retelling, or subsequent *imitations*. And that leads us to a significant distinction: these are *rhetorical* scenes—not performative scenes, or dramatistic scenes—and it is the method's relation to the tradition of *imitatio* that legitimizes the use of "rhetorical" as a modifier. As we explain in the next section, the significance of crafting rhetorical scenes is about more than performative writing; it is about crafting scenes *as* and *for* imitation, which unifies the drive to reflect what occurred in the field with the *telos* of improving rhetorical activity.

Scenes as and for *Imitatio*

Imitatio's central role in rhetorical studies stems primarily from the work of Isocrates, Quintilian, and Cicero. These ancient rhetoricians conceived of *imitatio* as the key lever for rhetorical pedagogy. In the wake of these rhetorical luminaries, citizens have long been taught that emulation of great speeches is the surest route to their own rhetorical excellence. Although the Greek word *mimesis* is often translated as "imitation," which evokes visions of faithful reproduction, the possible relationships between model, copy, and imitator are more subtle. John Muckelbauer's nuanced discussion of the three relations between model and copy generated by an imitative encounter—"repetition-of-the-same," "repetition-of-difference," and "difference and repetition"— illustrates how *imitatio* necessarily enfolds reproduction, variation, and inspiration.[13] As Muckelbauer notes, these three relations—different rhythms of *imitatio*—often converge in a "chorus" around a single act of imitation but can be disentangled for analytical purposes.[14] Each relation is present in our effort to capture the rhetorical dynamics of Occupy Lincoln.

Repetition-of-the-Same in Rhetorical Scenes

The first kind of *imitatio* traced by Muckelbauer encourages the exact replication of the original, or "repetition-of-the-same." In this relation between model and copy, students of rhetoric are encouraged to repeat a discourse, remaining faithful to the model in order to duplicate the best features of the exemplar in future rhetorical situations. While recognizing the impossibility of creating exact replicas, Plato tolerates this kind of imitation in Book X of *The Republic* because the intent is to come as close to the ideal form as possible.[15] Erasmus similarly attempted to develop the tongue's muscle memory when he instructed students to recite passages four separate times with the hope that the stylistic and moral proficiencies embedded in the text would become habit.[16] In "repetition-of-the-same," any deviation from the original is grounds for correction to align students with the cultural orthodoxy forwarded in the model.

Isocrates, according to Robert Hariman, likened this type of imitative practice as mindless reiteration on par with the forced regurgitation of the alphabet.[17] Nonetheless, repetition-of-the-same has a rich legacy in rhetorical education because this rhythm of *imitatio* familiarizes students with a cultural encounter. Cicero famously identifies the moral stakes of exact imitation by pointing to the process of matching texts and qualities to the needs of each student. Cicero does not consider *if* imitation should take place, but instead poses the question, "Whom should we imitate?"[18] For Elaine Fantham, Cicero's *De Oratore* underlines the importance of careful text selection because, in order to "realize the maximum potential of the young orator, a fusion of his [sic] natural tendencies with the right kind of imitation was needed."[19] Thus, replicating discourse with an ethic of fidelity to the original is useful insofar as it allows the student to become consubstantial with a discourse, "until certain voices . . . feel familiar."[20] Inhabiting others' voices runs the risk of "speaking for others," yet it can also expand critical horizons and empathy as it literalizes perspective-taking—especially when the models for *imitatio* are expanded beyond the privileged and institutional.[21]

Our crafting of rhetorical scenes embraces "repetition-of-the-same" insofar as we include select pieces of dialogue, discourse, and performance of participants, drawn verbatim from our field notes, into the written language of the text. For instance, in the above excerpt, the initial questioning about the devil's costume by Occupier 2, and the chant toward the end of the scene, both repeat material exactly as it was recorded in the field. In the original piece, the beginning of our second scene is a transcript of the first General Assembly from a video recording made accessible to us. In our fourth scene, we reproduce various status updates and comments from Occupiers copied from Facebook posts. Thus, through precise repetition, reproductive imitation resonates with the goal of field methods to capture in greater detail live rhetorical activity that actually occurred in the field. Readers, then, are subsequently invited to repeat the discourse exactly as it happened in the field. As Dwight Conquergood notes, there is traditionally a disjunction "between the Being There of performed experience and the Being Here of written texts."[22] The crafting of rhetorical scenes *as performances* that repeat communicative fragments with the aim of precision attempts to bridge this disjuncture, facilitating an imitative encounter between the rhetors in the field and the reader-performers of our scenes.[23]

Repetition–of–Difference in Rhetorical Scenes

Although the imitative relation of reproduction, or "repetition-of-the-same," acknowledges the infeasibility of creating identical copies (since the reproduction at least takes place in a different time and space), it still lionizes fidelity. A second relation of imitation explored by Muckelbauer actively values differentiation. Rather than approaching variation as a detriment, "repetition-of-difference," or differentiated imitation, embraces the modification of the model as a rhetorically and politically vital activity. This relation between model and copy emphasizes *iteration*. For Jacques Derrida, iteration refers to the capacity of written language to simultaneously repeat and to become different; to imitate an original utterance with some distinction ties "repetition to alterity."[24] Indeed, differentiated imitation permits a speech act to be, in Derrida's words, "abandoned to its essential drift," preserving the ability to function differently in new contexts.[25]

In the ancient world, Quintilian was perhaps the most eloquent advocate for a practice of *imitatio* that creatively adapted the original text. Quintilian's ideal orator does not simply copy a speech. Instead they modify it, because, as Quintilian notes, there is no need to be "immediately convinced that everything that great authors have said is necessarily perfect; for they sometimes make a false step, or sink under their burden, or give way to the inclination of their genius."[26] For Quintilian, the imitation of multiple speeches expands the rhetorical repertoire of citizens by encouraging adaptation: "Since it is practically impossible for mortal powers to produce a perfect and complete copy of any one chosen author, we shall do well to keep a number of different excellences before our eyes, so that different qualities from different authors may impress themselves on our minds, to be adopted for use in the place that becomes them best."[27] Thus, through alteration, iteration, and improvement, the goal is to recognize that the original model has to be made different and can be adapted to fit emergent situations.

How might field methodologists produce scholarly texts from observations of vernacular rhetoric while embracing the differentiation inherent to this mode of *imitatio*? The process of crafting rhetorical scenes follows this imitative rhythm insofar as written scholarly texts are considered workable *iterations*. The potential for such an intervention to generate theoretical insight is profound because, as Rob Pope suggests, "the best way to understand how a text works is to change it: to play around with it, to intervene in it in some way (large or small), and then to try to account for the exact effect of what you have done."[28] Crafting rhetorical scenes combines actual instances of dialogue with inventions from the critic, which occupies a middle ground between fabrication and duplication in order to locate "instances where spaces can be opened up."[29] In our case, because Young's confrontations between activists and deliberative democrats served as a theoretical backdrop, each scene was a creatively nonfictionalized conversation between two or more characters that reflected the presence of these observed tensions in Occupy Lincoln.[30] Whereas some parts of the scenes engage in repetition-of-the-same by repeating actual words/phrases uttered in the field, some of the other dialogue in the excerpt above is invented in the spirit of creative nonfiction. For instance, we witnessed the devil mask episode in the above excerpt, but the extended observations between Anda and John about the value of spectacle in social protest are largely crafted by us (though supported by additional events in the field). Each time the scene is performed it repeats the Occupy march, making it "live" again, but does so differently, self-consciously inflected by our reading of Iris Marion Young's work. It is, without a doubt, a *differentiated* imitation of the original event, an iteration invested in embracing the political and textual potentiality that accompanies indeterminacy.

Given the tradition of *differentiated* imitation, we should note that our own rhetorical scenes can and should be refined and improved. Subsequent iterations—readings, performances, and rewritings in different places and times—can themselves become imitations of our inscription of the scenes and could similarly be anchored to an ethic of differentiation: How could Anda and John have acted otherwise when confronted by the devil mask? Or, more radically, are the "activist" and "deliberative democrat" even the right subjectivities to capture the tensions of Occupy? How can their rhetoric be repeated differently, made better? Rhetorical scenes like the excerpt provided are not static artifacts: they are written to be remixed and revised in the tradition of *imitatio* itself. This kind of reconstructive-performative practice of reporting fieldwork usefully complements the deconstructive-analytic processes of much scholarly writing.[31]

Difference and Repetition in Rhetorical Scenes

"Difference and repetition" is the final dimension of imitation, which Muckelbauer describes as a moment of inspiration that "transmits itself through a kind of infectious quality."[32] Whereas "repetition-of-the-same" privileges fidelity to the original through the act of reproduction, and "repetition-of-difference" emphasizes differentiation through variation, adaptation, improvement, and iteration, "difference and repetition" draws attention to how *imitatio* inspires the subject. Importantly, this third relation of *imitatio* is immanent to the other two, as "this [inspirational] encounter only happens through these other movements of imitation."[33] For the ancients, the explanation for this transformative power of *imitatio* lies in the activity of the muses: the model inspires through some divine power—not fully explainable, but potent nonetheless.[34] This relation highlights how imitation does not just aid a rhetor in producing rhetoric, for it produces the conditions of responsiveness itself.[35] Thus, whereas repetition-of-difference focuses on how the rhetor changes the text, difference-and-repetition highlights how engaging with the text through *imitatio* reconfigures the rhetor as an affectively and strategically differentiated subject. At its best, then, *imitatio* produces or enhances the capacity of rhetors to respond in ways that strengthen the communicative infrastructures of democratic public culture.

Although the temporality of inspiration is one of futurity, to be actualized in one's responses to subsequent situations, even the most basic processes of imitation can instill a capacity for responsiveness. The mimetic exercise of memorization, for instance, is instructive of the process of transformation at the center of "repetition and difference." Memorization was not merely a cold informatic practice for the ancients, but a "learning by heart" wherein the student becomes consubstantial with the material they have internalized.[36] Robert Terrill points to the inspirational force of memorization when he claims, "A discourse that has been memorized does not simply reside within the student as an inert or benign parasite, but instead actually exerts a transformative impact, altering the discourse produced by the student, much as the DNA of some viruses intermingles with their hosts."[37] Following the logic of *imitatio*, subjectivity is not a reflection of an internal essence, but is instead woven from the threads of favored movie quotations, song lyrics, adages, lines from speeches, and *topoi* that citizens rely on and turn to for identity, purpose, and direction. These symbolic resources both change the subject and travel with them, "spontaneously appearing, as it were, out of their hoarded treasure."[38] Memorization of speeches similarly funds the composition of the subject, potentially intensifying the capacity to respond to future situations.

Thus the *telos* of *imitatio* is transmutation, a call to make the text, reader, and rhetors in the field differently consubstantial with one another. We think producing rhetorical scenes can instill a different kind of responsiveness, a responsiveness to the conditions of power that we seek to reconfigure and to the rhetoric capable of generating and sustaining such reconfigurations. A reader of rhetorical scenes, engaging the text with a different voice and emphasis within the rhythms of *imitatio*, "doesn't so much *learn* rhetoric," in David Fleming's terms, "as *becomes* rhetorical."[39] For us, becoming rhetorical means becoming a subject that imitates persuasive vernacular discourse, thus expanding one's imaginative horizon, responsiveness to the conditions of power, and corresponding communicative repertoire. A rhetorical scene is not a playbook, but a playhouse where the motivation to change can take form. Claiming that our rhetorical scenes about Occupy Lincoln are inspirational is more than a bit self-aggrandizing; however, we think that the practice of reciting and modifying these scenes of vernacular discourse activates a constitutive *praxis*—a consideration of what *did*, *could*, and *should* happen, and perhaps a motivation to see that change take place. In the context of the above excerpt, in becoming-Anda or becoming-John, the reader becomes, however momentarily, a vernacular subject considering the value of spectacle in contemporary protest.

Toward a Vernacular Tradition of *Imitatio*

Crafting rhetorical scenes is a method of rhetorical analysis that uses field-work to develop a *vernacular* tradition of *imitatio*. The turn to rhetorical field methods offers an opportunity to rearticulate *imitatio*—to imitate *imitatio* differentially—in a way that privileges vernacular rhetorical activity over the traditional exemplars of the powerful. The notion of vernacular *imitatio* is quite distant from Greco-Roman pedagogy, given that the focus is predominantly on everyday citizens who may have no specific claim to fame, social notoriety, or rhetorical training. Indeed, there was no proto-Pericles or Caesar-to-be in Occupy Lincoln, which is precisely the point of the horizontal organizational structuring and nonrepresentational politics of many contemporary social movements. Rather, rhetorical scenes are a form of vernacular imitation, a "bottom-up" and polyvocal embodiment of live rhetorical activity that displaces the centrality of the liberal humanist subject to be endlessly emulated. Yet, at the same time that vernacular imitation elevates the voices of everyday activists, it maintains a *telos* of revision alongside reverence, suggesting that we not uncritically substitute genuflection to the established and powerful with veneration of the everyday and unknown.

What kinds of methodological and pedagogical insights can be gleaned by turning the imitative impulse to vernacular rhetors arguing for social justice? All three rhythms—"repetition-of-the-same," "repetition-of-difference," and "difference and repetition"—are required to develop a robust tradition of vernacular *imitatio*. First, repetition-of-the-same creates textual fragments worthy of repetition. One key challenge for the study of vernacular rhetorical fragments in the tradition of *imitatio* is that there is often no text to be mimicked. For example, how is a student of rhetoric supposed to imitate protest discourse utilized during a march? Indeed, one can watch old protest marches in documentary films, but writing materializes discourse in such a way that it can be studied, scrutinized, performed, and revised. Because the audience may never be able to directly observe the field, repetition-of-the-same positions the critic in the role of a translator responsible for producing texts that repeat with some fidelity what happened in the field.

If repetition-of-the-same positions the critic as translator, then repetition-of-difference situates the critic as an iterator. In order to develop a tradition of vernacular *imitatio*, field scholars must also embrace the iterability of differentiated imitation: the writings we produce are inevitably going to be, and might be purposefully composed as, different from that which was originally observed and documented. The critic-as-iterator frame requires scholars to acknowledge that what participant observers produce are selective accounts *and* that the very process of scholarly production affects the continued existence of the rhetorical event through its textual inscription. When critics write about the symbolic behaviors of social movements, for instance, their texts become part of the extended life of the movement, a material emerging from the interactive forces of the movement, which allows for the event's continued existence in a different medium (an archived writing instead of, for example, a live oral performance) that in turn becomes part of the repertoire of future movements. Scholarly texts are not just representations or windows onto live rhetoric: they are repetitions, making the rhetoric "live" again every time the text is read, but with the differentiations born from authorial inscription and new contexts.

Of course, this kind of textual intervention, reliant on differentiated *imitatio*, can be problematic when discourses are divorced entirely from their original context and meaning. But, again, the tradition of *imitatio* justifies creative liberties taken by hybridizing different rhetorical forms with distinctive experiences. Fantham argues that the ancient mimetic practice of paraphrasing was not simply a process of rewording or reinterpreting speeches from ancient speakers; it was a type of friendly competition where students attempt to surpass the model.[40] Quintilian instructs that the duty of paraphrasing is to "rival and vie with the original in the expression of the same thoughts."[41] Therefore, paraphrasing requires loose commitment to the original while also inviting consideration of rhetorical strategy and appropriateness to bring new life to the model. If the critic is an iterator, then composing rhetorical scenes will invariably repeat, alter, and—in the tradition of *imitatio*—perhaps *improve* on the original rhetorical activity. For instance, our scenes contained the suggestion that Occupiers needed to make more explicit, so as to recognize and address, the confrontation between activist and deliberative subjectivities that ultimately contributed to a dissipation of the movement.

The key benefit of creating a tradition of vernacular *imitatio* derived from rhetorical field methods is to produce models that aid the emulation of discourse transformative of the subject, increasing responsiveness to the conditions of power and social justice. When producing imitative copies of field rhetoric, the critic is both translator and iterator, inspired by the activity of the field. When the criticism is completed as translation and iteration, it becomes the model for imitation, potentially functioning as a muse for increasing the capacity and compulsion of citizens to respond against future injustice. We typically insist that our students learn theory, which, as D. Soyini Madison writes, is itself an imitative performance: "You keep trying on the language, again and again, listening, until some parts of it begin to fit your tongue."[42] And our goal in producing scholarship is almost always to advance the theory we have internalized. Both of these traditional expectations just as easily connect to the vernacular symbolic activity of the field. Turning the rhetorical activities of citizens into a text suitable for imitation allows their strategies to be theorized and improved on by our readers. In the tradition of inspiration, rhetorical scenes allow readers to imitate differently, to listen to and embody the words of those communities of rhetors so that both the words and subjects who experience them are transformed. Vernacular rhetorics can thus animate an inspirational imitative encounter.

Conclusion

Contemporary rhetorical critics often acknowledge the need to produce texts out of fragments, to study vernacular rhetorical activity, and to enter into the field to observe "live" rhetorical activity. We have argued that, as we make these methodological turns, we should maintain our discipline's commitment to *imitatio*, allowing our texts to function as facilitators of imitative encounters between the audience and the vernacular rhetors in the field. How might we intensify the imitative force of rhetorical field methods such that our research not only imitates rhetorical activity from the field but invites subsequent imitation as well? As we have illustrated, one way of doing this is to produce rhetorical scenes that respond to John Sloop's observation that we scholars have "talked ourselves out of thinking of the publication of criticism as a performance, one that alters our world in the telling."[43] If we are to utilize a field methodology that embraces imitation as its *telos*, it must also recognize that the writing of the text is a performance *and* one that invites performance, specifically performances of reproductive, differentiated, and inspired imitation. This approach is not, however, without ethical concern.

The ethical challenges involved with differentiated imitation, of observing the rhetorical activity of a vernacular community in order to extend it, alter it, and make it live again, are as profound as they are inevitable. Scholars adopting rhetorical field methods with an eye toward crafting rhetorical scenes ought to be familiar with the intense controversies and best practices in the qualitative research literature regarding informed consent, vulnerable populations, data access, and member checks—among a plenitude of other ethical issues associated with such fieldwork. The specific ethical issues related to crafting rhetorical scenes of a "creatively nonfictional" variety raise specific questions about the ethics of a textual inscription strategy that borrows freely from vernacular rhetorics without feeling bound by exactitude. How reliable are rhetorical scenes in the tradition of *imitatio*? Does embracing creativity necessitate playing fast and loose with what "actually" happened, with the attendant risk of playing too fast and too loose? Does this permissiveness risk problematic representations of participants and their rhetorical activity? Might scholars' own terministic screens produce an interpretation of an event at odds with others' observations of events in the field? Does the compression of time and dialogue sequences inherent to creative nonfictionalization disservice the richness of the phenomenon? Does compositing characters and events mar the unique singularity of a scene's constituents? These questions, and surely many more, beg more in-depth treatment than we can provide here. Nonetheless, we offer three initial lines of response to further this conversation about ethics vis-à-vis rhetorical field methods in the tradition of *imitatio*.

First, most critiques that can be levied against *imitatio* can be levied against any written analysis of field observations (and, indeed, to qualitative and even critical-rhetorical scholarship *writ* large) because every act of textual inscription *is* an act, at some level, of imitation. We would go so far as to say that *all* scholarship participates in imitative logics as they creatively and critically disassemble an artifact to aid a subsequent reassembly into a scholarly product. As Stephen Ramsay argues, "The artist and scientist both endeavor to place the phenomenal world into some alternative formation that will facilitate a new seeing."[44] There may be degrees of imitation that merit different levels of ethical scrutiny. For practitioners of rhetorical field methods, the greatest danger lies not in writing imitations creatively but in eliding the inevitably imitative dimensions of scholarly texts in favor of a social scientific model premised on less reflexive claims to accuracy.

Second, we concur with the observation by this volume's editors that transparency about research processes, related to both the activity in the field and the process of textual inscription, aids in accountability. We see a unique opportunity afforded by digital publication to aid this transparency and accountability. Digital depositories hosted by universities, independent third-party websites (e.g., Academia.edu), or scholars' personal websites can be used to archive field notes, images, and other relevant data that shaped a particular research project. Publicizing field notes makes visible the intricacies and complexities involved with rhetorical field methods and serves as raw material that other scholars can examine to see the choices that were made as observations are winnowed down in the process of preparing a scholarly publication. From the perspective of a method grounded in *imitatio*, making field notes available also aids in the rearticulation of rhetorical scenes. For example, scholars could draw on our publicly available field notes to replace the episode with the devil mask with a similar conversation we observed about the effectiveness of putting Margaret Thatcher quotations on protest signs.

Third, rhetorical field methods in the tradition of *imitatio* could be accused of "speaking for others," which would be an unfortunate reversal of prevailing rationales to use field methods as a way to stand beside, advocate with, and learn from vernacular communities.[45] Field methods in the tradition of *imitatio* imply that some cultural figures—like academics—have the power and privilege to imitate with an end goal of improving the rhetorical activities of others. This presumption risks positioning researcher and researched in such a way as to reproduce historically problematic power relations. Of course, a critic iterating a scene can be held accountable in all the ways that researchers are and should be held accountable—the question of power relations in research contexts is hardly unique to rhetorical field methods. We must also admit that *imitatio*-based field methods may not be appropriate in every situation—for example, on "trigger" topics or with especially vulnerable populations. However, the shift from representational fidelity as the purpose of scholarship to a *telos* of improvement actuated through iterations of performance, criticism, and a recrafting of scenes does provide an opening to reshuffle the ethical relation between studier and studied. After all, part of the goal is to trade in negative critique (you didn't get this detail right; why didn't you include this perspective?) for the affirmative rhythms of *imitatio* to improve the scene (by adding the right detail, including another perspective). Ideally, crafting and recrafting scenes is a constant cycle of subjective improvement wherein multiple rhetors participate in what Celeste Condit calls "strategic criticism" that underscores the "constructive activity of making something better."[46]

The very method of crafting rhetorical scenes that we have described here is itself open to the logics of *imitatio*. For instance, some of the ethical issues we have raised might be ameliorated by developing scenes through dialogical co-construction with participants. Such a process might further reduce the distinction between critic and participant while making the critic more accountable to the opinions of field rhetors. Alternatively, scholars might draft rhetorical scenes and then ask rhetors in the field to work in an imitative vein to revise the scene. To demonstrate the benefits of this robust kind of participant-checking, and to enact our call for perpetual improvement of rhetorical scenes, we asked Jeffrey Eggerss, the last Occupier of the Occupy Lincoln camp, to revise the excerpted scene that begins this essay. We conclude with his imitation; since he chose to modify the original scene through the addition of words and phrases, we have italicized his substantive contributions to aid detection of his amendments:

[Scene] Occupy Lincoln Protest, Downtown
Lincoln, Nebraska, October 15, 2011

OCCUPIER 2: [Approaches microphone set up on stairs of the Capitol.] Alright everyone, we are *going* to get started. First, thanks for coming today to join in solidarity with Occupy protesters across the country and *global uprisings around* the world! Remember, the people, united, will never be defeated! We are going to march downtown throughout the business district and then turn back and regroup at the governor's mansion. *Feel free to grab a sign to carry the message with us into the streets.* This is a peaceful protest so please don't litter, block traffic, or engage counter protestors at all. Be loud and be proud! Are you ready? LET'S GO!!!

ANDA: Alright John, get excited; this is where the real work begins. *Let's go change the world!*

> [As they march, they pass Occupier 3, dressed
> in black and wearing a devil mask.]

JOHN: Oh jeez . . .

ANDA: Hey, what's your costume about?

OCCUPIER 3: I'm supposed to be a corporate devil.

ANDA: Oh, that's cool.

OCCUPIER 3: Yeah . . . not many people get it.

ANDA: Well it makes for good discussion. [Devil walks off.]

JOHN: You don't really think that do you?

ANDA: What do you mean?

JOHN: "Makes for good discussion"? That sort of stuff makes people think we should be laughed at and not listened to. You can't have a meaningful dialogue with someone wearing a costume. *Besides, if everyone were wearing masks people will think we are here to cause trouble and have a reason to hide who we are.*

ANDA: Come on, *you can have a real discussion with a man in a mask.* Relax John, it's fun. *If nothing else it's a conversation starter.* Besides he's expressing himself in a creative way. He's getting people to think about how they see things. He got our attention, didn't he?

JOHN: Yeah, but not in a good way. Drunken streakers get attention. Masked anarchists throwing bricks though Starbucks' windows get attention. But they don't get taken seriously. He has the right to dress and act how he wants, but let's be honest, that behavior only helps those who say this movement is just a bunch of crazy college kids with no message and nothing better to do. I mean what if a picture of that guy lands on the front page of the newspaper tomorrow?

ANDA: I dunno, no more Catholic supporters? *But at least we will have made the front page.*

JOHN: My grandma already suspects that Satan is behind Occupy Wall Street and *we'll probably make the front page regardless. The real question is what message and image are we sending?*

ANDA: Well, think about it this way: having diverse personalities gives us strength. It means we are flexible and inviting and then we can attract more people to our cause. That's what made this thing global. If we are too controlling and restrictive then people will choose to do other stuff *and in this global struggle we need a diversity of people and tactics. No one way alone will allow us to be successful.*

JOHN: Maybe . . .

ANDA: At the very least, it's important given our society's short attention span *and the corporate-controlled media.* Sometimes the only thing that gets the ball rolling is the spark that grabs the public's attention. *If people don't even hear or notice us then our message is completely lost.*

JOHN: Call me a *counterrevolutionary,* but I don't think weird leads to real discussion or *change.*

ANDA: Well—

OCCUPIER 1: SHOW ME WHAT DEMOCRACY LOOKS LIKE!

OCCUPIER 2–12: THIS IS WHAT DEMOCRACY LOOKS LIKE!

OCCUPIER 1: SHOW ME WHAT DEMOCRACY LOOKS LIKE!

ANDA: Come on John *it's ok, we don't have to agree about everything all the time or even understand each other. The key is that we are all in this struggle together and that we will win.*

OCCUPIER 2–12: THIS IS WHAT DEMOCRACY LOOKS LIKE!

From Guåhan and Back

Navigating a "Both/Neither" Analytic
for Rhetorical Field Methods

Tiara R. Na'puti

Guåhan (Guam), often overlooked due to its "small" size, is rarely covered by the mainstream U.S. media. Its infrequent moments of media attention are often accompanied by trivializing discourse.[1] This isolation and silencing contributes to a lack of knowledge about Guåhan, even though it is one of the "oldest colonial dependencies in the world"[2] and a major hub for U.S. military activity.[3] Ironically, in a region "so profoundly affected by American colonialism," Guåhan is "largely absent from the American imagination."[4] However distant from the public eye, Guåhan is a place where complex issues of national belonging, indigenous identity, colonialism, and securitization converge.[5]

Guåhan's existence at the nexus of colonialism demands attention from rhetorical studies and Pacific studies, where the region mistakenly named the Micronesian Islands has been profoundly absent from the fields of inquiry.[6] Communication scholars have argued that colonial relations are rhetorically naturalized and maintained, and therefore it is imperative to investigate colonial sites and rethink beyond dominant theoretical frameworks of communication rooted in the West.[7] Raka Shome calls for postcolonial interventions within the rhetorical canon that open up to alternative marginalized dialogues and voices.[8] Kuan-Hsing Chen argues that scholars must attempt to trace critical discourses generated "outside'" the imperial centers.[9] This move requires positioning communication studies as a decolonizing project.[10] Darrel Wanzer contributes to this project by arguing for rhetorical theory to better address epistemic coloniality.[11] In these views, decolonization is understood not simply as a political event but also as a cultural imperative. As Candace Fujikane explains, our connection by ocean currents holds us accountable for building on one another's struggles.[12] Thus I place Guåhan and its struggles at the center and extend the scope outward from our island to other areas where parallels or comparisons can be drawn.

By centering on Guåhan, this project works to destabilize national narratives about the Pacific and colonial forms of representation (military, strategic, security-related). Using Guåhan as a reference point enables rhetorical scholars to move beyond the imperial centers and toward reimagining different geopolitical sites.[13] I favor indigenous categories and understandings through local conceptualizations focused on the island, the broader ocean world, and indigenous identities. These movements reconfigure Guåhan and offer a remapping of the traditional terrain of rhetorical methods. Thus rhetorical field methods are needed in order to include the Pacific region while pushing forth critiques of the rhetoric of colonialism and expanding connections between local cultures, epistemologies, and histories of Oceania.

This project brings awareness of locally grounded struggles as possible models for decolonization elsewhere. In this essay I develop "Both/Neither" as an analytic that offers a way of navigating between self, place, and text when conducting rhetorical field methods. "Both/Neither" (hereafter B/N) is particularly useful for fieldwork that engages indigenous political identity and grapples with spaces always already marked by the settler-state and colonialist politics. I provide geopolitical and cultural context for Guåhan to situate and explain how B/N emerges from the cultural context itself. Then, using Guåhan as a case study, I illustrate how B/N destabilizes existing ideas of lands and peoples predicated on them and what this type of investigation in rhetorical fieldwork enables. Finally, I identify how the B/N approach contributes to rhetorical studies for analyzing structures and contexts of governance and charting identities across a range of resistances.

From Guåhan: Where American Colonialism Continues . . .

The Pacific island of Guåhan is a military colony of the United States. Centuries after Spanish colonial rule began in 1521, the United States took control of Guåhan in 1898 and established a military government through the Department of the Navy. During World War II Japan occupied Guåhan from 1941 to 1944, before the United States forcibly recaptured the island.[14] The island is now considered the most strategic military outpost in the Pacific Rim.[15] These waves of conquest and colonization have left an enduring legacy of settler colonialism and U.S. militarization that significantly affects the inherent collective rights of the Chamoru (Chamorro) indigenous people.[16]

The island's designation as an "unincorporated territory" imposes an ambiguous political status.[17] By only recognizing "states," the U.S. Constitution excludes Guåhan even as the issue of sovereignty remains contentious for the indigenous population of Chamoru people.[18] Furthermore, the discursive construction of the island through slogans such as "Guam: Where America's Days Begin," "The Edge of America," and "America's Unsinkable Aircraft Carrier" reveals the representation of the island as a *possession* of the United States, held in proximity, while simultaneously remaining exterior to the nation-state.[19] Mottos such as "Tip of the Spear" and "Fortress Guam" also illustrate how the United States frames its colonial relationship with Guåhan in overtly militaristic terms.[20] These examples of B/N rhetoric illustrate how U.S. maneuvers overdetermine Guåhan as a site understood only in relation to U.S. national security interests, while voices from Guåhan that challenge this colonial relationship remain peripheral.

Guåhan has increasingly become a site of military activities and buildup since September 11, 2001.[21] The air, land, and ocean have long been appropriated for Department of Defense (DOD) training exercises throughout the Mariana Islands; these environmentally destructive activities have largely evaded criticism from the United States despite the ruin they bring.[22] Militarization is a manifestation of the logic of settler colonialism, a structure of permanent invasion that focuses on usurping land rights of indigenous peoples and is fundamentally motivated by access to territory.[23] Settler colonialism displaces indigenous peoples from (or *re*places them on) the land.[24] Tracing the intellectual histories and methods of native peoples practicing decolonization, resistance, and survival helps theorize alternatives to settler colonialism.[25] This intersection reveals the complexity of Guåhan as a place that is in between, where the enduring presence of settler colonialism creates a seemingly impossible colonial bind that positions indigenous peoples as "domestic to the United States in a foreign sense."[26]

As of this writing, a controversial U.S. military buildup threatens Guåhan and the surrounding Mariana Islands as part of a sprawling military training complex.[27] The plans will impose more U.S. control in Guåhan, where the military already commands one-third of the island, and will maximize existing DOD leased lands on Tinian while also acquiring additional lands.[28] From this context, I build on Epeli Hau'ofa's argument for a holistic perspective that reconfigures Oceania as "a sea of islands," neither tiny nor deficient but rather a vast network of power.[29] This argument demands attending to people's daily experiences as interconnected exchanges and kinship, and using

Oceanic epistemologies to inform narration of indigenous cultural discourses in the Pacific.[30] Doing so shifts the focus away from disconnections integral to Western colonial perspectives, and the B/N analytic I explicate below provides rhetoricians a method for making this move.[31]

Launchings: A "Both/Neither" Analytic

B/N offers a path for rhetoricians to address the struggles of indigenous peoples in settler colonial spaces. This framework is particularly suited to field study since the construction of Guåhan illustrates how the B/N analytic emerges from the cultural context itself. This analytic recognizes that text *is* context, simultaneously produced and productive of the social world and capable of authorizing and culturally reproducing colonial logics.[32] B/N reflects the phenomenon of simultaneously *belonging to* while remaining *neither part of nor completely separate from*. This analytic connects with similar concepts proposed by postcolonial, decolonial, and feminist studies such as "outsider/within,"[33] "liminality,"[34] "mestiza consciousness,"[35] and "third space."[36] All share a sense of identity plurality that develops through positioning within, engagement with, and exclusions from a community. Patricia Hill Collins's outsider/within status provides a special standpoint for oppressed groups, and refers to the power relations implicated within duality and plurality.[37] Victor Turner's theory of liminality is captured by the phrase "betwixt and between," which describes the transition, place, and state effected through a rite of passage. Liminality emerges and erupts out of fissures that exist at and across borders and inside bounded spaces.[38] Homi K. Bhabha's use of "third space" and "hybridity" describe the construction of identity and culture within colonial conditions that open up possibilities for rearticulation of meaning.[39] These spaces are riddled with contradictions, imply instability, exist liminally, and reflect the multiplicity of being on the margins within interlocking systems of oppression.[40] These concepts are important because they explain refusal of constraints and boundaries imposed by the settler-state and nation, and articulate resistive possibilities. Kevin Bruyneel's "third space of sovereignty" explains boundary-crossing as another way to map out peoples' relationship to North America, and a discursive shift in the way indigenous actors articulate their relationship to the U.S. nation-state. These concepts are considerable for the Pacific, offering the possibility of a politics that moves beyond binaries and through ongoing productions of indigenous identity. B/N emerges with these key concepts, offering ways to speak back to the imposed Other, and launching in unfamiliar terrain.[41] This analytic is particularly useful to indigenous scholars and those engaging in work with and for indigenous peoples to challenge their relationship to the continental United States and to the politics of settler colonialism.

Being in motion, the B/N analytic attends to the productive tension between the conditions and demands of text and field. In rhetorical field methods we engage in data collection while also functioning as analysts of place, self, and text.[42] At times this work of collector and analyst occurs simultaneously ("Both"), as we are at once positioned in complicated ways within the field of analysis. Other times, this work is incongruous ("Neither"), as we remain "neither" part of the field nor completely separate from it as we conduct our rhetorical analyses of the collected data. Thus, as we engage in rhetorical fieldwork, we are always already moving between B/N rhetoric or B/N fieldwork. As an analytic, B/N complicates the idea that text and field are separate or sequential.

Data collection is "both" by virtue of *belonging to* place and self. The situatedness of this work depends on our connections and kinship with the local community, and our relation to the field as we experience emergent discourses. Fieldwork also *belongs to* text; as our artifacts are collected and analyzed through rhetorical methods we move back and forth through text, production, and reproduction. Thus fieldwork is both constitutive of, and a necessary component for our work in rhetorical studies which pays attention to how language functions to transform and persuade the identities, behaviors, and beliefs of others. "Both" reflects how rhetorical field methods "operate at the intersections" and involve a "commitment to utilizing and supplementing its practice with tools drawn from rhetoricians *and* critics in other communication subdisciplines."[43] Rhetorical field methods are also "neither." Our fieldwork is *neither part of nor completely separate from*, as text cannot be severed from place, nor can self be removed from rhetorical analysis. By engaging in rhetorical fieldwork we are always already drawing from elements of both ends of the spectrum of rhetoric and field methods. Below, I explain how B/N offers a means of moving between dimensions of self, place, and text in rhetorical field methods and back again.

Centering Place

The dependency on *place* in rhetorical field methods is complicated, as bodies, physical structures, and spaces converge and diverge.[44] Above, I connected some of the conceptual frames that attend to struggles over space and place. For "the border," Flores explains that Chicanas/os have "a sense of being neither truly Mexican nor truly American," and the unique experience of not belonging in either land.[45] These geographical influences can at once create isolation and separation.[46] While recognizing nuances in Chicana/o feminist theorizing, and the important situatedness of "the borderland," these seemingly disparate concepts share important features with the B/N analytic that enable us to consider the U.S.-Guåhan border as also a place of contestation. Here, the border is not understood as a land division, but rather in a more enlarged way where ocean figures prominently as part of a vast, surprisingly connected region.[47]

The B/N analytic builds from indigenous and Pacific scholarship that construes indigeneity and critiques of colonization that intersect with connections to land and peoples who define themselves in terms of relation to land.[48] Pacific Islanders and other indigenous peoples are bounded by a strong sense of place that is "neither immobile nor migratory."[49] Land as place lies at the heart of indigenous identity and belonging; these connections often invoke "storied land" whereby indigenous people make place through relating communal and personal histories to certain locations.[50]

The centrality of land also couples with a centering on the ocean. As B/N orients the ocean as place, the analytic enlarges the scope of *place* to demonstrate how the dimension of place is interconnected, multiple, ambiguous—it is all of these things at once, moving in this space that is neither here nor there. B/N offers a way to center on place without being confined to fixed boundaries. The B/N analytic builds from the perspective that the ocean links people in an expansive configuration where land and sky are joined in a contiguous environment; this vantage point follows Vicente M. Diaz's call for a critical rethinking of islands from indigenous epistemologies and cartographies that offer radically different indigenous conceptions of place, and "challenge colonial definitions of land (and self)."[51] This move also resists the land-centric view that islands are "small."[52] Considering ocean and land as place in this way prioritizes the maintenance of spatial relationships as one of the most important components of self and identity.[53] Indeed, as Hau'ofa argued, the ocean has always been intimately linked to survival and well-being for Islanders.[54] By using the ocean as a site of resistance, B/N works to destabilize settler colonialism in the Pacific. Attending to complexity of place and its discursive construction, B/N moves through shifting terrains and accounts for the rhetorical crossings within and beyond these locales.

Situating Self

The B/N analytic moves through dimensions of *self* and connects with analytical lenses taken up by rhetorical scholars. Here, I navigate among concepts of self to establish an existing scholarly conversation. Chela Sandoval described "differential consciousness," a way of self-consciously taking an ideological stance best suited for interrupting dominant ways and configurations.[55] Extending Sandoval's work, Carrillo Rowe casts "differential belonging" as a means of disrupting binaries; this understanding presents a sense of self that is "radically inclined toward others, toward the communities to which we belong," and is at times contradictory, multiple, and shifting.[56] Karma R. Chávez also explains differential belonging as moving us toward a coalitional subjectivity that offers agency to resist, unbound by fixed categories.[57] Bernadette Calafell's consideration of reflexivity and relationality also works to link across affects of Otherness regardless of our positionalities.[58] This framework for self suggests a "tactical maneuvering across resistive communities"[59] and enables decentering of dominant rhetorical styles.[60] Connecting these understandings, our critical reflexivity of subject positionings provides rhetorical strategies for negotiating multiple accountabilities.[61]

The B/N analytic parallels these concepts, and extends the navigational motif through tactical deployments of *self* and belonging in the Pacific, where scholarship has advanced primarily through ethnographic analysis. In Pacific studies, the success of this method couples with emphasizing Islander agency, local voice, and indigenous epistemologies.[62] For many indigenous scholars, self-identification is an important practice that "tactically functions to signify decolonization and can also be normalizing."[63] Our positionalities as researchers require us to be conscious of self-identification as a sort of B/N practice. We may employ politically engaged orientations to redress the representations of our indigenous communities. As Enck-Wanzer and Sowards explain, we may also engage in practices that operate at odds with our communities, but we are conscious of how these moves may grant us rhetorical power and agency.[64]

Hau'ofa argues the need for indigenously oriented work for Oceania that centers on our own histories, roots, and identities, to advance "our own distinctive creations."[65] As a Chamoru scholar, I center indigenous concerns to work toward understanding theory and research from our own perspectives and purposes as indigenous peoples.[66] The B/N analytic recognizes that engaging situated knowledge is key to revealing context and understanding dynamic relationships between structural forces and situated cultural practices as well as the articulations of identity, agency, and discourse.[67] This lens shifts rhetorical manifestations of *self*, considering the spectrum of discursive identity constructions of communities that are resistive to colonization and militarization. A B/N analytic asks how colonialism operates discursively through redefining our subjectivities as well as containing or often halting flow.[68]

B/N provides powerful transcendence across boundaries of belonging, identity, citizenship, and cultural practices. B/N navigates us through cultural expressions among diasporic communities and points of convergence or divergence in the formation of settler colonial subjectivities. B/N is particularly useful for analyzing the ongoing movement in Guåhan and the oscillations of identity and voice for activists against U.S. militarization.

Approaching Text(s)

Launching a B/N analytic involves navigating through elements of *text* in rhetorical scholarship. Barry Brummett explains text as discrete, "one with clear boundaries in time and space," or diffuse, "one with a perimeter that is not so clear, one that is mixed up with other signs."[69] The blurred boundaries of the latter open understanding of cultural and historical sites as texts. Bernard J. Armada argues for an expansion of text to attend to the materiality and symbolicity of rhetoric, and analyze forms of expression "not typically examined by scholars of rhetoric."[70] Along these lines, Greg Dickinson, Brian L. Ott, and Eric Aoki advocate for viewing diffuse "texts" as "experiential landscapes."[71] From these perspectives, critical rhetoric scholars have considered text in a variety of ways, shifting away from analysis of objectified texts to critique of "live" rhetorics and the consequences of lived experiences.[72]

The B/N analytic invites ways to speak back to the imposed Other, and provides a pivot point toward engagement with "transnational spaces, hybrid identities, and subjectivities grounded in differences related to gender, class, race, and culture."[73] *In situ* rhetorical analysis works through such spaces, identities, and subjectivities and engages the voices of marginalized rhetorical communities that often evade critical attention.[74] Pushing rhetorical scholars further, Wanzer charges that we should be "*hearing* these marginal voices and moving toward theoretical changes that avoid complicity with modern/coloniality."[75] This is especially important for indigenous voices, which have been overwhelmingly silenced in the Western academy.[76]

The B/N analytic helps to understand critically (con)texts of colonialism, settler colonialism, and militarization. It reveals complex interrelations of place, self, and text. It allows scholars and activists to understand and analyze the rhetorical construction of identity and in-betweenness that permeates our (con)texts. It examines situated rhetoric and offers insight on how people accept, coordinate, establish, negotiate, and reject meaning.[77] And a B/N approach attends to discourse, releasing the critic beyond boundaries of traditional texts and to consider the context in uniquely constitutive ways— through iterations of place as text, as self, and back again. The preceding sections have used *place*, *self*, and *text* as conceptual tools. In launching a B/N analytic, these dimensions are not entirely separable or completely connected. Analytically, B/N provides a way of moving through malleable and mutually reinforcing elements of place, self, and text in rhetorical field methods. Below, I return to Guåhan as a robust case study for working through the B/N analytic.

Back to Guåhan/United States: A Case Study in Navigating "Both/Neither"

My fieldwork begins in Guåhan, conceptualizing the island as both a landscape and a seascape. This expansive consideration of "field" challenges externally imposed understandings of Guåhan *from the U.S.* perspective, and instead focuses *from Guåhan* before navigating outward. Centering ocean interconnectivity demonstrates how Guåhan is multiple and ambiguous elements simultaneously—a field outwardly constructed as extremely connected through ties to the United States yet also remote, distant, and beyond the field of vision.

I center here because Guåhan and surrounding islands are threatened by militarization. In 2013 the DOD announced revised buildup plans for a large-scale military training complex that will include one-third of Guåhan, two-thirds of Tinian, and the entirety of Farallon de Medinilla and Pagan.[78] Yet the situation facing our "island has registered little to no protest on an international or national level."[79] In my fieldwork, Guåhan serves as "both" text and field, as the island context is so saturated and rooted experientially. It is extremely important to be here, to work from here, not only to understand Guåhan as a "field," but also to center on local texts that are overlooked due to ongoing settler colonialism. This positions Guåhan as "neither" text nor field by predominantly constructing the island as intelligible only in relation to the *U.S.* nation-state and the *U.S.* military.

Grounding fieldwork in Guåhan challenges these external constructions. I conducted ethnographic work, collecting interview data that emphasized local voices in Guåhan, and focused on indigenous perspectives about the buildup. This emphasis led to conversations with community organizers, activists, and my family. I spoke with local residents, Chamorus, and community groups such as We Are Guåhan (WAG). My experiences provided key sources of data because so much was happening *here*, so centering on these local voices offered much more insight than would attempts to collect data from afar. I am also situated as part of the data. My fieldwork engages a complexity of *texts* within the Chamoru culture that has a strong oral tradition. Thus my consideration of text expands to places as texts, self as text, and events as texts. Data analysis occurred while I was in Guåhan and also continued after I left. This analysis moves between questions about place, self, and text as interconnected components of B/N, reflecting how phenomena in rhetorical field methods *both belong to* and are *neither part of nor completely separate from*. I moved through these questions, at times blurring the boundaries among the place/self/text dimensions, and always in transit with my analysis of "field" and "text."

Ginen Guåhan: A "Both/Neither" Place

Every summer since 2011 I have taken a seventeen-hour flight traveling 7,200 miles across the International Date Line to Guåhan—a place I call home despite growing up in the continental United States. After arriving I go through U.S. Customs and Border Protection. I must show my passport although I have not left the U.S. nation-state; this customs process is a physical reminder of the contradiction that exists in Guåhan. The popular tourist slogan

"Guam, Where America's Days Begin" communicates the complexity of place in Guåhan-U.S. relations.[80]

Guåhan, in similar and distinct fashion with Hawai'i, is figured as a cultural, economic, military, and political possession.[81] Political dependency reflects the dispossession inherent in the outside construction of Guåhan as a place that is "simultaneously being embedded yet peripheral."[82] This place is "Both," a political landmass with U.S. citizenship status afforded to the inhabitants. Yet its political status is also "Neither" because Chamorus and other native inhabitants are prohibited from voting in presidential elections, and we have yet to fulfill our inherent right of self-determination. This phenomenon affects local politics, which are embedded within global colonial structures while also "being 'remote-controlled' by an outsider nation-state."[83]

Local organizations, voices, and perspectives in Guåhan challenge these external constructions of place. From 2010 to 2011 WAG organized "Heritage Hikes" as part of continued efforts to educate and engage the community about the military relocation.[84] The hikes are a local example of how B/N connections to *place* articulate resistance through a vernacular way of making Guåhan meaningful on its own terms, beyond the military presence. The Heritage Hikes series had Chamoru titles, provided an opportunity for the local public to get to know the land, and were rooted in Chamoru cultural practices. Hikes offered experiential data within the "field," functioned as their own "texts" situated in storied land, and provided understandings of self as connected to place. The hikes themselves articulated belonging to both text and place by telling the story of the land through embodied and experiential practice. Hike leaders also imparted knowledge about these places, produced by the terrain that is culturally and spiritually rooted.

A key feature of the hikes as texts connects to the Chamoru cultural practice of "asking permission." When passing through the tano' (land) it is important to pay respects to elders and spirits who have come before and to request permission to enter their land. Asking permission at the outset of the hikes also recognizes land as a living connector to our past and future, and recenters these places within our vibrant cultural and genealogical contexts. Hikes also educated people through the experience of place, embodying the shared responsibility of inafa' maolek (to make things good for one another) that is based on the assumption that mutual respect must prevail over individualism. A representative from WAG explained the hikes as "really trying to strengthen the connection to our culture, and our heritage, and our land—which kind of gets lost in this whole process. Doing things like the Heritage Hikes, the [*Manenggon*] walk that we did just a few weeks ago. And, even before the military buildup, the story that's always been told is the American story."[85] Here hiking is understood as an active process of respectful connection within an experiential landscape that blurs the boundaries of text, place, and field. Place is articulated as a collective local identity ("our culture, and our heritage, and our land") that is *distinct from* the United States. However, place is also characterized by *belonging to* the U.S. nation-state and by virtue of the repeated "American story" in Guåhan. B/N foregrounds how place is figured prominently in everyday acts of resistance to the U.S. military's claims to place. Each hike included brief lectures about the history and current landscape to strengthen connections with natural resources and reinforce inafa' maolek values of mutual respect and caring. They mobilized people to reconsider the buildup in relation to U.S. militarization and its effects on the island over the past century, and navigated future concerns about the island.[86] For example, the first hike series, Tungo I Estoriå-ta (Know Our Story), situated place in deeply rooted contexts of sacred land and history of sites previously threatened by military expansion. It told the story of Guåhan on its own terms by offering "Our Story" about place as a challenge to the military views of land as merely ahistorical, disconnected property for claim without permission. Through telling stories of the locales, sharing information about the buildup, and using the Chamoru language, the hikes reinforced cultural significance of place and community through grassroots organizing. Hikes reimagined Guåhan as a place not belonging to U.S. military frameworks where land is merely property; they strived to "educate ourselves on our true history" and perpetuate Chamoru cultural values to change Guåhan's story.[87]

The B/N analytic reveals complicated constructions of *place* and grapples with discursive and material implications often overlooked within these spaces. Here B/N uncovers how troubled conceptions of *place* emerge even as the Heritage Hikes sought to directly challenge the DOD process for military buildup and the U.S. government's disregard for indigenous and sacred land.[88] B/N foregrounds this phenomenon of in-betweenness manifested by the literal distance from the United States, and its overlapping proximity to the United States through military and security policy. It clarifies contradictions in place and rhetorical constructions of space by providing a means of analyzing the structures and contexts that govern, preside, and determine Guåhan as a place that *both* belongs to and is *neither* completely part of the United States. The B/N analytical framework also provides understanding of the unique struggles of rhetorical fieldwork and the challenges for activists and scholars who face a perplexing rhetorical situation when working in Guåhan.

Hita: Situating (My)Self/(Our)Selves

Continuing to move through the fieldwork, I tread among considerations of *place* and *self* and remain centered on Oceanic understandings. As Hau'ofa reminds us, an identity grounded in the sea provides ways of knowing connected to our ancestors that explored the oceanic unknown and made it "their home, our home."[89] Our landscape/seascape approach to *place* intertwines with *self* in ways that complicate our efforts to distinguish them. In my fieldwork I consider *self in place*, as the field of Guåhan is so contextualized—I cannot separate my understanding of self from this place. B/N explains my understanding of self in relation to this project, and the shifts I experience between my primary home spaces.

My position as a member of the Chamoru diaspora directly informs and contributes to the field methods. Diasporic Chamorus often experience cultural and political identity crises, as we are detached from our homeland geographically but remain within the boundaries of the U.S. colonizer.[90] When I heard of the U.S. military buildup plans for Guåhan, it was a wake-up call. I was simultaneously connected and isolated as I searched for more information and engaged in conversations with family and friends from thousands of miles away.

Enacting the B/N framework entails recognition of how my position as a member of the Chamoru community offers privilege of access to local community groups. I am also, however, keenly aware and conscious of my particular kind of spatial relationship with the land. I live primarily at a distance from my home/landscape and draw on powerful conceptions of space that deploy land strategically as a mechanism for resisting imperial geographies and settler colonial realities.

B/N navigates back and forth through these experiences of identity and belonging, and of space as expressions of self and community. Advocating with the ongoing work in Guåhan is an important factor as I engage with community groups. Accountability for this work is deeply connected to *self* as rooted in *this place*, and these connections reflect the unique ways of forging resistive agency and possibilities for tactical maneuvers across communities.[91]

My participation with community groups highlighted the benefits and the challenges facing activist work in Guåhan. Connecting field methods and rhetorical studies has unfolded opportunities for further community engagement and advocacy. Field experiences were initiated through my early connections with the local population in Guåhan and have transitioned into opportunities to strengthen my community work and praxis. These moments reflect positive elements of rhetorical field methods, but they are also B/N manifestations of my identity and articulations of resistance. Chamorus do not neatly situate within any specific identity category with regard to the nation-state or the transnational arena, and this phenomenon results in an ambiguous rhetorical and cultural identity that corresponds neither to the exclusively national or international, or the vernacular or local experience. Thus B/N rhetoric is vexed by its mixture of strategies that depend on U.S. nation-state institutions while concurrently articulating a distinct indigenous identity as a challenge to the United States.

B/N as an analytic helps map the rhetoric of identity and "Americanness" across the spectrum of resistance that spans decolonization options (from U.S. statehood to Free Association, to Independence) and opposition to the buildup.[92] Those challenging the U.S. military buildup utilize rhetorical strategies that are *neither* advocacy nor in favor of full decolonization. There is a tension of simultaneously pushing *away from* the United States while also drawing near to the United States through an American identity. Everyday conversations in Guåhan reproduce a range of evaluative discourses of self, often relating to U.S. nationalist sentiment in complex ways. While talking about political status for Guåhan, one of my family members spoke incredulously: "Decolonization? I did not know that we were a *colony!*" They were amused and satisfied by the quip; out of respect for my elders I kept quiet. Our conversation lulled, but it began shortly thereafter with their complaints about the "American" government and various problems that result from our island being an "unincorporated territory" that "belongs to someone else." This example shows how the community uses and appeals to both the law and the culture of the broader U.S. colonial entity (Both) while at the same time insisting on its own difference from it (Neither). These B/N identities relate to the ironies of the United States, together hiding and revealing Guåhan. On the one hand, U.S. colonization *hides* its violence through ingrained discourses of civilization and sacrifice; on the other hand, soldiers from Guåhan and the Pacific are significantly overrepresented in the U.S. military.[93] The B/N analytic moves through contradictory elements of discourse about the U.S. nation-state in relation to, and opposition from, the island; it operates at the intersection of these issues of self with place, and helps address the texts and contexts emerging from our work.

Tuge': Texts and Local Tactics

In November 2009 the DOD released its Draft Environmental Impact Statement (DEIS) on the military buildup, which revealed its intentions to acquire more control in the largest single project ever proposed, totaling an estimated $15 billion. The people of Guåhan were granted only ninety days to review and comment on the nine-volume, eleven-thousand-page document.[94] The DEIS release was a catalyst for WAG's creation. Working collectively, activists split up the complex text and conducted information outreach for Guåhan, the region, and among the diaspora.[95] Everyone scrambled to read, process, and respond to the DEIS during the DOD's public hearings and "review and comment" period.

Text figures significantly due to the length of the DEIS and the system of submitting written comments as public engagement with the document. The discrete text of the DEIS functioned as a restraint with imposed restrictions for response (eleven thousand pages, limited meetings). Simultaneously, the DEIS provided a release sparking significant organizing, public outcry, and response, with hundreds attending every public hearing and the submission of over ten thousand written comments.[96] Beyond submitting written comments, the Guåhan community navigated the DEIS by creating an experiential seascape at public meetings that simultaneously challenged the text-centric comment process as a farce. Although the comment period purports to allow the public's voice to be heard, U.S. policy decisions about the buildup were already decided without consulting Guåhan. Thus, relevant texts extend beyond formal written documents (DEIS, submitted comments) to include the practice of local engagement at the public meetings. Similar to the hikes, the meetings themselves functioned as "texts" where residents drew on vernacular articulations of Guåhan to challenge external constructions of place as exclusive military property. People gave oral testimonies, told stories, created art, and performed poetry, Chamoru chants, dances, and songs. These performances reconfigured place as inseparable from deep cultural, genealogical, and historical contexts. Land, people's deep ancestral connections to place, and arguments against the DEIS review process also figured strongly in performed commentaries opposing the buildup. These live responses reimagined Guåhan as a place with a non-militaristic future, providing an alternative format to resist the ways the DEIS had "virtually ignored the social and cultural implications of the [buildup] plans."[97] These performances were B/N texts falling outside the written comment forms that belong to the U.S. federal review agencies, while also not completely separate from the U.S. security policy for Guåhan. Understanding these meetings as texts captures performances of people's daily experiences woven together both within the U.S.-imposed comment system and against it.

In 2014 I attended a public meeting at the University of Guam organized by several community groups presenting findings from the DOD's Supplemental Environmental Impact Statement (SEIS) about the revised buildup plans.[98] In contrast to the DOD public meetings, these groups had organized their own meetings to address issues of the economy, environment, cultural sites, and public services. The meeting was an experiential seascape where speakers performed what would be discernable as rhetorical criticism of the thousand-page SEIS for the public audience. They distributed handouts titled "Twelve Things You Should Know," containing information taken directly from the SEIS. They organized small group discussions with the audience participating to generate lists of buildup concerns from the information they had just received. These participatory elements centered on people's lived experiences and kinship ties with the land, privileged oral performances about the cultural context, and situated Guåhan as a place separable from the United States and militarization. By focusing on Guåhan's sacred and protected places, such as Pågat and Litekyan (Ritidian), the meeting foregrounded deep cultural connections throughout the Marianas archipelago as arguments against the buildup.

Experiential emphasis on cultural sites and the oceanic environment situated Guåhan within a living seascape incapable of being captured by the SEIS and static constructions of land. Speakers also discursively depicted the dilemma of militarization without representation by questioning the centrality of American security concerns in the Pacific, thus bringing decolonization issues to the center. At the end of the meeting, organizers critiqued the DOD review and comment system while also distributing SEIS comment forms for the public audience. This move both informed audience members how to submit comments and participate in an externally imposed process of belonging to the United States, while also challenging the SEIS as an exclusively text-centric system that is *neither part of, nor completely separate from*, the dynamic relationships within lived cultural practices and contexts.

B/N reveals how the DEIS/SEIS texts draw connections to and belonging with the United States; it also highlights how these texts dislocate Chamorus from the United States and the discussions on sovereignty, land, and resources. Local engagement functioned through a motif of motion; participants simultaneously experienced the work of analyst and collector of texts, while they remained neither completely separate from the field nor part of it. B/N uniquely contributes to an understanding of text and field by blurring the distinction, moving between local discourses, texts, and experientially connected contexts and events.

Concluding the Voyage

Given the lack of international attention directed at Guåhan, B/N helps critics address the dynamic elements of social movement struggles occurring in otherwise marginal places and is particularly important for critiques of militarization and colonization in rhetorical studies. This project offers to communication studies an extended orientation toward the Pacific and a particular mode of engaging in interdisciplinary connections with indigenous and Pacific studies. Using fieldwork to enable considerations of indigenous epistemologies and indigenous cultural politics within the study of rhetoric, I explained how rhetorical field methods are paramount for analyzing and understanding the complexity of territorial politics.

I centered on Guåhan as an extended example to demonstrate how a B/N analytic reveals the complexity of place, self, and text in opposition to U.S. militarization. From this case I considered how everyday discourse and language constructs and positions spaces, identities, and texts in opposing ways. These examples illustrate how B/N attends to the linguistic and discursive constructions that inform and perpetuate settler colonial ideology. B/N also reveals how groups issue rhetorical claims of identification and connection to and against the U.S. nation-state. It illustrates where cultural practices and creative aspects of identity narratives are situated within constraining and enabling structural dimensions (e.g., the nation-state, the United Nations, military bases). Finally, B/N recognizes the dialectic between the structural and the cultural. It allows us to uncover the deep connections and shifts of political and material forces that restrict agency and subjectivity while also pushing toward consciousness and active negotiation of meaning within and against those structures.

At the end of the summer, I have to leave Guåhan and travel back to the continental United States. Leaving home is difficult for me. The long airplane ride over the Pacific Ocean provides an unavoidable physical reminder of the distance I will have to travel when I return. I will experience the back and forth, and complex articulations of self, place, and texts (created, collected, and performed). My experiences further illustrate the B/N concept in rhetorical field methods. It is an embodied expression of how people who feel entirely possessed by distant centers of power, as in Guåhan, are further motivated to challenge "the bases that purport to justify possessions of this magnitude."[99]

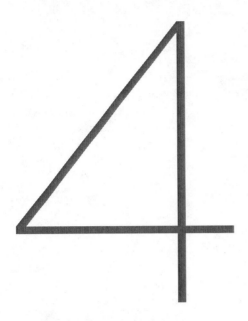

Feeling Rhetorical Critics

*Another Affective–Emotional Field
Method for Rhetorical Studies*

Jamie Landau

"The muscles look like chicken, so I feel gross like a cannibal." "I gasped when looking into the bottle labeled 'ectopic pregnancy,' because I could see the fingers." I wrote those statements in my field notes while conducting research one summer at "Bodies: The Exhibition," located at the South Street Seaport in New York City. At first glance they are the only recorded notes about my feelings in the now single-spaced five-page typed document. Another rhetorical scholar who accompanied me took separate field notes that run just as long, but they do not include an utterance about her feelings.

Like my colleague and me, most rhetorical scholars hold back feelings. It is all too common to block them from criticism, whether at the stage of analysis or when writing and revising for publication. The failure to feel is disingenuous for a discipline that distinguishes itself from the objective lens of the sciences. Aren't we embodied scholars with hands, hormones, and hearts that feel alongside other bodies in society? Don't you sense me right now while reading this essay? Insights from affect theory suggest that personal bodily feelings are intertwined with other people and society as we are alive and interact with one another in the world.

By *feeling rhetorical critics*, I argue that we can more fully embody the political practice of rhetorical criticism, expand the object of analysis beyond traditional symbolic texts, and take seriously the possibility of another participant in rhetoric. Michael Osborn recognized the stakes of embodiment when he introduced the notion of the "critic as participant" in a close criticism of a Martin Luther King Jr. speech: "If we follow traditional academic directions, and attempt to objectify, disembody, and distance the subject of criticism, we run the risk—at least in rhetorical criticism—of losing that subject."[1]

For the remainder of this essay, I flesh out *feeling rhetorical critics* by first discussing rhetorical studies that theorize the critic as political and integral to the text and the act of criticism, arguing that these same scholars still hesitate to express emotions or are disciplined when they do. To more fully account for the bodies of scholars, I turn to contemporary affect theory and explain how it cannot be subsumed into a phenomenological or (auto)ethnographic perspective. Finally, affect theory informs my development of a new affective-emotional field method for rhetorical studies, which I apply to an explorative study of "Bodies: The Exhibition" that moves people to feel fetal personhood.

(Dis)Embodying the Critic and Burying Feelings

The political performance of rhetorical criticism laid the groundwork for embodying the critic. Giving up the idea of a detached observer, however, did not result in *feeling rhetorical criticism*. A logic-and-text-based standard for conducting analysis and writing has long reigned and still reigns in the discipline as proper rhetorical criticism. This is a rationalist approach that too often omits pathos, even in overtly political critique, or at least evaluates feelings as a weaker form of argumentation. As I also document below, another tendency today is for rhetorical scholars who emote in print to be marked as *other than* rhetoricians (e.g., ethnographers), a gesture that disregards how their work speaks to the discipline. Ideological rhetorical criticism and critical rhetoric may open the door to the bodies of critics but they have not let feelings in, a classic case of logos trumping pathos.[2]

I imagine that Michael McGee, Philip Wander, and Raymie McKerrow experienced an intense rush of feelings when they argued that the rhetorical critic was a "performer," "ideological," and an "inventor."[3] In a bold move that earned scorn from colleagues,[4] they dropped the façade of a disinterested scholar and debated what this new contemporary critic did. McGee described how the old critic was portrayed as an "entirely independent agent."[5] In contrast, the criticism envisioned by McGee was "on its face that sort of action which intervenes in the world."[6] He continued, "The answer, I believe, is a more active, performative attitude toward analysis and criticism. Rhetoricians are performers, and our public badly needs us now."[7] Wander decried the "ivory tower mentality" to advocate for an ideological perspective that "recognizes the existence of powerful vested interests" and enables "the efforts of real people to create a better world."[8] Building on McGee and Wander, McKerrow outlined a critical orientation for a specific intellectual who engaged in political performance itself, which he explained functioned like academics who took to the streets as practicing revolutionaries.[9]

The next generation of rhetorical scholars proudly identified as doing "critical rhetoric," continuing to conceive of criticism as far from innocent. John Sloop writes, "As critics and activists, we must utilize criticism as a way to envision and encourage other ways of being."[10] He continues, "Critical rhetoric forces us not only to function as critics, then, but to function as rhetoricians, to read the material discourse of everyday life and write about it in such a way that our encounters with the world are thereafter altered."[11] Critical rhetorical scholars coming from feminist and queer perspectives often express commitments to the embodiment of the critic and reflexivity; one example is Charles Morris, who says that "critics not only constitute texts by their assemblage of fragments and close readings, but are too integrally and consequentially inscribed in text and context."[12] In that same essay, which is dedicated to the state of the art of rhetorical criticism in 2010, Morris reinvigorates a charge from the 1990s by postulating and enacting "critical self-portraiture," where a critic reads oneself. Phaedra Pezzullo's rhetorical studies that involve participant observation are another model, although she concedes in the introduction to her book, "I do not dwell heavily on my personal experiences."[13] Finally, Debra Hawhee recently documented how the past one hundred years of the *Quarterly Journal of Speech* exhibit a concern with a locus of feeling she calls the "sensorium."[14]

Nevertheless, when scholars have the guts to share their feelings in print as part of the political performance of rhetorical criticism, they are frequently disciplined. The response to an article written three decades ago by Thomas Benson exemplifies not only the obscurity but also the negation of a feeling critic. Benson published "Another Shooting in Cowtown" in the *Quarterly Journal of Speech*, in which he wrote, "My own study of political rhetoric cannot simply remain content with an armchair examination of texts and situations recorded from a distance. . . . Only by involving myself as a participant can I be a useful observer, because by risking a double investment of myself—both as a media consultant and an academic critic—I encounter feelings that I would not encounter as a mere observer."[15] Peter Simonson says that only recently did he discover Benson's essay, which he describes as "written in narrative, journal-like style, and blending elements of documentary, first-person reflection, and criticism into a striking variation on autoethnography before its time, and a signal example of non-paradigmatic rhetorical criticism."[16] I suggest that this oversight is an outcome of the discipline's standardization of what counts as scholarship. In fact, Benson recently shared that his essay provoked explicit complaints from reviewers and readers that the *Quarterly Journal of Speech* should not have published it.[17] Thomas Nakayama and Robert Krizek's article on whiteness as a strategic rhetoric received considerable acclaim, but at the same time its reflexivity is ignored or is not considered "normal" rhetorical criticism.[18] Feminist scholars have had varying degrees of success as well, since publications that call attention to themselves are frequently relegated to book chapters or regional or interdisciplinary journals, or, like what happens to a lot of feminist arguments, they are "labeled as 'new' material and thus placed after 'traditional' material in most textbooks for rhetorical studies."[19]

Joshua Gunn's work is another illustration of how the feelings of rhetorical critics are tamed even when a concerted effort is made to release them.[20] In the opening to an essay, Gunn transcribes the orgasmic yawps from the climactic scene in the hit movie *When Harry Met Sally*, in which Sally fakes sexual pleasure. Gunn says that these words read on the page of an academic journal violate mandates of scholarship, yet at the same time he exclaims, "We've all made similar sounds (or at least faked them) . . . *except for the fact that she is releasing them in public.*"[21] This writing persuades viscerally, as does the insertion of songs in this essay and throughout much of Gunn's work, since, he says, "it is in song that screams and cries approach the edge of emotive anarchy."[22] While I laud Gunn's efforts to be affective, he does not go far enough, at least in the published version and in the analysis section specifically.[23] That is, Gunn gets emotional in the introduction to the essay but then he withdraws; there is no longer an embodied sense of the scholar when he analyzes presidential oratory. A similar critique that Gunn eventually makes about Barack Obama's presidential campaign rhetoric is my critique of Gunn as a rhetorical critic here: Gunn ultimately holds back feeling.

There are a number of reasons why rhetorical scholars bury feelings. At the theoretical level, for centuries pathos has been pitted against logos, the latter of which is privileged given the discipline's ties to classical philosophy and rational argumentation.[24] Additionally, in studies of the discourse of the discipline, Gunn and Jenny Rice found that speech scholars defined themselves *against* the "effeminate" elocutionists,[25] and later abandoned speech because it was "aligned culturally with the body and the feminine. . . . Speech was killed because it echoes the softness of the maternal voice in the steely, manful corridors of the academic industry."[26] I suggest that this echo of the feminine and its connection to feelings has not disappeared in the early twenty-first century, nor has privileging the masculine (and its connection to the rational) diminished in the discipline.[27] At the methodological level, approaches that call attention to the researcher can also make scholarship seem overly self-focused and indulgent.[28] For example, in her rhetorical analysis of the names of Chinese women, Wen Shu Lee expresses feelings of exile when Americans urge her to use a different name.[29] She says this experience influenced her research and therefore she is obliged to comment on it, but she also notes that this reflexive move "has been criticized as confessional therapy for the author."[30] And at the pragmatic level, when scholars express feelings in research, it exposes them to retribution by putting their bodies and jobs at risk. Female rhetoricians were "disciplined" when writing about and celebrating feelings in our profession, which is implicated in sexist beliefs that denigrate women and emotions.[31] Similarly, I sensed that a review of one of my co-authored essays submitted a couple years ago to a leading rhetoric journal "disciplined the feminine" when the reviewer rejected the essay and wrote, "But, bless your hearts, there's nothing particular about your personal reactions that adds much to the critical reading." This reviewer may have devalued "personal reactions" no matter the gender of the scholars. Even so, I interpreted the comment, "bless your hearts," as a backhanded insult that invalidates lived experiences and infantilizes women, especially since my co-author and I identified in the manuscript as junior female faculty.

Turning to Affect Theory

My call for *feeling rhetorical critics* is influenced by contemporary affect studies that conceptualize and analyze affect along with emotion. Affect and emotion are not discrete, as they are closely related to each other. I join a chorus of scholars within and outside of the discipline who distinguish affect and emotion while recognizing their complex relationship. *Affect* is a visceral bodily sensation that is physiological but social, and for which we do not have language since it functions beyond semiotics. On the other hand, *emotion* is a symbolic attempt at capturing an intensity of affect. Emotion is directed at an object while affect is unfixed, with no predetermined direction. For example, Gunn stresses "the distinction between affect as the event of a bodily intensity, and its signification, which delivers it over to the signifier as emotion."[32] Brian Massumi acknowledges that affect is often used as a synonym for emotion, but then claims that "emotion and affect—if affect is intensity—follow different logics and pertain to different orders."[33] In what is perhaps his most frequently cited sentence, Massumi writes, "Emotion is the most intense (most contracted) expression of that *capture*—and of the fact that something has always and again escaped."[34] Elsewhere he describes emotion as "sociolinguistic fixing," or a "qualified intensity, the conventional, consensual point of insertion of intensity into semantically and semiotically formed progressions, into narrativizable action-reaction circuits, into function and meaning. It is intensity owned and recognized."[35] For some affect scholars, including me, *feeling(s)* is an umbrella term that encompasses both affect and emotion,[36] which I will often label in this essay as *affect-emotion*, too. However, placing *affect* before the hyphen and *emotion* does not suggest that the relationship between them is linear or that there is chronological movement from one to the other. Affect and emotion are simultaneously at play because every capture always coincides with escape. Like Hawhee advises when thinking about feeling rhetoric, I do not want to "simply stall with the emotion/affect distinction."[37]

This theoretical perspective parts ways from phenomenology and (auto)ethnography even while they have similarities, like an appreciation for emotions. There is considerable debate and diversity within these perspectives. In general, the starting point for phenomenology is the mind and consciousness from the subjective or first-person point of view.[38] (Auto)ethnography shares some of these traits by attending to the individual researcher, such as through the practice of reflexivity, autobiographical writing, or personal narrative. Contemporary scholarship on affect and emotion calls attention to the researcher as well, often with similar writing strategies; however, personal feelings are understood as always already implicated in public feelings. As Sara Ahmed illuminates, affect might be best thought of as a "contact zone": "I do not simply interweave the personal and the public, the individual and the social, but show the ways in which they take shape through each other, or even how they shape each other. So it is not that 'my feelings' are in the writing, even though my writing may be littered with stories of how I am shaped by my contact with others."[39] Definitions and uses of (auto)ethnography as a method are contested in the field of communication, so its critiques and newer orientations resemble what I conceive as *feeling rhetorical criticism*. The work of Dwight Conquergood as well as Carolyn Ellis and Laura Ellingson demonstrates the rejection of binary oppositions between mind and body, reason and emotion, researcher and the researched, objectivity and subjectivity, self and others, and personal and cultural.[40]

In short, for rhetoricians who are interested in embodied field methods that take seriously emotional communication that does not follow conventional logic, affect theory foregrounds *public feelings* in contrast to centuries of relegation to the sidelines. What's more, this thinking suggests that the object of rhetorical study and the approach to examining it cannot be fully accounted for through traditional textual or symbolic analysis, especially not from the standpoint of disembodied critics.

An Affective–Emotional Methodology for Rhetorical Critics

I propose an affective-emotional field method with *feeling rhetorical critics*. This methodological heuristic is provisional, partial, and permeable because a step-by-step approach is theoretically at odds with affect itself. At least two registers of *feeling rhetorical criticism* include analyzing emotion words captured by rhetorical critics and analyzing affective bodily sensations that are felt by rhetorical critics but for which they struggle to articulate linguistically. To be clear, affective-emotional registers happen simultaneously and are intimately intertwined with each other even though I separate them here for purposes of description.

Emotion words are grammatical parts of speech with emotional meanings that come from their denotative definitions and connotative use in society. Gunn examines how media and political commentators (and himself) affix emotional nouns and adjectives to describe speeches given by Barack Obama and Hillary Clinton during the 2008 Democratic presidential primaries. Gunn says Obama's speech is "measured" and references *New York Times* journalists who declare Obama's speech "brave," "frank," and so forth.[41] In comparison, Gunn says Clinton's speech is "forceful and impassioned" and references BBC News and Politico.com, which describe Clinton's speech as "fierce" and "angry."[42] Emily Winderman's study of angry rhetoric in Margaret Sanger's notorious newsletters, *The Woman Rebel*, identifies anger at play in rhetorical figures and grammatical structures that are intelligible in print, such as fiery metaphors, anaphoric repetition, and copious listing.[43] With a comparable approach, Ahmed says that "my argument will suggest that 'figures of speech' are crucial to the emotionality of texts," and she is concerned in particular with metonymy and metaphor.[44] Deborah Gould reads emotive language in a social activist group's leaflets, speeches, chants, demonstrations, and other types of actions (e.g., lesbians and gay men in ACT UP [re]name a complicated constellation of feelings as 'anger' in publicity statements and personal reflections on political funerals they held).[45] *Feeling rhetorical criticism* follows these models but turns the analytical lens toward the emotional language of the critic. The primary object of study, then, is the emotional discourse of the researcher that is spoken aloud and written, yet this cannot be a self-centered project. "My" emotion words are not something that "I" think and write alone. Instead, it is only through interactions with other people in a social context (and by using language which is a cultural construct) that the symbolic capture of affect happens.

A rhetorical critic can "capture" emotion words in field notes, journal or diary entries, and multimedia recordings (e.g., video) from early stages of conducting research in the field to later when writing and revising for publication. The sociolinguistic fixing of emotion can also occur in e-mails and text messages with other people, postings online, academic conference papers and presentations, interpersonal communication and group discussion in meetings (whether held in person or via technology), as well as when preparing for and teaching students. This is a sample of recordings that might happen intentionally or not and most likely not in chronological order, but a rhetorical critic must at least strategically attempt to symbolically describe feelings with emotion words. As Thomas Lindlof and Bryan Taylor claim, writing "fieldnotes" is an important practice for "observing social action and reflecting about what it was like to be a participant. These acts create the foundation on which research claims are built. But this creation is not automatic. To achieve the status of evidence, participant observation must first be documented in text known as *fieldnotes*."[46] They conceive of *fieldnotes* as a "text" because they are concerned with describing and interpreting the symbolic qualities of social action.[47] In some sense, classical and contemporary rhetoricians already do this when studying the textual symbols of pathetic appeals. However, this approach calls the scholar to consciously attend to herself as a participant in emotional rhetoric since she is not separate from the text but part of it. To generate emotion words of rhetorical critics, it might be helpful to deploy the tools of qualitative communication researchers who have spent considerable time using and critically discussing field notes and other related practices such as scratch notes, head notes, journals, and diaries that two or more participants can even collaborate on together.[48] "Personal reactions" might be captured here and the first-person pronoun can be used as the critic asks and answers questions such as "How do I feel?" But this does not mean that what is said or written is only (or even predominantly) about the scholarly experience; this is not a solitary confessional. Remember that emotion is cultural and contextual, so awareness of and reflection on how the scholarly body bodes public feelings is imperative. For example, in a related essay in progress, my co-author and I write our feelings in the third person to illustrate how even personal bodily experiences of affect and the individual usage of emotion words are inextricably linked to the outside world.

At the same time that feeling rhetorical critics symbolically fix emotion in textual narrative, there will be a bodily intensity of affect that they feel and even express but which has no semantic meaning. Massumi theorizes this as an "affective residue" that escapes signification.[49] Like emotion, this visceral sensation is social and political. Unlike emotion, it is ineffable and free-floating. To study affect that theoretically defies description, Gunn analyzes what he calls "uncontrolled speech"[50] (e.g., the cry, the grunt, the scream, the yawp, and other involuntary blurts such as "Yaaaahhh!!!!" and "Ohhhh!"). Instead of "focusing on the rational march of meaning," Gunn writes, "uncontrolled speech gives one a glimpse of the unscripted, unconscious self,"[51] and "uncontrolled speech, of course, is *of the body*; it reminds the hearer of a body, *the body*."[52] However, uncontrolled speech is just one kind of affect for feeling rhetorical critics to analyze. Even with the empirical difficulties, Gould takes the affective curve in the emotional turn, too, for the purpose of "trying to preserve a space for human motivation that is nonconscious, noncognitive, nonlinguistic, noncoherent, nonrational, and unpredetermied—all qualities that I argue play a role in political action and inaction."[53] As a result, Gould recommends that scholars (whom she identifies as "emotional beings" with "introspective, emotional self-knowledge") closely read texts, speech, and bodily action in a manner that is attuned to the silences, to the inarticulable, to the inchoate, to the less-than-fully conscious, and to the repressed, of course all within specific historical conditions.[54] A representative chapter in Gould's book focuses on how "emotional undercurrents" or "unacknowledged feeling states" operated in the internal conflicts of ACT UP during its disintegration, along with how she and other activists struggled to figure out what happened and unconsciously blocked the conflicts out of their minds for many years after.[55] Almost as an addendum to Gunn, then, Gould accentuates silences and the repressed as unconscious affect that critics can access. This register of feeling rhetorical criticism will be more difficult for rhetoricians than the aforementioned analysis of emotion, not only because affect is opaque, unsettling, and often fleeting by definition, but also because the rhetorical tradition focuses on purposeful discourse (even when looking beyond conventional public address to the material rhetoric of protests, for instance). Analyzing visceral sensations that someone experiences but which are impromptu and intelligible values uncontrolled speech and other embodied nonverbal communication that is spontaneous, not symbolic, and often unconscious. In fact, in a radical departure from most presidential rhetoric scholarship, a recent object of inquiry for Samuel McCormick and Mary Stuckey is "presidential disfluency," a wide range of the president's "unscripted communicative actions—including, but in no way limited to—awkward pauses, verbal hiccups, botched colloquialisms, and confessional or overly personalized speech."[56]

Once again, methods already exist for feeling rhetorical critics to adopt or adapt to access affect. Although affect should not be subsumed under speech, per se, the sound emitted by someone's voice is one bodily expression that rhetorical scholars are uniquely trained to study.[57] Following communication (auto)ethnographers and materialist rhetoricians who assert that spaces and places "move bodies,"[58] we could also open up our sensing to the tastes, smells, touches, and so forth of the body of fieldworkers in the physical environment. These visceral sensations will be unconsciously felt throughout every stage of a research project, yet affect studies suggest the scholar should try to tap into these undercurrents. For instance, I suggest rereading field notes, journal or diary entries, and the researcher's other multimedia recordings of emotional words with a specific sensitivity to uncontrolled speech released by the rhetorical critic. Crucially, what I propose is not a rationalist symbolic critique of an individual's consciousness but rather an analysis of public feelings that engulf a researcher and ooze out of her pores, usually without awareness. Along the lines of what I envision is also Condit's new pathos-based rhetorical criticism that invites "*readers* of academic criticism [to] add to our assessments a deliberate reflection on what we feel when we read any piece of criticism, and a consideration of what those feelings imply about our affiliations and those on offer by the critic. For *authors* of rhetorical criticism, this analysis suggests that attention to one's own pathos, especially the affiliations one is crafting, should also be routine."[59] Condit's concept of affiliations is also significant since it stresses, like I do, how feelings are relational and not subjective.

Additionally, to tap into the collective unconscious, a feeling rhetorical critic could engage in *reflexive* analysis and alternative or creative writing formats (e.g., freewriting) that deeply embody the scholarly process, even during publication. The practice of reflexivity varies tremendously but is loosely defined as "accounting for the researcher's own role in social interaction."[60] In this case, I call for a reflexivity that "encourages consideration of that which has been silenced or invisible in academic conversations"[61] with affective rhetorical analysis that uses writing to bring forth the body of the critic as legitimate evidence, as (part of) a public argument even if that argument is illogical. Ellingson claims, "Writing is done with fingers and arms and eyes: It is an embodied act, not mental conjuring, and we should reflect on the experience of writing our research just as we reflect on our experience of being at a research site."[62] Although I similarly urge researchers to embody themselves in scholarly writing and reflect on it, the first emotional register of my method involves "mental conjuring" with emotional language, while this one focuses on unexpected bodily intensities that are precognitive but can be performed in writing. Stephen King, a prolific creative fiction writer who also published a best-selling advice book titled *On Writing*, similarly emphasizes that writers "*must not come lightly to the blank page*" (emphasis in the original) and seems to explain a process of writing from the unconscious when talking about his "far-seeing place" or "basement place" where he receives telepathic messages.[63] While this might seem strange to many Western thinkers, anthropologists have found that a mystical mentality coexists with the rational-logical in all human societies, the former of which is characterized by participation and involvement of all the senses and emotion.[64] I suggest that the creative writing practice of freewriting, specifically, could be useful for attending to affective bodily sensations that are inarticulate. Peter Elbow's work in English pedagogy explains freewriting as writing "without stopping, just write whatever words come out—whether or not you are thinking hard or in the mood."[65] Tellingly, he says that freewriting helps "make writing less blocked" and is a "raw" and "natural way of producing words" that gets at the "energy that drives the meanings," even though it "may seem crazy" and people accuse it of being "garbage."[66] There are a number of published scholarly prototypes to read for inspiration when engaging alternative or creative forms of writing, though they frequently take an ethnographic perspective.[67] I contend that actually how affect appears on the page is open-ended as long as it is not a self-centered soliloquy.

Analyzing "Bodies: The Exhibition" and Feeling Fetal Personhood

The enactment of a feeling rhetorical critic is akin to a long roller coaster ride with unforeseen twists and turns and ups and downs that are both exhilarating and exhausting. It is challenging to conduct an in-depth affective-emotional rhetorical analysis for those reasons alone. That task is more difficult here given that the main objective of this essay is to advance another field method grounded in contemporary affect theory and the politics of rhetorical criticism. Nonetheless, I return to the case study of "Bodies: The Exhibition" that opened this essay to provide an extra analytical sense (even if it is selective) of the approach.

Some context is necessary for setting the scene. "Bodies: The Exhibition" is operated by Premier Exhibitions Inc., a publicly traded company based in Atlanta, with a mission of being "the leading provider of museum-quality exhibitions throughout the world and the recognized leader in developing and displaying unique exhibitions for education and entertainment."[68] Premier Exhibitions' revenue for the 2013 fiscal year totaled $39.5 million with a gross profit of $20.7 million.[69] In particular, "Bodies: The Exhibition" is a multicity international commercial exhibit that opened in the United States in 2005. These exhibits are either stationary or they tour through cities for four to six months. As of February 2014, Premier Exhibitions concurrently ran seven exhibitions of "Bodies." The one located at the South Street Seaport in New York City was one of the permanent exhibits until its closure in late October 2012 due to complications from Hurricane Sandy and subsequent action by governmental authorities and the landlord; however, on April 9, 2014, Premier Exhibitions signed a lease to open "Bodies: The Exhibition" in a new permanent location in New York City.[70] Using more than two hundred specimens, each "Bodies: The Exhibition" features a collection of whole human bodies plus single human organs and body parts that are publicly displayed after undergoing the process of plastination which preserves them.

A common scholarly interpretation of my field notes from "Bodies: The Exhibition" might pinpoint only two observations related to my emotions and make little of their significance, as I initially did. But for a rhetorical critic now attuned to capturing emotion words and studying visceral sensations felt by people like herself, the text becomes much more complicated and compelling. With apprehension, I argue that the rhetoric of "Bodies: The Exhibition" at the South Street Seaport in New York City moves people to *buy* and *feel* the personhood of the fetus.

One way in which I literally bought fetal personhood was by paying money to visit the exhibit twice as well as traveling to its commercialized location in the South Street Seaport. Evidence of this purchase among the larger population is that fifteen million people worldwide, including me, have paid around twenty dollars each to enter "Bodies: The Exhibition," as of mid-2014.[71] I first experienced one of the exhibits in Atlanta shortly after it opened in 2005. Later in the summer of 2011 I joined a colleague at the exhibit in Lower Manhattan, which is when we took the aforementioned field notes. "Bodies: The Exhibition" at the South Street Seaport is organized around systems of the human body that are laid out in the following order on the second floor of the building and labeled as such: skeletal, muscular, nervous, respiratory, digestive, reproductive and urinary (with a supplementary section on fetal development), circulatory, treatment, and health and wellness. Resembling other commercialized destinations in Manhattan, a gift shop and photo booth bookend these parts of the exhibit. One level is a room with a ticket counter that serves as the exhibit's main entrance and exit. Emphasizing the commercial enterprise further is how this doorway opens onto South Street Seaport, a designated historic district along the East River and across from the Brooklyn Bridge that was renovated from an old mercantile fish market into a modern tourist shopping mall (e.g., a Banana Republic clothing store neighbors the building that houses the exhibition).

However, what "I" paid to experience cannot be attributed solely to me, nor did it remain a rationalist research project. Recall that emotion and affect are social. As a body feeling alongside other bodies that are alive and interacting with one another in the exhibit, and as people immersed in language and the sociopolitics of the early twenty-first-century United States, I became part and parcel of an emotive and affective American public that anthropomorphizes the fetus. Rereading my field notes reveals not only the involuntary statement of astonishment, "I gasped when looking into the bottle labeled 'ectopic pregnancy,' because I could see the fingers," but also gut reactions and emotionally loaded, uncontrolled speech released from other people: "That's sick"; "Wow, you can see the ribs"; "That's actually a real person"; and a handful of indecipherable references to "baby." We could not have been fully conscious given that many of these expressions are illogical. For example, I am a pro-choice feminist who has extensively studied the rhetoric of fetal imagery. Therefore I am aware of the rhetorical construction of the fetus as a "baby" and the erasure of the pregnant female body in history, from medical illustrations in the 1600s to sonograms and popular media in the contemporary moment.[72] According to the same scholarship, this representation of "fetal personhood" promotes pro-life ideologies, policies, and laws that I adamantly oppose. Thus my "gasp" was bodily affect over which I almost lost control; I was on the raw precipice of public feelings in favor of the personhood of the fetus that, cognitively and individually, I never intended to experience. More collective evidence of this affective-emotional rhetoric is another person's uncontrolled speech of amazement when s/he said, "Wow"; the person who linguistically articulated, "That's sick," a claim with emotional meaning about something that is unusual and disgusting; and the symbolic discourse of "baby" along with the personifying description, "That's actually a real person."

It is further telling that we felt this humanizing subjectivity of the fetus even though there was hardly talking or other noises, and the labeling of the glass jars by numerical "weeks" of "embryonic" and "fetal" development invited a more clinal response. This illustrates again how rhetorical critics must look outside the symbolic logical text. Put another way, critics need to pay attention to what is in front of the glass—the bodies of visitors like themselves—as much as what is behind it.[73] In particular, the glass jars were spotlighted in the middle of an otherwise dark room without sound. Even television screens that hung along one wall of this relatively small room displayed silent videos of cell reproduction with an egg and sperm, a sonogram, and camera shots of an infant crawling on a floor and children on a playground. In low lighting alongside two other walls of the room was the statement, "Birth begins when a woman goes into labor," next to a list of technical jargon such as "cells," "embryo," "uterus," and "zygote." But none of the people in the room with me spent time looking at these walls. In stark comparison, the majority of the exhibition included physically large spaces filled with bright lights and colors, featuring background music or sound playing with videos on television screens, and people had the option to listen (and many of us did) to "audio tour" recordings with earphones plugged into a handheld device included with the cost of admission.

Finally, as much as I am uncomfortable admitting it, we "bought into" the privileged person-status of the fetus not only when paying to enter "Bodies: The Exhibition" but also when walking into the "fetal development" gallery room, which was set apart by a partition wall within the "reproductive and urinary" section. Unlike the linear organizational flow of the rest of the exhibition, a directional sign is posted outside the "fetal development" room, giving people's minds and bodies another option: "Please pause a moment and consider if you want to enter this gallery. It displays the stages of embryonic and fetal development. All fetal and embryonic specimens in this gallery perished in utero from complications during pregnancy. If you wish to bypass this gallery, the exhibit continues to your left." Indeed, I physically and affectively paused before entering, as did two other people nearby. Yet I observed only one person bypass the room while more than ten people walked in while I was there. By moving with many other bodies into and through this part of the exhibit, people in some sense accepted that fetuses were human bodies just like the rest of the specimens. It seems impossible that rhetorical critics could ignore their bodily sensations when analyzing "Bodies: The Exhibit," but the field notes taken by my colleague and me nearly perpetuated that problem.

Letting Go, Let's Go

About five years have passed since I walked through "Bodies: The Exhibition" in New York City (more than ten years since I visited the Atlanta exhibit), and yet

I still feel what I felt back then. Perhaps many of you reading this essay can also still viscerally sense a study that you completed a while ago—the chills that ran up your arms or the uncontrollable words that came out of your mouth when analyzing a text? Quite possibly those feelings were rooted in your interactions with other people, as affect theory claims. Attending to such affect-emotion of rhetorical scholars not only further embodies the politics of criticism, but also denaturalizes the borders of rhetoric that are too often assumed to be rational, logical, cognitive, conscious, and symbolic. To better "listen to our guts," I developed and applied here a field method called *feeling rhetorical criticism.*

This approach is useful for moving away from evaluating symbolism alone, for comparing and contrasting another audience of rhetoric, and for rectifying the centuries-long myth of objectivity and preference for logos over pathos. Even though my case study involved an exhibition, this methodological perspective is suitable for examining a range of other subjects and objects, from public addresses delivered by presidents to digital media artifacts circulating through contemporary culture. This is not to say, however, that any of this will be simple or painless. For example, the autonomy of our selves will be theoretically threatened but at the same time difficult to actualize given conventions in the humanities that isolate researchers by training them to sit thinking at their desks by themselves. Female rhetorical scholars, specifically, might face backlash when they express emotion in a male-and-logic-dominated profession. As Ellingson aptly declares, "Academic research and life intersect; endeavoring to keep them artificially separated can lead to personal unhappiness as well as eliminating promising areas for research, but exploring the intersection is no easy task."[74]

In sum, Blair points out that bodies have become a more prominent concern in rhetorical criticism, but "the more personal (not to be read as 'subjective') character of criticism has emerged without nearly as much fanfare."[75] Indeed, there are many remaining questions about this kind of rhetorical criticism that I did not resolve. Nevertheless, nascent gestures toward an approach like this began in the discipline several decades ago, so isn't it about time that we let ourselves go?

Embodied Judgment

*A Call for a Phronetic Orientation
in Rhetorical Ethnography*

Aaron Hess

In turning toward field methods, rhetorical critics have taken to the streets to study social movements and localized community discourses. Various approaches have surfaced at this intersection of rhetoric and qualitative approaches, including rhetorical ethnography,[1] critical-rhetorical ethnography,[2] convergent critical rhetoric,[3] and rhetorical field methods.[4] Each shares similar commitments; rhetoric should be considered from an embodied perspective through which the critic, at the very least, witnesses the production of discourse. Yet they differ in how the critic should be positioned in relation to such discourse. On the one hand, some position the critic's identity as implicated within and integral to the study of rhetoric.[5] In this way, the critic is a direct participant in the production of rhetoric alongside other vernacular advocates. Similarly, Michael Middleton and colleagues construct a participatory epistemology that guides the research process,[6] while I have utilized *phronesis* as a guiding virtue.[7] In these cases, critics take part in discourse and learn specific strategies and praxes for advocacy. In contrast, others have maintained a critical distance from the performance within advocacy, positioning the critic as an observer of live rhetorics.[8] Looking across these considerations, I offer a conceptualization of the critic's role and how it informs rhetorical judgment potentially ascertained through an embodied and participatory approach to rhetoric.

Ethnographic and other *participatory* approaches uniquely position the critic to arrive at critical judgments about the performance of rhetoric. While criticism has long been about judgment pertaining to practices of identification, persuasiveness, and meaning-making, *embodied* judgment requires new theorizing in consideration of the critic's involvement in the production of discourse. Ethnography offers vital insight into rhetorical strategies that are otherwise difficult to realize, especially from a textual purview. Positioned within the field of argumentation, critics take up inventive practices and are directly affected by their successes and failures in advocacy. They comprehend advocacy through embodiment and as intrinsically tied to space and time, offering critical judgments that may differ from a textual perspective alone. I call this positioning a phronetic orientation that is realized through affective involvement within advocacy, which I outline through this essay. To begin, I discuss how advocacy can be understood from an ethnographic and embodied perspective, connecting it to the judgment of rhetors, audiences, and critics. Then I offer *phronesis* as a virtue that is tied to advocacy and deliberation, and especially pertinent to judgment. Finally, I outline a phronetic orientation within field research, implicating it within the performance of argument, as dialogic reflexivity, and as affectively embodied.

Advocacy and Judgment

Understanding *phronesis* and the situated character of rhetoric requires a conceptualization of rhetoric that is particular to embodied moments of advocacy. Admittedly, my characterization is somewhat limited, insofar as I primarily use examples from my own fieldwork experiences. By no means is this characterization exhaustive of all instances of rhetoric, although *phronesis* could be adapted to include a diverse array of rhetorical performances. As I have argued elsewhere, participatory approaches to studying rhetoric offer a robust set of tools and novel comprehensions of advocacy.[9] I follow Barry Brummett's conceptualization of rhetoric as "the advocacy of realities."[10] Rhetoric, in this sense, can be understood as a means of creating intersubjective realities; people come together and share perspectives via language, thus forming new realities. The goals of community-based advocacy often include the active persuading of publics toward their preferred conception of reality; in other cases, advocacy is performed in the public articulation of subjectivities. In my own work I have explored the nature of these "realities" in a number of contexts, including drug use with the harm reduction organization DanceSafe, public memory at the tenth anniversary of September 11, reflections on public deliberation practices at late-night host Jon Stewart's "Rally to Restore Sanity," and natural childbirth and home birth advocacy by midwives at a local birthing center. Each of these contexts constructs reality in varied and particular ways.

For Brummett, rhetoric is the human ability to make meaning out of the essentially ambiguous character of reality, a claim founded in a postmodern sensibility. In this sense, rhetoric enables humans to share ideas about their reality and find moments to challenge others. As a foundation, this definition—"the advocacy of realities"—provides a starting point for seeing the nature of rhetorical exchange in local, everyday places, or within vernacular contexts. Rather than focusing on official, privileged discourses, critics of vernacular discourse consider where and how unofficial discourses—those discourses "written out of history"—struggle and resist dominant discourses.[11] Critics turn their attention to the smaller, mundane instances of rhetoric, often found on the street, in coffee shops, and on picket lines. These expressions are not contained in spoken words alone; indeed, vernacular speech includes the use of pamphlets or newspapers,[12] digital media,[13] or photography.[14] In short, vernacular discourses offer a robust opportunity for realizing rhetoric and judgment. In my work, I have explored the localized realities and judgments traded between advocates and the public, appearing in the form of creative expression, judgments about political issues, and calls on the government to alter legislative structures. The strategies and tactics deployed in these moments of advocacy include myriad forms of discourse, but at their core they are understood in opposition to existing structures of governance and power.

By approaching advocacy at the vernacular level, I engage an adversarial model of rhetoric. Rhetoric is a contested art and an art of contestation—contested in its desire for audience, its varied crafting of messages, and its reflection on the role of bodies, language, identities, and power.[15] Advocacy, then, is at the heart of vernacular exchange as ideas crystalize within particular moments of discursively constructed realities. Localized communities seeking to establish a sense of identity and community that resists dominant logics engage in rhetorical performances that seek to shift the intersubjective comprehensions of reality. My research spans a range of vernacular judgments, from the nature of drug use in society to the over-medicalization of childbirth. The identities of "drug user" or "midwife" carry specific meanings both inside and outside these communities. For vernacular and out-law discourses, rhetorical advocacy serves as an outward expression and instantiation of the "loosely shared logics of justice, ideas of right and wrong that are different than, although not necessarily opposed to, a culture's dominant logics of judgment and procedures for litigation."[16] John Sloop and Kent Ono suggest that out-law and vernacular judgment should be understood at a fundamentally material level of discourse, which has more direct political consequences and impact, and requires critics to consider participatory and ethnographic methods.[17]

To understand the judgments within drug culture, I joined DanceSafe and traveled to desert raves across Arizona, enacting the localized judgments regarding drugs by interacting with volunteers and users alike within arenas of active drug use.

For participatory rhetorical methods, advocacy can be conceptualized as the purposeful expression of a subjective construction of reality, utilized for social change, the recognition of identity, or resisting power structures. Advocacy includes decorous and indecorous acts, depending on the nature of the rhetorical situation, and may carry strong commitments to democratic processes or a belief in radical action. In defining advocacy in this way, I seek to underscore its rhetorical and material foundation; it is a contest rooted in language, body, space, and time. Advocates express themselves through embodied practices tied to specific places and moments and through nonverbal, verbal, corporeal, and mediated expression. The kairotic character of advocacy recognizes that speaking requires due attention to decorum and the opportune moments where tactical invention might alter larger social structures.[18] While many of my examples attend to the deliberative nature of advocacy—as in, those moments that feature advocates engaging in strong democratic action[19]—a phronetic orientation is not limited to this nature of advocacy alone. In other examples, interlocutors engage in a variety of rhetorical actions, including protest activities, performative outbursts, and creative dialogue.

Two examples illustrate the drastic differences in rhetorical action. Jon Stewart's carnivalesque "Rally to Restore Sanity" attempted to challenge existing deliberative practices by gathering in front of the Capitol Building on the National Mall.[20] Attendees at the rally sought to challenge their representatives in Congress by speaking directly to them through mainstream democratic means—that of large-scale protest. As a critic at the rally, I took part in the atmosphere by engaging in dialogue with those around me as well as singing along with a somewhat off-key Jon Stewart. Quite differently, DanceSafe members and ravers are inherently embracing an illegal act, one that can potentially strip a citizen of his or her democratic rights through incarceration.[21] Moreover, many ravers are under the voting age and may not be interested in the politics of drug use. Strong democratic processes, such as voting or protest, were not perceptually present for many youth attending a rave. Yet DanceSafe finds opportunities to advocate for better health choices among this younger population, and as a critic inside of the organization I stood alongside other volunteers, passing out drug pamphlets, conversing about contraindications between drugs, and, when possible, finding time to dance. A phronetic orientation invites a practical sensibility that is guided by the demands, needs, and opportunities found in each instance of advocacy. In some cases, such as the rally, advocacy may be guided by a strong deference to democratic order or through official channels. In others, such as DanceSafe, advocacy may take on a very radical stance that exists largely outside of traditional legal avenues, very much in violation of democratic decorum. Nevertheless, such action may be deemed necessary in order to be heard or to reach the appropriate audience. Advocates inherently recognize these competing social and political judgments, navigating the choppy waters between existing belief and new realities created through their outcries. In essence, then, rhetorical ethnography is an attempt to apprehend the nature of judgment as it is gained and performed by vernacular advocates.

Judgment, Rhetoric, and *Phronesis*

The nature of political, social, and critical judgment continues to be a difficult theoretical question. Rhetoric has always been concerned with judgment, especially as it is received in the moment of speaking. The nature of judgment in criticism remains contested in rhetorical scholarship. On the one hand, for Aristotle, the "object of Rhetoric is *judgment*," something to be gained by the audience upon the hearing of the speech.[22] Judgment, in this case, is contained within the speaker and audience, passed on or altered by the act of speaking. On the other hand, judgment is something that critics have regarding the nature of speech, which has long been a point of contention for literary, art, and rhetorical criticism.[23] In the distancing of rhetorical criticism from its neo-Aristotelian roots, Edwin Black outlines the nature of critical judgment arrived at through the reading of speeches, establishing that "rhetorical transactions are not things; they are processes."[24] The act of judging a speech requires, then, a concern for context, history, and ideology—a well-established turn in rhetorical methods.[25] Criticism that includes a variety of theoretical perspectives can provide insight into the motivations, ideologies, and indeed judgments of speakers and audience, leading to a deepening of knowledge about the nature of power in discourse. Another concern regarding critical judgment is the relationship between theory and method, with some believing that method exists as a way to support the critic's evaluation of speech and, in turn, produce "better" judgments of the text.[26] The establishment of *rhetorical* methods served early disciplinary needs; yet the trappings of formalizing neo-Aristotelian criticism proved inadequate and faulty, finding flawed or partial judgments.[27] Similarly, criticism only partially fulfills its aim in understanding judgment, especially through its distancing of the critic from embodied speech.

The critical turn in rhetoric invited myriad perspectives and stances toward the production of discourse.[28] Consequently, the nature of judgment was troubled by a host of theorists, including Derrida, Baudrillard, and Foucault. As James McDaniel and John Sloop put it, "The status of judgment in 'postmodern' thought is highly problematic, and leans rather heavily toward the negative."[29] Indeed, the critical turn in rhetoric leads to persistent critique, interrogating the nature of knowledge, truth, and power. In these instances, critical rhetoric may struggle to rely on universal or strong judgments, believing that they are, in actuality, mere passing figments. That said, out-law and vernacular discourse theories provide a framework for understanding materialist judgments as they are enacted in localized levels. In this sense, judgments between dominant and marginalized logics are rhetorically contested in both public and private places.[30] Critics seeking to understand these competing judgments should "cultivate an interest in cultural artistic expressions, ways of living, and principles of survival" found in out-law and dominant logics.[31] While working with DanceSafe I found the nature of "artistic expression" and "survival" fascinating. Ravers often spoke of the need to attend raves because of the sense of family found there, as if the dominant logic had excluded them from participation. Moreover, interviewees spoke of survival through self-medicating with marijuana or weekend ecstasy use to avoid "zombifying" corporate pharmaceuticals. These alternative logics and judgments illustrate the competing realities—perspectives even—found in raver culture and dominant society.

James Jasinski indicates that the "nexus of rhetoric and judgment is perspective; advocates craft arguments and appeals that shape the way audiences perceive and, in turn, act in the world. Criticism contributes to or thickens our grasp of political and rhetorical judgment as it reveals the way perspectives are crafted, circulated, and subverted."[32] Certainly, perspective can be at least partially gained through the criticism of the textual products of advocacy. Websites for DanceSafe or the pamphlets distributed by volunteers may provide clues into the localized judgments. While criticism has led to evaluations of judgment, the *in situ* demands for persuasion or identification differ significantly from judgment gained through textual reflection alone. When working with advocates, participatory critics require a new sense of judgment. Judgment "attains conceptual solidity or substance as it is vibrated against a particular case—a materially embodied episode of discursive action and choice—and becomes refined and instantiated in an interpretation of that case."[33] During my "embodied episode" with DanceSafe, ravers spoke of *how* they used the drug pamphlets offered and the ways in which they interpreted the health organization's central message. In this way, the division between spectator/critic judgment and rhetor judgment becomes blurred, especially at the point of an embodied phronetic orientation. When critics step into the role of rhetor, they embody the decision calculi inherent to that context and advocacy. Simultaneously, critics can investigate the position of the audience through interviews and participant observation, which offer a new vantage point for apprehending the judgment of those witnessing the act. Between these positions, the critic serves as a conduit of competing judgments and perspectives, all of which can be understood through embodying each rhetorical role. Being able to interview both volunteers and ravers illuminated the *exchange* of the educational materials offered by the volunteer organization. A textual perspective alone on those materials would not reveal how DanceSafe volunteers take care in their arrangement across the table at a rave, or how ravers collect and adorn their bedroom walls with drug education.[34]

In another episode, during protests regarding home birth regulations, a textual perspective might reveal the importance of children to the protest as living examples of the efficacy of home birth practices. Yet the textual product cannot account for the embodied, affective experience of holding a baby while also holding a protest sign, chanting to the windows of government bureaucrats in the Phoenix heat. Engaged critics learn of the competing judgments of government and midwives during protest conversations about the use of drugs in labor, while chants of "My body, my choice!" can be heard in the background. The adoption of a phronetic orientation in rhetorical ethnography can illuminate affective and situated knowledges in ways that criticism cannot. More traditionally, locating *phronesis* entails "an attempt to find a cultural/ community, local, based model of judgment."[35] From an embodied perspective, *phronesis* can be understood through direct performances of advocacy by the ethnographer, which provide entry into the localized and grounded judgments of vernacular advocates.

When examining localized instances of controversy, deliberation, or commemoration, participatory critics can acquire an interpretation of judgment that is tied to the particulars of individual vernacular communities. In so doing, the dividing lines between rhetor, critic, and audience blur. Working with DanceSafe positioned me as critic and rhetor, and empathic interviews with ravers offered insight into the audience of the campaign. The relationship between political agent and spectator illustrates the "duality inherent to the concept of judgment."[36] The interplay between audience and speaker often entails competing judgments and perspectives coming together through discourse. The critic, however, is often seen as separate from this process, offering critical yet distant judgment. Rhetorical ethnography and other field-based methods bring together the three positions at the moment of advocacy joined with critical reflection. Certainly, the rhetorical ethnographer cannot fully appreciate and apprehend the unique positioning between the three; yet, with due attention to the rhetorical praxes enacted both in body and voice, the rhetorical ethnographer can provide an accounting of each. As such, I argue that the virtue of *phronesis* should serve as a guide for rhetorical scholars in the field as they seek to gain perspective.

As a virtue, *phronesis* is quite elastic but carries key components that guide my own fieldwork and participatory rhetorical research. Indeed, the virtue has been recently taken up by researchers across the discipline of communication and other social sciences.[37] The Aristotelian virtue of *phronesis* has long been related to the concept of judgment.[38] Initially offered in the *Nicomachean Ethics*, the virtue has been defined in many ways, including "practical wisdom,"[39] "wise deliberation,"[40] "practical intelligence,"[41] and "prudence."[42] In my conception, I maintain some Aristotelian elements while also expanding the virtue with a contemporary theoretical and methodological grounding. As Lois Self concludes, "Rhetoric is an art, *phronesis* an intellectual virtue; both are special 'reasoned capacities' which properly function in the world of probabilities."[43] In contrast with *sophia* (eternal wisdom), which operates external of human affairs as divine contemplative knowledge, *phronesis* is fundamentally understood as the practical wisdom of human affairs operating within the contingent relations between rhetors and leaning toward action.[44]

Given that the rhetorical field requires due recognition to human custom and culture, *phronesis* also requires situational adaptability. *Phronesis* is set apart from other intellectual virtues because "it puts special emphasis on the practical and the particular."[45] However, understood as an ethical framework, the construction of *phronesis* is both practical and universal. While seemingly contradictory, *phronesis* combines knowledge of the larger human good with an application of that larger understanding toward the individual and practical case. As a virtue, *phronesis* entails an oscillation between recognizing larger, ethical ideals and the practical needs of a particular situation.[46] The virtue can be refined for expression in all cases but is applied in the particular. Christopher Lyle Johnstone argues that "two key elements figure in the acquisition and exercise of *phronêsis*: knowledge of the 'first principles' of praxis, the final ends or causes of human action; and knowledge about means to attaining these ends, which rests on excellence in deliberating."[47] These two elements figure directly into the rhetorical production and the acquisition of practical knowledge in fieldwork. *Phronesis* functions at a material level for field researchers, who strive toward recognition of excellence in rhetorical action through experiential and embodied approaches. To do so, rhetorical ethnographers should adopt a phronetic orientation that focuses on performative action, dialogical reflexivity, and affective involvement.

A Phronetic Orientation

From an embodied perspective in fieldwork, *phronesis* can be understood as a dialogic political performance that shares attention between larger contextualizing ethics, morals, and principles and the particulars driving rhetorical exchanges. As I articulate the concept here, I hope to bridge the gap between scholarly knowledge and practitioner knowledge, while also recognizing that they entail and occupy two relatively different subject positions. Indeed, Scott Welsh contends that the desire to bridge scholarly reflection into political agency leads to a nearly irresolvable antagonism between the two.[48] The antagonism surfaces largely because of the subject position inherent to each; as soon as the pull of one overtakes the other, the equation becomes unbalanced. Welsh believes that the academy is an impediment to producing viable democratic action in the public.

Phronesis serves as a corrective and connective virtue between the types of knowledge developed at the advocate and critic level. While the two subject positions (practitioner and researcher) appear distinct and possibly in opposition, *phronesis* invites consideration of the many characters of advocacy. In evaluating the wisdom in advocacy, the *phronimos* constructs an empathic character in research[49] that requires participatory perspectival training. Put another way, a phronetic orientation toward rhetoric invites the scholar to reflexively consider her or his position relative to other advocates and audiences alike. Stepping into the position of advocate foregrounds the needs of the organization over the academy. Along the way, researchers may find avenues of support and democratic action through their participation with the group. The voices of individual participants can be elevated through traditional academic publishing or through alternative means that support the cause. For example, while filming a documentary project in New York, I met many people who experienced the horror of 9/11 firsthand, including a survivor who narrowly escaped the World Trade Center as floors were burning above. Before interviewing, she asked if we were a part of the 9/11 Truth movement and about the purpose of the film. We explained our intent regarding public memory and disavowed conspiracy theories regarding 9/11. During the interview she explained how survivors are somewhat lost in the media narratives of 9/11 while conspiracies have gained traction. Subsequently we featured her story in the documentary and shared clips of the interview via YouTube and Facebook in an effort to promote localized truth regarding the events and the memory of survivorship. Because of our attention to the localized wisdom of those involved, we found ways to expand our critical judgment about the memory of the tragedy. This new sense of critical judgment is what can be gained by the participatory critic who embraces a phronetic orientation.

Phronesis *and the Performance of Rhetoric*

First, *phronesis* is a virtue that is gained by sustained performance of rhetoric or argument in the field, embodied through "practical action by ordinary decision-makers possessing common knowledge and conventional skills."[50] For example, during the aforementioned film project, much of the city was commemorating the anniversary of the 9/11 attacks. Participating in those events included the practical action of affective memorializing—meaning that I performed the epideictic practices occurring in that space and at that time. During a hand-in-hand moment of silent commemoration I joined those who encircled Battery Park to reflect on the anniversary. During that same trip I participated in the

"Ribbons of Hope" memorial by offering my own voice alongside others who authored messages on the ribbons attached to the display. Working in the field requires attention to the contingent character of the advocacy at hand and the researcher's relationship with it.

Phronesis is also driven by the contingent context of speaking about a particular case: "It involves comparing the relative advantages and disadvantages of alternative courses of action, finding evidence to support one or another judgment about these things, making arguments that will reveal one set of outcomes and costs as more or less likely than others and one course of action as more efficacious than the alternatives, and then deciding on that one action."[51] This means that *phronesis* will differ between research projects, yet the core understanding of "wisdom" remains. To be "wise" in the field means that the participatory rhetorical scholar has achieved some experienced status in the field, a status that is not necessarily related to academic credentials. With DanceSafe I was often considered an "expert" on particular contraindications of drugs, such as taking ecstasy and antidepressants. Beyond "book smarts" I also learned how to identify the types of drugs users were on by examining their behaviors, which directly affected interactions with them. These moments are difficult to put into words; often, I could just sense that this person was on ecstasy or that person was on acid. Being wise entails experience and intuition—the "gut feelings" about how advocacy is performed—in the context of speaking, likely gained through a learning curve. This means that *phronesis* is something that can be "acquired through choice and training" and "deliberation about choice and action is the way to cultivate this superordinate virtue."[52] It is bound up in our character and how we personally develop and change over time.[53] In other words, *phronesis* is achieved through the practice of adaptive invention, through which the participatory critic learns new avenues for creative expression and argumentation. Charting one's personal growth within an organization and the successes and failures in performing the advocacy illustrates how *phronesis* can be acquired.

Phronesis is also an embodied virtue that opens up new forms of deliberation. As Daniel Smith contends, *phronesis* can be "understood as cultivating ways of inhabiting the social differently, with an aim of 'disrupting' the familiarity and common sense that is the very fabric [of] everyday life. Such disrupting would seek to destabilize the stability of the spaces, *doxa*, habits, practices, norms, signs, narratives, concepts, subject-positions, and social institutions that are the very 'ground' of communal life."[54] In other words, a phronetic orientation connects the *phronimos* with the contingent conditions of possibility in everyday life through dialogue. Importantly, this conception of *phronesis* allows for an oscillation between what it is and what might be, which can open spaces for invention that tend toward the common good. Maurice Charland expresses concern about this element of an Aristotelian *phronesis*, that it becomes a conservative ideal insofar as "it unproblematically follows the community standard."[55] Potentially, then, *phronesis* can fall into the trappings of those communities, effectively blinding the critic from alternative possibilities or more radical forms of invention. Charland also invites critical rhetoric to engage in "disassembling (deconstructing) certain formations to try out new constructions."[56] Toward this end, a phronetic orientation should embrace the ethnographer's insider/outsider position, which provides the vantage point for seeing and opening more possibilities within rhetorical action. For Smith, *phronesis* involves both the living in the context of deliberation but also being able to recognize spaces where *doxa* can be opened and destabilized: "Phronetic disruption is not the transgression of habits, norms, and conventions but the amplification of 'other' forces and movements within those social practices and relations, which may enable them to operate in different ways."[57] Put another way, a phronetic orientation relies on both a dialogic position inside established communities and their practices, as well as the wisdom to find outside, inventive avenues for deliberation.

This disruptive nature of *phronesis* can be seen in fieldwork, in terms of both rhetors and critics. In my work with DanceSafe I witnessed the planning that goes into the performance of political argumentation within health advocacy contexts. During an interview, one volunteer portrayed raves as countercultural and rebellious, but also thought that DanceSafe could find opportunities to speak to ravers about political issues not typically heard in clandestine desert raves. She spoke of voter drives and discussing legislation as a part of the advocacy of the group. While typical of other political organizations, the *doxa* found in a rave is far removed from politics. Yet, in her estimation, raving had a politics to it that should be shared and discussed, even in the midst of thumping music and chemical indulgence. This wisdom is gained through the unique position of those who embody *phronesis*, saying that "the special knowledge of the *phronimos* comes clear in his or her departure from what the rules seem to dictate."[58] As a virtue, then, *phronesis* provides both an impulse to take stock of the extant norms of speaking *and* a desire to find new avenues for communicative action. Know the rules, *and* know how and when to break them. During my research at the Rally to Restore Sanity, for example, participants in the study expressed a desire for both rational deliberation and ironic subversion of those principles through political humor. In seeking to embody a phronetic orientation, my research engaged the dual judgments of attendees through an embrace of both the seriousness of political change and the spectacular comedy of the stage. This led to the production of a short documentary that features two intelligent interlocutors conversing about the history of political satire while dressed as Dr. Seuss's Thing 1 and Thing 2.[59] Overall, phronetic research must account for the relationship between tradition and disruption, decorum and change, self and other.

Phronesis exists at the level of interpersonal interaction through dialogue. Steve Schwarze acknowledges the complex temporalities that compose the dialogic moment: "Rather than face a situation 'cold,' deliberators rely on past experiences to discern the repeated aspects of a situation from the new, the relevant aspects from the irrelevant."[60] The moment of advocacy draws together past experience between multiple speakers who dialogue about rightness, wrongness, and a course of action. Even in specific events, where participation is limited by time, dialogic wisdom can be built through active reflection on interactions with participants. For my work in 9/11 public memory I interviewed roughly sixty people in Lower Manhattan regarding their memories of the events.[61] Every discussion regarding the morality of specific memory practices, the interpretations of the official memorial, and judgments about the historical significance of 9/11 served as a learning moment for the next interview. Through an empathic stance, I strived to understand the dual impulses of vengeful violence in response to the death of family members on 9/11 and exasperated peace due to a decade of war since the events. Over time I found myself identifying with them and with other residents of New York in unexpected ways.

Critics who embrace a reflexive stance toward deliberation can recognize the nature of this learning and development, understanding that *phronesis* is a virtue that is built over time and through sustained engagement in the field: "The recognition (by Aristotle) that all judgment involves prejudice, both 'blind' and 'enabling,' lends urgency to the attempt to develop a kind of knowledge (*phronesis*) capable of critically evaluating both the internal and external conditions of its own deployment."[62] In other words, *phronesis* provides a critical stance that evaluates the conditions of advocacy from the perspective of the advocate *and* the critic. McGee would concur in this estimation of *phronesis* as a reflective and reflexive virtue. Drawing from Gadamer, he remarks that "the *phronimos* must constantly 'go back to school' to be sure that what resulted in a degree of goodness last time will have the same effects this time, in this particular circumstance."[63] The constant reevaluation of knowledge and wisdom speaks to the contingent character of advocacy as performed in various places. This means that those engaged in rhetorical ethnography should pay close attention to the ways in which they succeed and fail, to the new empathic identifications with those around them, and to how they grow in their advocacy.[64]

As a locally situated virtue, *phronesis* also requires an ongoing recognition, evaluation, and critical examination of inherent social and moral characteristics involved in rhetorical situations. The critic takes careful consideration of the actions within both research and activism, finding instances when the two perspectives can simultaneously inform each other. As a cyclical model of self-reflection, "phronesis adds clarity to the nature of the relationship between reflection and actions—that is, actions are derived from reflection, and reflection is built through the practice of reflective actions."[65] The participatory actions carried out by the critic embody the roles of researcher and community advocate, much like the nature of insider and outsider status in ethnography. Reflexivity bridges the two, as those in the field can reflect on their role of researcher juxtaposed with the role of advocate, and vice versa. In my own work with DanceSafe, I found that the wisdom gained through advocacy directly affected the research I was producing. For example, while in the field I learned of drug support websites, such as Pillreports.com (now Pillreports.net) and Erowid.org, dedicated to sharing information to provide users with better experiences and healthier drug choices. Learning of these as an advocate extended my research into the digital realm.[66] It was not only that I gained knowledge of the existence of these websites; I also learned how much of the harm reduction philosophy extends online and how raves and the websites share a community ethos about drug use. When I returned to the field, I was able to carry lessons learned from online users into my work as an advocate.

This give and take of *phronesis* mirrors the self-reflexive accountability common to critical-qualitative researchers and ethnographers. D. Soyini Madison recognizes the importance of critical reflexivity in research, focusing attention on the representation of identity and the Other.[67] Drawing from Norman Denzin's work,[68] Bryant Keith Alexander outlines six levels of ethnographic reflexive engagement: subjectivist, methodological, intertextual, standpoint, queer, and feminist materialist.[69] To these I add phronetic reflexivity, which exists at a rhetorical level within advocacy, meaning that the judgments arrived at through dialogical interactions require specific reflection different from and on top of existing reflexive commitments. It provides a moralizing yet interrogatory force within participatory rhetorical approaches and is specifically tied to rhetorical practices, which require attention to the discursive and affective embodiment of argument.

From a pragmatic perspective, embodying phronetic reflexivity means taking note of the development and training of the researcher-advocate. Being phronetic means practicing *phronesis*. While seemingly tautological, this means that the virtue is acquired in the process of doing and reflecting, and then doing anew. Those scholars reporting on the development of *phronesis* could recall instances of failure and success, consider moments when advocacies were altered to fit different audiences, and chart the personal trajectory of training. In this way *phronesis* builds on other qualitative reflexive approaches, such as the vulnerable observer in anthropology, who bears witness and is implicated in the power dynamics of the narratives of others.[70] The vulnerability in *phronesis*, however, is tied more specifically to the successes and failures in rhetorical practices. As mentioned above, success can be measured in a variety of ways, but it should be apprehended through the localized judgments of the organization or group under study. For the individual rhetorical ethnographer, reflexivity through a phronetic orientation requires admissions of fault and fallibility within those spaces of judgment. It is being ethically and epistemologically vulnerable to how the advocacy is *supposed to be* performed and whether the critic is living up to those expectations. Working with DanceSafe I found myself struggling early on with personal questions from ravers about my own drug use. I also found that, in some cases, knowledge gained from ravers' personal experience overpowered medical arguments offered by the group. DanceSafe's informative approach paled in comparison with simple experiential arguments offered in deliberation. I had to learn and develop my personal deliberative character over the course of my time with DanceSafe, balancing cold drug facts with warm drug stories.

While other critical ethnographic approaches implicate elements of demographic *identity* and privilege—which certainly also apply here—a phronetic orientation questions the *character* of the advocate, tying wisdom and experience to argument. This does not mean that *phronesis* is merely about wins and losses; it is about those learning moments in the field that provide insight to successful argumentation, with success measured in a variety of ways: "For Aristotle, phronetics as an intellectual virtue was not gained by stepping back and contemplating reality from an objective distance, as if that was possible, but it came from getting one's hands dirty by actively confronting the problems of the day."[71] It is the process of becoming a seasoned advocate in the field. This could be conducted by personal journaling throughout the research process, where reflections on early attempts provide clues to the growth of the advocate, or by member-checking with other advocates about successes in the field.

Embodiment and Affect

As a virtue, *phronesis* "is judgment that is embodied in action."[72] The practical moment of speaking calls forth the dialogic characters and bodies of speaker and audience. As an embodied virtue, *phronesis* can include wisdom as felt or intuited, as well as wisdom understood cognitively. Consideration of this virtue can open up participatory critics to a critical affective understanding of rhetoric,[73] a sense of deliberation and dialogue as simultaneously corporeal and felt as well as cognitive and spoken. Interviewing 9/11 first responders who witnessed the towers falling, holding hands with strangers during a ceremony, and feeling the personal malaise inherent to being witness to the repeated recounting of the "worst day in my life" all hint at an affective element of *phronesis*. During one conversation, an interviewee gave her "flashbulb memory" of 9/11, narrating how she was on the phone with the investment firm Cantor

Fitzgerald when the first plane hit the towers and the line went dead. The shivers and goose bumps accented the interview with a lasting affective sense. In another interview, a first responder also gave me chills as he recounted watching people who had to make the decision to "jump or burn." These powerful moments are informed, in part, by embodied and affective elements.

As an experiential virtue, *phronesis* requires affective involvement of the self through its dialogic positioning of bodies.[74] Bent Flyvbjerg sees the intuition built through *phronesis* as "the ability to draw directly on one's experience— bodily, emotional, intellectual—and to recognize similarities between these experiences and new situations."[75] Being in the field of advocacy means *passionately* performing argument by activating an affective level of perception, leading to embodied understandings of argument. During my time in Lower Manhattan there was a sense of unease in the air. The community advocates who organized local commemorative events expressed concern about the warnings of potential terror attacks on the city again, especially on the bridges and tunnels. The eerie feeling of raised terror levels in the background, coupled with narratives of death and destruction, marked the occasion with an intensity that is difficult to put into words yet was shared among volunteers and researchers alike. Feeling in the field entails reflection on bodily and sensory exploration of the sights, sounds, and smells of the research site while appreciating the corporeal highs and lows of performing vernacular advocacy.

Conclusion

In this essay I have offered a phronetic orientation toward participatory and ethnographic methods in rhetorical research. *Phronesis* provides a virtue that illustrates the complexity of gaining practical wisdom in the field of argumentation. Through it, critics can ascertain new forms of materialist judgment that are directly tied to the lived experiences of advocates in their everyday lives. Departing from traditional textual approaches, the virtue compels questions about the nature of the body, and requires a reflexive response that challenges the role of the critic. At the individual research project level, inquiries into *phronesis* can be made regarding the practical action and outcomes of advocacy. Phronetic rhetorical scholars can ask about the *doing* of advocacy, the types of tactics, strategies, and/or arguments that are deployed. As an embodied virtue, *phronesis* questions how the body can be implicated into the field. Finally, a phronetic orientation invites a reflexive and affective positioning experienced in dialogue with those in the scene, always seeking to act and reflect on our advocacy in the field.

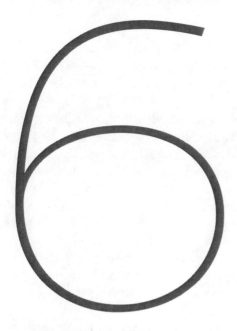

"Pa' que tú lo sepas"

*Experiences with Co-presence
in Puerto Rico*

Kathleen M. de Onís

A plane flew over the camp of Playas P'al Pueblo in Isla Verde, nearby the San Juan Luis Muñoz Marín International Airport. It was la Noche de San Juan, an event replete with bonfires, live music, and other festivities. Ariel Hernández, the camp's lawyer, looked up at the aircraft flying overhead and shouted over its loud hum: "Estamos aquí, pa' que tú lo sepas." ("We are here, just so you know.") The assembled beach-goers cheered!

—FIELD NOTES CONCERNING A GROUP THAT HAS BEEN
OCCUPYING THE AREA SINCE 2005 TO DETER THE MARRIOTT
HOTEL CHAIN FROM PRIVATIZING THE PUBLIC BEACH

*Thank you to the *Text + Field* editors for their insightful and encouraging suggestions on this chapter. Thanks, too, to Phaedra C. Pezzullo, Kirstin Wagner, and Lindsey Campbell Badger for reviewing earlier drafts of this essay, and to the ardent activists I met in the field. This project was funded by Indiana University's Office of Sustainability, the Organization for Research on Women and Communication, and the Waterhouse Family Institute. The author received an Environmental Communication Division top paper award for this essay at the 2015 International Communication Association convention.

"Pa' que tú lo sepas" is often invoked by boricu@s[1] to signal their unique cultural and linguistic roots despite living in a U.S. unincorporated territory. The cultural idiom is derived from a song titled "Yo soy boricua, pa' que tú lo sepas" / "I am Puerto Rican, just so you know." This saying is also used in environmental struggles seeking to protect public beaches from private development: "Las playas son p'al pueblo . . . pa' que tú lo sepas" / "The beaches are for the people . . . just so you know." This utterance constitutes a cultural performance and an act of resistance that constructs a counter-narrative to the official ethno-racial, nationality, and citizenship designations imposed on Puerto Ricans by the U.S. government. Given that "labor, education, language, and health policies were instituted to fix what was 'wrong' with Puerto Rico, to take control of human matter out of place and relocate, contain, and reshape it," staying *in* place has become a mode of protest and defiance for many boricu@s.[2] These discursive, embodied performances, as exemplified by Hernández, direct attention to the important role of language, ideology, and corporeality in everyday encounters. Being in place, or *in situ*, also speaks to the fieldwork possibilities available to rhetorical critics. I appropriate Hernández's declaration—"We are here, just so you know"—to evince the importance of "*here*-ness," or being physically present in the field. This *co-presence* is central to ethnographic studies.

Michael Middleton, Samantha Senda-Cook, and Danielle Endres offer "rhetorical field methods" to communicate the approaches guiding *in situ* research.[3] They maintain that "by accessing embodied and 'live' elements of rhetoric suppressed in textual representation, and by focusing on communities often excluded from critical analysis (e.g., the mundane, the oppressed, the oppositional) rhetorical field methods both challenge *who counts* as a rhetorical community worth studying, and *what counts* as a form of rhetorical action worthy of scrutiny."[4] Gerard Hauser issues a similar claim in his "plea for an ethnographical rhetoric"; he explicates that such a methodological commitment "holds the promise of revealing how ordinary people engage in the ongoing struggle between those in and out of power by which society continually produces itself."[5] Informed by these methodological insights, this essay details how co-presence facilitates the study of otherwise undocumented cultural artifacts and communities by charting rhetorical practices of oppression and resistance.

In 2014 and 2015 I completed eleven weeks of participant observation and environmental and climate justice advocacy in Puerto Rico's archipelago, which includes the Big Island, Vieques, and Culebra.[6] While certainly not exhaustive, the following activities offer a glimpse of my interactions with/in the field: I attended numerous government-sponsored public hearings and grassroots meetings; volunteered at a weeklong youth camp; marched in a pro–Puerto Rican independence demonstration; participated as an interviewee on *Radio Vieques*; and attended two community tours offered by a microbusiness dedicated to educating the public about polluted water. To participate in these events, I ventured to numerous municipalities throughout the archipelago. Co-presence also allowed me to converse with and interview environmental activists, professors, historians, filmmakers, Department of Natural Resources officials, and fossil fuel and renewable energy experts. I completed seventy-five interviews, during which I asked interviewees about a range of topics, including nationality and ethno-racial self-identifications, sustainability concerns regarding the financial and environmental effects of the archipelago's electric energy crisis, and to what extent anticolonialism and environmentalism are entwined in Puerto Rico.[7] I also took daily field notes that highlighted discursive patterns, key terms, and other rhetorical insights I observed in media and in everyday personal exchanges, including during interviews and participant observation. Additionally, in these notes I often described my liminal feelings as a light-skinned U.S. American of Puerto Rican descent who speaks Spanish with a noticeable accent.[8] These documentation and reporting practices created opportunities for and often required engagement with multiple cultural artifacts, viewpoints, and environments.

Rhetorical field methods have allowed me to ask and answer questions about environmental and colonial injustices related to and yet different from the conversations enlivening easily accessible news media reports and extant scholarship about Puerto Rico. Accordingly, predicated on my *in situ* experiences, I consider the following questions in this essay: *What are the ethical entailments of co-presence, and how do particular judgments enable and constrain scholarly and political goals? To what extent does co-presence change how critics encounter, read, and understand cultural artifacts, and in what ways and for how long might interactions with the field continue? How might imagining rhetorical field methods as a coalition (re)shape existing assumptions about the role(s) of critics?* In response to these queries, I explore various dimensions of relationality between critics and the field. Informed by extant rhetorical scholarship, I read this latter term capaciously to include human and nonhuman animals, landscapes, and the cultural artifacts shaped by and found in manifold environments.[9]

This essay focuses specifically on co-presence, which Phaedra Pezzullo describes as being physically present in the field.[10] Foregrounding co-presence invites critics to consider various ethical and epistemological considerations, including what might be gained by envisioning critic-community relationships as a coalition, particularly when working with subaltern groups. Drawing on scholarship by María Lugones and Karma Chávez, I perceive the coalitions created by critics and the communities they engage as "the horizon of possibility . . . the space where two seemingly different things [or people or groups] merge and remain separate. It is also the space where the distinction between entities blends and blurs."[11] Importantly, coalitions vary in duration. Some may be temporary, while others may endure for long periods of time. Imagining fieldwork encounters as a coalition carries important implications; while field experiences need not have a political tenor, they can serve as "a space of convening that points toward coalitional possibility."[12] Thus, even exchanges that are not political in nature have the possibility to become so, should it be desired by critics and those they encounter in the field. This co-presence can assist both researchers and their interlocutors. For example, scholars may request input on manuscript drafts from community members prior to publication and may also assist them with social movement efforts (e.g., volunteering, posting public comments, grant-writing). One way to better understand the collaborative and reciprocal dimensions of this co-presence is via what I term the *field-text*. This critical heuristic recognizes the interactivity between the text and the field and calls for heightened awareness of rhetoric's materiality and the ways in which critics and different components of the field interact.

In the following pages I highlight extant rhetorical scholarship that serves as a foundation for my claims about co-presence, the field-text, and coalition-building. Next, I share a few representative anecdotes from my field experiences in Puerto Rico by documenting and analyzing various cultural artifacts, conversations with interlocutors about their rhetoric, questions of presence vis-à-vis translation concerns, and opportunities for conjoining rather than isolating activist and academic endeavors. Finally, I conclude by considering the possibilities and limitations posed by *in situ* studies and the stakes of approaching this methodology with a coalitional commitment. While the insights illuminated in this essay are derived from co-presence in a predominately Spanish-speaking country, these experiences are broadly applicable, including for the U.S. mainland; after all, encounters with intercultural rhetorics, as well as diverse languages and ethnic communities, are increasingly common in the United States.[13]

Foundations: Co-presence and Coalition in Puerto Rico

The fieldwork experiences discussed in this essay are informed by Pezzullo's research on counterpublic resistance, embodied rhetorics, *in situ* observation, archives, and environmental justice.[14] Her call for participant observation invites us to consider what is gained through *in situ* studies and what might be obscured when scholars select research methodologies not conducted in the field. Pezzullo and other scholars committed to rhetorical field methods have addressed the importance of presence to better understand communicative practices and to eschew alienation.[15] While also interested in this concept, this essay extends that work by focusing primarily on the ways *co-presence*, or being physically present in the field, can facilitate feelings of presence that would otherwise be impossible (or at least unlikely) through other research approaches.

It also emphasizes the importance of collaboration with the communities in which we, as critics, conduct our studies.

Presence is a polysemous term. In some instances it refers to a rhetorical effect that aligns form and content and magnifies particular claims.[16] The term also serves as "a mode of advocacy" that makes injustices and other communities more "present" to critics during various encounters and exchanges.[17] Pezzullo asserts that the term "indicate[s] when *we feel as if* someone, someplace, or something matters, whether or not she/he/it is physically present with us. Presence also refers, then, to the *structure of feeling* or one's *affective* experience when certain elements—and, perhaps, more importantly, relationships and communities—in space and time appear more immediate to us, such that we can imagine their 'realness' or 'feasibility' in palpable and significant ways."[18]

These feelings and affective encounters often emerge from and are facilitated by decisions to be co-present with people, places, and/or things. However, Pezzullo notes that "physical co-presence does not guarantee a sense of presence, and vice versa."[19] This essay is interested in exploring the ways in which co-presence *can* heighten opportunities for a sense of presence. Rather than assume that being physically present in the Caribbean nation was sufficient for grasping the stakes of surviving and thriving in the U.S. commonwealth, I strove to live like a local by eating typical foods (especially "arroz y habichuelas" / "rice and beans"), traveling via car (the primary mode of transport) and ferry, consulting popular periodicals and radio programs, and visiting the neighbors of my family and those I interviewed, all the while speaking as much Spanish as possible. I could have chosen isolation from the culture around me, limiting myself to reading texts from the National Archives and visiting restaurants and historical landmarks frequented by English-speaking tourists. Instead, I chose co-presence via cultural immersion, which prompted me to conceptualize the field-text.

I find that engaging "live" rhetorics encourages critics to reimagine "the text" and "the field" as fluid and experiential.[20] Approaching these terms from a both/and orientation via the field-text helps us to consider the ways in which rhetoric might become inseparable from the field because, in many cases, it *is* the field. While the text and the field should not always be viewed as one and the same, ethnographic studies require a more nuanced, embodied recognition of how co-presence enhances our understanding of rhetorical materiality.[21] In my own fieldwork, the "texts" I collected (e.g., handouts, newspapers, and books—sometimes out of print), transcribed (i.e., interviews and field notes), and experienced (e.g., encountering tourist signs and other cultural artifacts while using public transportation, hearing boricu@s debate economic, energy, and political status anxieties, feeling the ocean breeze and inhaling toxic smells, tasting local tap water, experiencing the effects of water rationing and the conversations it evoked) profoundly shaped my relationships with community members, environments, and the ways I understood discourses circulating in and about the archipelago. Thus, through my *in situ* encounters, these manifold texts and the problems and possibilities they posed felt present.

Ethical and epistemological concerns about critic-community relationships and the discourses we study also emerge from co-presence. A turn to this idiom's prefix assists in situating the term within a coalitional register. According to the *Oxford English Dictionary*, "co-" denotes in common, together, in company, jointly, equally, mutually, and reciprocally.[22] These definitions call attention to the co-production of meaning-making that critics and community members construct together, as well as the importance of striving for mutually beneficial interactions and reciprocity if/when possible. As historian Kirsten Weld writes, we should consider how to make our "research useful" for the communities and groups we study.[23] In this spirit, I conceptualize co-presence as a coalition between critics and those we encounter in the field.[24]

In step with long-standing efforts to reimagine the role of interlocutors in qualitative research, rather than refer to interviewees and others with whom I interacted during my fieldwork by the social science terms of "subjects," "informants," or even "participants" I prefer "compañer@s," which in Spanish means "partners," "companions," and "colleagues." I use this term to challenge binaries (e.g., activist-scholar, insider-outsider, expert–lay person) that reduce the complexities and multiple commitments of social movement actors, critics, and others.[25] Similarly, this moniker also seeks to diminish hierarchies that traditionally position researchers and "subjects" in relationships not unlike that of colonizer and colonized.[26] During my fieldwork, activists frequently invoked "compañer@s" to reference their peers and sometimes even me. By using boricu@s' preferred term, in their preferred language, I seek to disrupt the colonial injustices that punctuate everyday life in Puerto Rico, many of which implicate ecological concerns.

Puerto Rico's status as a U.S. commonwealth has resulted in innumerable deleterious consequences for boricu@s and the environment. The local Puerto Rican and U.S. governments have exploited resources and people by deploying discourses of economic necessity and racial inferiority to legitimize colonialism in the name of "development" and "progress."[27] These colonizer campaigns have been and continue to be fought in tandem with environmental degradation concerns in Puerto Rico.[28] After all, efforts to exploit the natural world and marginalized groups are fueled by the same conqueror ideologies.

Extant rhetorical scholarship has engaged the intersections of colonial and environmental injustice, revealing "the discursive [colonial] apparatus" that fuels logics of conquest and domination toward the planet, places, and people.[29] In the case of Puerto Rico, boricu@s are always already becoming with colonialism and the toxic chemicals produced and discarded on and around the archipelago by the U.S. government, military, and corporations. This practice, which treats particular environments and people as disposable, epitomizes what I term "colonial wastage." As a result of this injustice, many Puerto Ricans live in "sacrifice zones" that are "toxically assaulted" by disproportionate exposure to pollution and other toxins.[30] To better appreciate the possibilities and merits of co-presence for eroding these barriers to human and nonhuman well-being specifically and for enhancing rhetorical studies more generally, a turn to specific fieldwork experiences is in order.

Experiencing Co-presence

I offer two representative cases from my *in situ* encounters in this section. These exemplars assist in revealing the stakes of co-presence, coalition-building, and the ways in which the field-text serves as an instructive heuristic for rhetorical field methods. The first anecdote chronicles my visit to the Puerto Rican islet of Vieques, where I interviewed a compañer@ who shared her testimonial with me. Our encounter and my other co-presence experiences helped me to better apprehend the exigencies confronting local community members, especially regarding inadequate medical and transportation services and the troubling effects of island paradise discourses to attract tourists to the area. The second instance examines cultural and linguistic translation considerations and the ways in which these concerns might emerge during *in situ* studies to help inform rhetorical field methods and to cultivate a more just, decolonial imaginary. Both cases reveal the ways my physical presence in the field heightened my commitment to a coalitional approach, as the injustices I documented felt increasingly present and urgent. This effort also offered additional texts and context to enhance my research. I begin by recounting my co-presence in Vieques.

"Preocupaciones muchas" / "Many Concerns"

Viequenses, the residents of Vieques, confront a quotidian reality characterized by "preocupaciones muchas," as Zaida Torres Rodríguez informed me during a personal interview. My encounter with this community activist, former nurse, and cancer survivor was serendipitous; both of us happened to be at the local museum and community center at the same time. During our fifty-minute interview this compañer@ frequently interacted with others in the room. Rather than viewing these additional conversations as interrupting our time together, I found that Torres Rodríguez's warm exchanges with others provided a glimpse of her interpersonal interactions and the ways she communicates her role as a community leader. For example, at one point she exclaimed, "¡Hola! ¡Ven aca, Carmen!" / "Hello! Come here, Carmen!" On another occasion, she discussed contacting a community member via e-mail about participating in a local event. While these conversations might seem inconsequential, they point to this compañer@'s enactment of leadership and the quotidian communication practices of community activists.

Not all of our time together was punctuated by moments of excitement and happiness, however. During our interview, I asked Torres Rodríguez for her reaction to my observation that local newspapers in the museum's archive referred to Viequenses' experiences as a "genocide." Torres Rodríguez agreed and insisted, "Es un genocidio. . . . Aquí es el que duele, el que sabe." / "It is genocide. . . . Here are the human beings that hurt, the human beings that know." This localized knowledge of inhumane conditions stems from more than six decades of brutality at the hands of the U.S. government and military in the name of "national defense."[31]

From 1941 to 2003 Vieques was (ab)used as a military training ground by the U.S. Navy and allied NATO forces. Seventy-five percent of the fifty-one-square-mile island was "cleared" so the U.S. Navy could conduct "live fire practices, air-to-ground bombing, shelling, artillery fire, ship-to-shore bombing, and maneuvers."[32] From 1980 to 2000 the U.S. military dropped just shy of three million pounds of explosives annually. Records reveal that nearly half of the fired shells missed their targets—targets that were only nine miles away from where Viequenses lived. To realize this militarized invasion, 4,600 residents were evicted from their homes, sometimes with only a day's notice, and pushed to the middle of the island. Another 3,000 people fled Vieques during the first twenty years of occupation.[33] Later, the navy devised "Plan Dracula," which would have expropriated *all* Viequenses and mandated the exhumation of the islet's cemeteries to deter locals from returning to visit the deceased.[34] The plan did not come to fruition; however, years of hyper-militarization continue to haunt local residents.

While the U.S. Navy left the island in 2003, after years of dogged protest from Puerto Ricans across the diaspora, including Torres Rodríguez, the toxic legacy of the U.S. government and military remains, and it is deadly.[35] According to a recent study, the cancer rate on Vieques was "27 percent higher than among those living on the main island. The prevalence of other illnesses was also higher: hypertension rates were elevated 34 percent; asthma, 16 percent; diabetes, 28 percent; epilepsy, 116 percent; and cardiovascular disease, 130 percent."[36] Infant mortality is also disproportionately high. The consequences of the monstrous and persistent disregard for human rights and dignity on the island point to the environmental justice saying "The wind blows and the water flows,"[37] and in Vieques locals know where the toxicity goes . . . into bodies of water, land, and human beings.

Part and parcel of treating the islet and its inhabitants as colonial wastage are the discursive deceptions and erasures promulgated by the U.S. and local tourism industry. For example, as I stepped onto the Vieques ferry dock,

FIG. 6.1 Signage greeting ferry travelers arriving in Vieques, Puerto Rico. Photo by Kathleen M. de Onís.

I glanced up. My eyes were greeted with a bilingual sign: "Like waking up in para- dise" / "Como despertar en el paraíso." While the residents of Vieques are proud of their beautiful island as well as their individual and community resilience in the face of tremendous challenges, the ferry sign perpetuates an untenable utopic narrative that obscures the colonialism, poverty, hyper-militarization, and other interlocking forms of oppression that shape everyday life in the area, as evidenced in Torres Rodríguez's remark during our interview: "Somos una población en riesgo demasiado de grande y nadie quiere darse cuenta que esto está pasando." / "We are a population very much at risk, and no one wants to realize that this is happening." The sign's erasure of the island's history further aggravates the legacies of colonial, environmental, and military violence.

It also occurred to me that the ninety-minute ferry ride, which required standing in a long line to purchase tickets followed by more waiting, could be very debilitating for those with a disability, sickness, and/or who are elderly. This ferry trip is necessary for many Viequenses because, as I would discover from Torres Rodríguez, the island lacks a formal hospital; residents have lim- ited access to very basic treatment options without specialist care. Echoing her aforementioned genocide claims, during our interview Torres Rodríguez asserted, "Los servicios de transportación son malísimos. Es inadecuado . . . está muriendo gente por la falta de servicios." / "The transportation services are very bad. It's inadequate . . . people are dying because of the lack of services." This injustice, among others, has moved the compañer@ to write about the ongoing brutality inflicted on her people and land.

Toward the conclusion of our interview, Torres Rodríguez handed me a document. This gesture not only offered me an otherwise inaccessible text but also afforded an opportunity to talk to the rhetor about why and in what ways she felt compelled to author a testimonial. She mentioned her inability to sleep at night and the desire to write as a means for assuaging her restlessness. I also inquired about her reliance on particular terms (e.g., "salud"/"health") and their community and cultural resonance. When offering me the two-page text, she asked that I excuse any grammatical or spelling errors. She explained to me that though she hopes readers will feel welcome to draw their own conclusions while reading her essay, she also wants them to recognize that Viequenses live and die amid appalling conditions.

Torres Rodríguez's testimonial and call for action is titled "Genocidio u olvido involuntario" / "Genocide or an Involuntary Oversight." In the text's peroration she writes, "Yo no quiero un hospital nuevo grande, quiero servicios donde el paciente no tenga que salir de Vieques a recibirlo, que el paciente de diabetes sea evaluado por un endocrinólogo, el alta presión sea evaluado por un cardiólogo. . . . La salud de los pueblos no es un negocio es un derecho. Cuando a un pueblo enfermo con estadísticas como las de Vieques se les niegan los servicios es como matarlo poco a poco. . . . Recuerden que PUERTO RICO ES MAS QUE 100 × 35" / "I don't want a new big hospital, I want services where the patient doesn't have to leave Vieques to receive it, that the diabetes patient is evaluated by an endocrinologist, the high blood pressure [patient] is evaluated by a cardiologist. . . . The health of the people isn't a business it's a right. When sick people with the statistics like those of Vieques are denied the services it's like killing them little by little. . . . Remember that Puerto Rico is more than 100 × 35 [miles]." Torres Rodríguez emphasizes the imperative of adequate health care services; she elucidates that her request is not extravagant or superfluous, but essential. The compañer@ points to residents' prolonged experience with genocide, as health and well-being are sacrificed in a businesslike transaction ("negocio") that kills residents "poco a poco" / "little by little." According to Torres Rodríguez, this injustice stems from a lack of specialized care and the elision of Vieques and Viequenses from public discourse. She mentions that Puerto Rico is more than the Big Island's dimensions ("100 × 35" miles), enjoining readers to recognize this important fact to challenge the quotidian reality that she and her fellow residents encounter. Torres Rodríguez highlights this problem by uppercasing a section of her concluding statement, revealing both her frustration and commitment to changing dominant perceptions, which have proven deadly for her community. She implies that Viequenses should not be excluded from decision-making processes, as their very survival hinges on contributing to important health, political, and other conversations. Of course, for adequate public participation to unfold, community members must be allowed to express themselves in their preferred language—in this case, Spanish. Since colonial logics underlie English monolingualism and U.S. monoculturalism, I feature Torres Rodríguez's interview responses and written prose in her language.[38] This effort seeks to resist colonialism's discursive dimensions and to convey more accurately the multilingual and intercultural contexts that sometimes emerge as a result of co-presence.

My *in situ* encounters with riding the ferry, interviewing Torres Rodríguez, and studying her testimonial offered me a variety of texts that demonstrate how they were bound to, and in some cases were, the field. For instance, my transportation experiences constituted their own text for studying the mobility and well-being constraints imposed on Viequenses, many of whom are in poor health, by communicating various dimensions of precarity. Thus, sharing the same environment may serve as its own cultural artifact that leads to deeper understandings of more accepted, traditional texts (e.g., interview transcripts and printed documents, such as a testimonial). This co-presence can also motivate political engagement.

Learning of Vieques's history and its ongoing crises makes Torres Rodríguez's claims difficult to ignore and moved me to write an entry for EJOLT .org, a website that offers an interactive map charting different environmental injustice cases across the globe. Having observed the deadly erasures and falsehoods shaping life on Vieques, I felt compelled to share the island's story when I found that Viequense experiences were absent from the map.[39] This modest coalitional effort allows researchers, students, teachers, and others who peruse the site to learn about the island's assault and to question colonialism and the U.S. military's toxic practices. Without my co-presence in Vieques, including my conversation with Torres Rodríguez—who emphasized the imperative of sharing her community's story—and my encounters with troubling erasures and lies characterizing everyday life on the island, my interest in writing about this case for the EJOLT.org project would have been unlikely. Entries for this website are solicited and written in English, which brings us to another important dimension of rhetorical field methods: translation concerns.

Translation: A Reality of Co-presence

Co-presence often uncovers communicative tensions resulting from the process of trying to make something (e.g., a term, concept, or phenomenon) feel present for community members, critics, and others. This challenge is particularly complex in multilingual and intercultural fieldwork contexts. Extant scholarship about rhetorical field methods tends to be in English and address English-speaking communities and places. But what happens when critics enter different cultural and linguistic milieus that disrupt normative assumptions and communicative practices shaped by English monolingualism and U.S. monoculturalism? To engage this question, I share my experiences from a personal interview and a public hearing to evince both the diverse settings in which co-presence might unfold and the problematics of cultural and linguistic incompatibilities.

About one month after arriving on the Big Island I interviewed Puerto Rico Sierra Club chapter director Adriana González. I inquired about the challenges she faces in trying to translate Sierra Club agenda-setting for the environmental and cultural realities of Puerto Rico. With little hesitation González, who is bilingual, offered a communication incongruity. She explained that the term "grassroots," often used in U.S. movement-organizing discourse, does not translate in Spanish-speaking cultures. González remarked in English:

> I always laugh because in the Sierra Club we use a lot of the word "grass-roots organizing," and there's not really a direct translation in Spanish—you can say "organización de base," but it doesn't really have that appeal. . . . And throughout the years we've been here [at the Puerto Rico Sierra Club chapter] translating them [Sierra Club documents] to be able to provide knowledge about organizing to people here [in Puerto Rico] and in that transition of translating things, the language when we're talking about these things initially is totally different. How we use different words, and how we approach people, and the examples that we give. In the [Sierra Club] trainings, for example, there is a lot of things about the civil rights movement or other things that although are general knowledge . . . people [in Puerto Rico] might not have had the privilege of having all that education and knowing that history. (Field notes)

González's remarks reveal both linguistic and cultural translation incompatibilities as well as the complexities accompanying trans/national coalitional efforts often necessary for movement organizing.[40] Absent this compañer@'s comments and experiences, the term "grassroots" likely would have been uncritically used in my scholarship. As evidenced by this example, co-presence allows critics insights into the constraints involved when seeking to make an issue or exigence feel present for various audiences. Recognizing the troubling effects of English monolingualism and U.S. monoculturalism is key for studying the resonance of particular language terms[41]—an acknowledgment that was impossible to ignore not only in personal interviews but also during public forums.

My co-presence often involved attending "vistas públicas" / "public hearings." One of the more memorable meetings occurred in Ponce, Puerto Rico. The U.S. Coast Guard (USCG) organized the meeting to discuss the proposed Aguirre Offshore Gasport, a project that, if approved, will increase Puerto Rico's reliance on imported gas. Local fishers and other community members are very concerned about the proposed gasport because coral reefs and fish populations will be adversely affected by the heavy ocean traffic needed to transport the fossil fuel. Moreover, the area is already heavily polluted by a petroleum refinery and a coal plant—the Big Island's two largest carbon and toxic chemical emitters.[42]

The following is an excerpt from my field notes written during the meeting:

> At 9:30 a.m. USCG officer José Pérez convened the meeting half an hour late. Donning a blue uniform complete with big black, shiny boots, he asked if the hearing could be conducted in English because they had a few U.S. visitors attending who were monolingual. He inquired in Spanish if that was a problem. Several local attendees responded by explaining that the majority of the audience was Spanish-speaking, so the discussion should be conducted in their preferred language. Ruth Santiago, a lawyer and environmental justice community leader, also chimed in, expressing her frustration with the meeting's lack of planning and the USCG's irresponsibility with returning phone messages. She showed Pérez her cell phone, proving that she had called the USCG several times without any response. After this somewhat tense exchange, Pérez proceeded with the introduction in both English and Spanish to accommodate all audience members.

This experience reveals the way in which English monolingualism can violate the legal right to know. Without resistance to Pérez's initial preference for communicating in English because of "a few U.S. visitors," the audience's Spanish-only speakers would have been denied this democratic principle of transparency.[43] Furthermore, these notes point to how Santiago refused to accept the USCG's deceptive practices and failure to communicate. As I would discover, the (mis)management and injustice characterizing this gathering were just beginning.

Public participation at the hearing was also curtailed via the violation of the legal right to comment. According to my field notes, "One of Pérez's colleagues, Efraín López, began his very brief presentation about the Aguirre Offshore Gasport. He explained that people could make comments about the project in the U.S. Federal Energy Regulatory Commission's (FERC) register. All commentary had to be in English, he said. Pérez suggested he could help with translations, but with the lack of instructions offered, it was clear that Spanish-only speakers were on their own to negotiate writing and posting their comments." This passage places into relief a fundamental injustice of Puerto Rico's occupation by the United States: the mandate that public commentary should be expressed "in English." By explaining "that people could make comments," while simultaneously rendering such commentary impossible for non-English-speaking Puerto Ricans, the USCG and the U.S. government violate the legal right to comment and the democratic principle of direct participation through institutionalized linguistic oppression.[44]

The aforementioned experience is indispensable for understanding the ways in which the U.S. discursive colonial apparatus functions to constrain possibilities for a more just Puerto Rican imaginary that values public deliberation and local, renewable energy alternatives. Furthermore, this incident serves as an exemplar of how co-presence allows critics access to traditionally unobtainable texts and the opportunity to gauge different audience responses (e.g., community members, USCG officials, and U.S. energy representatives). Thus, being co-present with different dialects and/or languages provides the critic with additional insights about the ways in which various communities communicate, the cultural and linguistic barriers they encounter, and the stakes of their claims for achieving a more livable life.

My co-presence at this meeting has allowed for continued engagement with the gasport controversy. Two months following the event, I submitted a public comment to FERC's register detailing my opposition to the project. I also signed up for e-mail messages alerting me of every new post. The decision to continue my involvement with this controversy signals a coalitional effort that seeks to advance the cause of compañer@s politically *and* allows me to track various project responses that inform my academic work. This experience exemplifies the ways that collaborative, reciprocal efforts between critics and compañer@s might continue as a result of co-presence.

"Activist critics," as we might call them, serve a key role in "addressing the politics of knowledge production and working to decolonize our research process."[45] They reimagine the compañer@-critic relationship so that both parties might benefit, albeit differently, from their field encounters and co-presence. Articulated by Lawrence Frey and Kevin Carragee as "communication activism," this "scholarship is grounded in communication scholars immersing themselves in the stream of human life, taking direct vigorous action in support of or opposition to a controversial issue for the purpose of promoting social change and justice."[46] Such a coalitional commitment is key for maintaining a generative "tension between critical analysis and political pragmatics" and, in my case, constitutes a form of Puerto Rican diasporic solidarity.[47]

Echar Pa' lante / Moving Forward

Co-presence "changes rhetorical criticism" and, I would add, it changes critics.[48] It alters the ways we communicate about and experience our environments and interactions with human beings, structures, and landscapes. This essay foregrounds these embodied encounters to consider the coalitional possibilities that co-presence makes possible. It also explores the field-text, a heuristic widely applicable to various ethnographic research settings because of how this perspective highlights the ways these fieldwork components are entwined and integral in shaping critic observations and claims. This interconnection is predicated on embodied encounters, ranging from verbal and nonverbal exchanges during personal interviews to interactions with sounds, smells, tastes, sights, and tactile sensations that, together, create a unique archive.

While I focus on Puerto Rico, the insights offered in this essay extend beyond the U.S. commonwealth, as attending to the possibilities of co-presence matters for all *in situ* studies. This essay's two analytic sections point to the importance of experiencing the realities confronting subaltern communities, uncovering otherwise inaccessible cultural artifacts, conversing with compañer@s about their rhetoric, addressing translation concerns that facilitate/ inhibit presence, and considering the fusion rather than the isolation of activist and academic endeavors. For those working at the intersections of multiple cultures and languages, this essay is particularly instructive, given its interest in intercultural and transnational rhetorics.

Co-presence carries the potential to profoundly influence our critical judgments during and after our fieldwork. Thus we would do well to consider rhetorical field methods via co-presence as a vital approach for expanding the possibilities of rhetorical studies. I write this not to diminish more traditional forms of rhetorical criticism (e.g., close textual analysis of cultural artifacts already in circulation). Instead, I seek to underline the significance of rhetorical field method labor and problematize rhetorical field rigidities that dismiss, reduce, or underappreciate co-presence—a troubling tendency that this anthology seeks to rectify.

Scholars also should consider the ways in which being physically present facilitates civic engagement and collaboration, as these *in situ* practices require that we leave our manuscripts, lecture halls, and seminar tables to interact with communities beyond academia. By doing so, co-presence allows matters of public concern to feel present and may move us to become more invested in these causes, both academically and politically. In my own research, which would have been impossible without compañer@ collaboration, I offered resources (e.g., documents and photos), volunteered my time, and shared information about other community groups and upcoming events. Together, compañer@s and I employed a coalitional approach predicated on reciprocity in the quest for environmental and climate justice.

Another component of this collaborative effort centers on requesting "feedback"[49] from compañer@s both pre- and post-publication. Anticipating this essay's inclusion in the *Text + Field* volume, I e-mailed an early draft to several community members. Those who replied were pleased overall with what they read. Santiago, mentioned earlier in this essay, shared the following: "I think the article is very good. Thanks for sending it and your solidarity." Hernández, whose rhetoric animates this essay's epigraph, offered helpful feedback on a footnote and assured me that I was "boricua de pura cepa" / "pureblood Puerto Rican." He also inquired about why I had not focused on beach privatization struggles in this essay. I replied that I would write about these concerns in a future study.

While my experiences sharing this essay were positive, given the contingencies of our work as critics, compañer@s may not like what they read for a host of reasons and may even request that some content not be published, although that was not my experience. We are especially likely to elicit such a response from those we encounter in the field if we are critical rather than sympathetic toward their rhetoric. When considering the possibility of soliciting feedback for this essay, I carefully contemplated what was to be gained or lost by sharing my work and with/for whom. I reflected on who would (1) be most helpful in holding me accountable for any colonial or U.S. mainland assumptions I might be perpetuating and (2) benefit most from having my essay as a resource. After all, the communities we study must come before our academic aspirations.[50] In my case, I selected lawyers representing local community members and environmental concerns, given that I featured their discourse and that this essay might be useful for their work. In contrast, I chose not to share this essay with the USCG, FERC, and other pro–fossil fuel entities because I do not seek to forge political coalitions with these agencies, nor would have their response, should I have received one, dissuaded me from making the decolonial environmental and climate justice arguments I express in this essay.

As Puerto Rico marks yet another year of U.S. colonial invasion, opportunities for continued study and struggle abound. *In situ* encounters, like the ones discussed in this essay, assist in uncovering and intervening in practices of colonial wastage by examining the ways in which injustices are discursively (re)produced, translated (or not), and resisted. It is with this commitment to coalitional co-presence that I contribute to this volume's conversations while simultaneously advocating for health, dignity, and justice for one of the world's oldest still existing colonies and its people. "Estamos aquí, pa' que tú lo sepas."

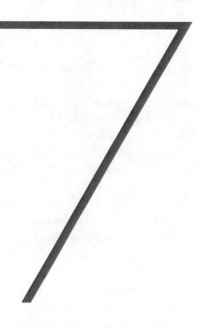

It's Like a Prairie Fire!

*Rhetorics of Trust and
Reciprocity in the Texas Coal
Plant Opposition Movement*

Valerie Thatcher

Most coal-fired facilities are situated in or near communities of color, sparsely populated, impoverished areas, and developing nations, in particular. Coal emissions create what health and environmental experts now consider a global human rights issue.[1] While much of the United States experienced a decrease in coal production and usage between 2010 and 2011 due to an increase in the cost of the U.S. Environmental Protection Agency's (EPA) new pollution controls, Texas increased coal production by 32.3 percent.[2] Texas leads the nation in the amount of carbon emissions from stationary fossil-fuel combustion sites, which primarily use coal. Texas ranks first internationally in CO_2 emissions compared to other states or provinces[3] and releases more mercury than any other U.S. state.[4] Although Texas places third nationally in coal-fired power production, many of its numerous old-technology plants are larger than other U.S. coal plants; thus the state's CO_2 emissions outpace those of states that are home to even dirtier plants. For these reasons, Texas became the site for a contentious battle over coal-fueled energy plants—between an alliance within the state government and its energy industry cronies versus a patchwork band of anti-coal grassroots activists beginning in 2004.

A large number of Texas citizens directly affected by these plants participated in discrete groups to oppose these facilities due to their adverse affects on health, natural resources, and local economies. Local anti-coal groups attracted and united a diverse membership to agitate against the broad implications of pollution created by coal plant emissions, many of whom had previously never engaged in activism or were not connected to the environmental movement. While each group had its own unique identity and issues, the argument upon which all agreed was the negative effects of plant emissions upon human and nonhuman health. Each group agitated against differing phases of coal plant development—proposed, under construction, or operational—often within local cultures that were averse to activism generally and environmentalism specifically. Anti-coal activists challenged corporate overreach within sparsely populated or marginalized communities that promoted a don't-rock-the-boat complacency and a don't-stand-out cultural homogeneity. Members entered into their specific anti-coal group with existing individual identities that remained intact (such as small-town dweller, low-income African American, gay Latino, or conservative Republican), despite becoming involved with a group that presented its own distinct identity, and often rejected overt identification with the environmental movement. The smaller, localized groups then formed coalitions with other like-minded anti-coal, environmental, social justice, and civil rights organizations, broadening the sense of sociability within and awareness of an expanding movement.

The five geographically dispersed sites researched within this study seem to have little in common besides their locations in Texas, a shared desire of each anti-coal group to not live near a coal-fired power plant, and many activists that did not identify as environmentalists. The sites differ in population, phase of coal plant development, type of anti-coal organization, and local issue focus upon which the organization built its argument. Each of these factors determined different cultural norms, what type of group was created, what rhetorical strategies were used to educate the public about their efforts, and how they identified the group and framed rhetorical appeals within their respective communities. What also united them was their concerted response to the social injustice inherent within the siting of toxic plants in regions with scant political power, making the movement's purpose not only about addressing health and environmental degradation but also one of environmental justice.

The members of anti-coal groups are highly organized and motivated; they worked with other coal opposition and social justice groups in their region, around the state, and with larger non-profit environmental organizations. Certain coalitional strategies used among the various unassociated groups were also unique within environmental activism. In addition to contributing to a growing arena of work on activist coalition building,[5] this essay furthers existing scholarship on the coalitional aspects of counterpublics by illustrating the ways collaborations may exist between non-normative organizations that differ in scale, ideology, and identity. Such a nuancing further illustrates Robert Asen's[6] call to see counterpublics as interconnected and differentially situated within dynamics of power.

Scholars have identified several types of publics, including specialized publics or subpublics,[7] counterpublics,[8] subaltern counterpublics,[9] identity publics,[10] and affinity publics.[11] Felski first used the term *counterpublic* to describe an oppositional public sphere that "consciously and unapologetically concerns itself with the emancipation of particular identities/groups rather than orienting itself to the goal of universal human emancipation."[12] Through publicity, minority counterpublics contest societal disadvantages as a means to persuade the general society that their concerns should be a matter of public consideration, that societal norms should be changed, and exploiters are pressured through legislation, regulation, or legal limits to reflect a more equitable norm. Counterpublics are always aware of their subordinate status; they circulate texts that are essential to maintaining membership through "ways of imagining stranger sociability and its reflexivity"[13] through divergent means, such as the Internet, printed materials, dyadic conversations, and small group meetings.

The anti-coal movement was subordinate not only to the State of Texas pro-business environmental policy but also to local opposition and attitudes of indifference or hostility toward environmentalism in general and anti-coal campaigns in particular. "Citizen groups engaged [in] 'citizen action' spark public renewals by revitalizing the scenes of local politics,"[14] and these new efforts included more women, people of color, and the economically disadvantaged, essentially strengthening the community along the lines that originally created fractures within it. Eric Doxtader argued that counterpublics theory requires a rhetorical turn in which scholars focus on "the 'middle voice' of human relations, the bonds of the 'in-between' that are occasioned by controversy, invented in speech, and that establish the basis for collective action,"[15] and identify the junctures at which counterpublics articulate their identity, challenge predominant discursive conventions, and instigate communicative action; in this essay I attempt to address these intersections of counterpublicity. Next, I describe how "lived texts" of the Texas anti–coal plant counterpublic were collected and used as a foundation for rhetorical analysis. I then analyze an ethnographic study of trust building and reciprocity in the rhetoric of Texas coal plant opposition groups.

Field Research, the Interview Process, and Rhetorical Analysis

Each anti–coal plant group in this study maintained its distinct local identity while creating new connections with one another in a shared fight against coal plants. Not only did members of local groups agitate against the plant closest to them, they joined in solidarity with the struggles of other coal-opposition groups, forging a new collective identity within their shared efforts. In essence, each discrete organization within the Texas anti-coal movement became a combination of its local culture and a more dispersed environmental activism. Riesel, Fayette County, Bay City, Austin, and San Antonio, Texas, were selected as sites for this fieldwork research for their divergence in both phase of coal plant construction and population size. The variety of sites substantiates my claim that, collectively, they represented a counterpublic. In addition to interviewing members of the anti-coal organizations, I also met with and interviewed residents in Bay City who were either supportive or apathetic about their local coal plant. Fieldwork included on-site observations of coal plant resistance campaigns, attendance at organization meetings and governmental public hearings, recorded interviews with plant proponents and opponents, e-mail and telephone correspondence with anti-coal activists, field notes written during my research, and a search of newspaper archives from 2009 to 2012.[16]

Research included participation with Sierra Club Lone Star Chapter's Austin beyond Coal (ABC) campaign as a volunteer for one year. I participated in local events, facilitated an educational campaign focused on presentations to civic and neighborhood organizations, and established personal relationships with many volunteers and paid staff. Direct involvement with ABC expanded my understanding of how strategies differ for opposing an existing plant and for a campaign spearheaded by a larger, established nonprofit organization, compared to the messaging used by local grassroots groups to agitate against proposed plants, such as the White Stallion Energy Center in Bay City, and how strategies differ in urban areas compared to rural and less populated areas.

I made several three- to five-day visits to San Antonio, Bay City, Fayette County, and Riesel. Personal interviews with informants were conducted over a six-month period. Questions and interview styles were based upon Geertz's development of Ryle's concept of thick description.[17] Thick description is an ethnographic approach, yet it is also a rhetorical endeavor with its focus on an interpretation of culture, its symbols, and systems of meaning. Thirty-two informants participated in audio-recorded interviews; all but four informants gave permission to use their names. Informants' responses were not limited to the sets of questions constructed for this research project. Rather, each interview was conducted "organically" and conversationally. No matter the level of informants' trepidation or eagerness to participate, by the end of the interview they all unwittingly let down their guard and revealed something significant about themselves, their perceptions of the coal plant controversy, and/or their attitudes about environmentalism.

Interviews were transcribed and, along with newspaper articles and letters to the editor pertinent to local coal plant controversies, organized, catalogued, and analyzed. I conducted a close reading, which "is [a] mindful, disciplined reading of an object with a view to deeper understanding of its meaning."[18] Close reading of interview transcripts and newspaper materials allowed me to discover distinct patterns and select the appropriate method of rhetorical analysis. In the next section I analyze identified patterns of coalitional and reciprocal relationships among anti-coal activists to show how actions and processes rhetorically define a counterpublic.

Reciprocity in Coalitions

Coalitions work best with others who share similar goals, sometimes as the helper and other times as the one needing assistance, but always within a reciprocal relationship. Joint efforts gave structure to individual articulations and public enactments of coal plant resistance within a sense of belonging to a broader imagined community. Robert Cervenka, founder of Riesel's Texans Protecting Our Water, Environment, and Resources (TPOWER), observed how the synergy of collaboration born from a shared threat quickly grew the movement: "It's like a prairie fire! We threw a match in the grass and it just burned from there. It has to start at that part, the match."[19] Reciprocity is a culturally embedded tradition within sparsely populated and marginalized communities that dates back to earlier times when farmers and village residents were, by necessity, "embodied in mutual claims and responsibilities."[20] Due to geographic dispersion, citizens of rural areas are accustomed to traveling long distances to interact with others to create a regional community; these efforts challenge claims that "social and geographical isolation discourages collective action,"[21] and demonstrate how coalitions that are not geographically co-located function successfully. Acts of reciprocity are rhetorical expressions of duty not only to local and nearby communities but also to the coal-opposition movement and its supporters, whether locally situated or as a public of like-minded strangers interacting through social media. Moral obligations to justice and fairness motivated civic-minded actions and behaviors that were then extended beyond local battles to publicly assist other communities engaged in similar anti-coal endeavors.

In the following subsections I analyze instances of trust and reciprocity in coalition-building within the Texas coal-opposition movement in five areas: first, the shared effort among the environmental nonprofit organizations (NPOs); second, an alliance between the nonprofits and local organizations; third, connections among groups from sparsely populated communities; fourth, connections among groups from urban communities; and fifth, coalitions that ultimately were unsuccessful due to incompatible organizational styles and also, in part, the lack of a shared core purpose and identity.

We're All Willing to Compromise: The Structure of Successful Anti-coal Campaigns

Within the broader environmental movement, various organizations address different aspects of a particular issue or problem, and each is convinced that its perspective and rhetorical plan of action is the correct remedy to the situation. Power struggles may ensue within this amalgam of organizations when certain groups or group leaders feel adjunct to factions more powerful, better funded, or larger, or certain proposed approaches are ignored or remain invalidated. These factors often lead to fractures in collective efforts and a failure to achieve success. Overwhelmingly, this was not the case within the coalition of Austin-based NPOs Sierra Club Lone Star Chapter, Greenpeace, Public Citizen-Texas, and Sustainable Energy and Economic Development (SEED) in their joint effort to eliminate coal-fired power plants in Texas. Beginning in 2000 Karen Hadden's organization SEED worked with director Tom "Smitty" Smith of Public Citizen-Texas in a combined effort to address various environmental concerns in Texas and helped organizations around the state launch local campaigns through their joint Stop the Coal Plants campaign. Sierra Club launched its national Beyond Coal efforts in 2006–2007.[22] Greenpeace began its global Quit Coal campaign in 2008, which was the organization's foray into community-based organizing.[23] Ryan Rittenhouse of Greenpeace discussed the rare collegiality between the NPOs allied within the Texas anti-coal movement:

> I hear the same thing around the country and even within Greenpeace, a lot of my fellow organizers going, "We're very jealous of you because of the coalition partners you get to work with." I feel very lucky to be a part of the coalition work done here. I think a big part of it is that we all have been working in it for so long and a lot of us . . . consider ourselves friends. And we're very respectful of one another and even when we disagree we are all willing to hear each other and we're willing to all compromise.[24]

While each organization had its own anti-coal campaign, they worked together toward the same goal in an extraordinarily harmonious fashion. Engagement within coalitional efforts thus rhetorically encouraged sociability, which "may be discerned in the collective character of ostensibly individual activities and the perspective-taking entailed in critical judgment."[25] The combined discursive and performative efforts of the various anti-coal campaigns both inside and outside of Texas led to a significant reduction of existing coal plants and the cancellation of numerous proposed plants. In the next subsection I analyze how collaborative efforts between the four Austin-based NPOs translated into working alliances with smaller, localized anti-coal groups.

Just Do a Lot of Listening: Coalitions between Austin–Based Nonprofits and Local Groups

The first issue that most newly organized local anti-coal groups faced, particularly in sparsely populated regions, was the accusation by coal plant proponents that they were unduly influenced or "indoctrinated" by the big-city environmental groups. This was not the case in any group included in this study; in each location, participants met on their own accord about the local coal plant, realized they needed organizational assistance, and through Internet research connected with at least one of the four Austin-based environmental NPOs. Eva Malina of No Coal Coalition (NCC) began looking for help as soon as she and her husband, Robert, found out about the plans to build the White Stallion Energy Center outside of Bay City: "When I first read that they were going to build a coal plant here, Bob said, 'We're gonna live in an industrial zone.' So I said, 'Not if I can help it!' I got online and did some research and found Smitty [Smith]. I e-mailed Smitty and said, 'Please help us. They're trying to put a coal plant down here. This is the last place that they should be doing this. And we need your help.'"[26] Public Citizen's Smith and Rittenhouse,[27] along with Hadden, answered Malina's call and traveled to Bay City to meet with the fledgling organization. Malina recalled, "I just really don't think we would've gotten much off the ground without Public Citizen. I mean, as our initial contact, and their help. They gave us a tremendous amount of help at the beginning. They furnished us with materials. They would come down here and meet with us. I think without them that we probably wouldn't have gotten the impetus to continue."[28]

Soon afterward Sierra Club sent organizers to Bay City. This created some tension and dissonance within the NCC membership and was fodder for coal proponents, since Sierra Club is a widely known environmental organization. NCC member Robert Lee confessed that he was "a little leery of a strong association with Sierra Club. Not that I disagree with Sierra Club. I think I understand the organization and their motivations, but I also think for a lot of people, Sierra Club is a red flag and if you're associated with the Sierra Club you're in that extreme, not to be trusted, you know. I'm a little reticent to make a strong association with our organization and Sierra Club."[29] Lee clearly articulated dissonance within his concern that NCC would be stereotyped as an environmentalist organization that needed assistance from the environmental NPOs. Chávez argued that dissonance necessitates resolution or completion and "promotes a heightened awareness of, and attentiveness to, the need for constant work and reflexivity."[30] While "dissonance potentially causes problems for relationships within movements . . . it also instigates, agitates, and informs; dissonance disturbs and creates energy around some issue so that it remains altered in our consciousness; dissonance produces the necessity for movement."[31] Using music as a metaphor to describe dissonance as a "disagreeable sound," Chávez also observed that dissonance may be used to create new "sounds" that can be integrated into a harmonious work.[32] Despite his suspicions that Sierra Club would taint the reputation of NCC in the community, casting it as an extremist environmental organization, Lee also acknowledged that Sierra's help was invaluable and that a trust-based relationship was built between NCC and Sierra Club. I will return to the concept of dissonance within the subsection on unsuccessful alliances to demonstrate how discord and tensions between coalitional organizations often remain irresolute.

According to Sierra Club organizer Flavia de la Fuente, the process of building trust is vital to establishing a connection with individuals who are new to environmental activism.[33] To trust heretofore unknown others implies engagement with risk and "is only possible in a situation where the possible damage may be greater than the advantage you seek."[34] Building relationships through involvement in voluntary organizations has the potential to "teach trust and social understanding because [these relationships] allow a variety of people, sometimes with disparate backgrounds and different values, to work together. . . . They breed and enforce reciprocity."[35] Trust is the "social capital" upon which participation in a deliberative democratic process depends and a rhetorical construct that implies a confrontation of uncertainty and risk, since "the model of civil society is predicated on exchanges that occur within its network of associations. Its character is inherently rhetorical."[36] Trust is created and strengthened not only in the belief "in the intentions of others not to cheat us" but also in the belief that the newly trusted entity will "perform adequately over and above their intentions."[37] Establishing and maintaining shared trust created a connection between NPO organizers and local activists, which inspired a mutually beneficial relationship. De la Fuente described her personal process of earning the trust of local coal activists:

> I just stayed with some folks and got to know people for two weeks. They would ask me, "What are you here to do?" I would say, "Not much right now! Just hearing about the issue and hearing from you, and why people are involved and why they care about it so much." Just to get people to trust me. And there's definitely that breaking-in period for the first couple months, I would say, where even before you can actively get involved in a campaign, you want to have people trust you. And share some values with them so that they know that you're there for the right reasons. As a career organizer, that's something that I definitely try to do whenever I'm going into a new space, just do a lot of listening, share my motivations, and usually that smoothes most things over.[38]

Hadden also utilized the rhetoric of trust through listening to the concerns of the newly formed local groups and avoiding polarizing environmentalist language. She explained that it is best to not "go in the door with an aggressive attitude and not listening to people—you're certainly going to get nowhere. And so we would just try to listen to where their concerns were and talk about it from there."[39] Hadden mentioned that she was introduced to polling data at a national environmental organizing conference that presented what terms to use and which to avoid, such as *climate change* or *global warming*, when working with rural and small-town communities. She discovered that avoiding discussions of big environmental issues was unnecessary, even while environmental terminology was used judiciously.

It was a mutually advantageous arrangement for most of the groups involved in the Texas coal-opposition movement. Sierra Club, SEED, Public Citizen, and Greenpeace provided fact-based literature and information to educate smaller communities, and they provided a legal team, since the fight was also waged in courtrooms; the local groups mobilized volunteer labor and made sure that the opposition was recognized as an effort born of that area. Hadden reminisced about working with Riesel's TPOWER when they first organized in 2004:

> We have tried really, really hard to always make sure there is a local face on everything. It's not that we don't like getting quoted sometimes. But we've tried to let that be the local people as much as possible. We train people and we educate them. Basically, just give them the facts and after that, they can take it and run. That's one of the huge, great joys of doing the work we do. . . . It's much, much stronger if it's not us. They can isolate you and destroy your credibility by calling you an outsider.[40]

To establish and maintain credibility, all of the anti-coal groups situated the coal plant issue within a rhetoric of the local to gain community support and to fend off accusations of outside influence by coal plant proponents and wary members of the community. For example, Charles English of East San Antonio knew Hadden and Smith through an earlier alliance formed to protect San Antonio's aquifer. At the same time English worked on the water issue, he was also involved with the social justice group Neighborhoods First Alliance (NFA). Hadden and Smith searched for ways to establish trust with NFA, and, according to English, SEED "started sponsoring through their organizations literature, because I think at the same time, they too was at a loss. They couldn't come into this area and just make those claims."[41]

Inherent within shared anti-coal efforts was the dialectical tension between what I argue is one of the strongest motivators toward activism, betrayal by authorities and "protectors," and the fulfillment of that betrayal: to establish mutual trust with like-minded others. Having worked with numerous small communities organizing against local coal plants, de la Fuente saw what she called a "running theme" of betrayal: "All of the small communities in Texas where they want to bring coal plants, people are always like, 'We trusted them. We believed them when they said that they would be nice to us and protect us! They would do all these great things for us! We had no reason not to believe them! And then they screwed us over.' . . . They fit your stereotype of nice, humble, hardworking country folk. And someone comes in and wants to take advantage of them! That's wrong!"[42] Dialectic signifies the development of opposing perspectives that influence one another. Dialectic functions to "perfect" one form by establishing its opposite; within the process of resolution between two absolutes is produced a "'resultant certainty' of a different quality, necessarily ironic, since it requires that all the sub-certainties be considered as neither true nor false, but *contributory*."[43] Dissonance may also be seen as a dialectical form in which trust is the harmony created from the discord of betrayal. In the coal plant opposition movement, anti-coal activists resolved their sense of betrayal by establishing trust in those they considered worthy. After local group members became well versed in the facts about coal plants, established strong ties with the Austin NPOs, strengthened their organizations, and rhetorically built for themselves positive reputations within their respective communities, they formed supportive networks with other anti-coal groups around the state and created coalitions with organizations that were more indirectly linked to coal opposition; these reciprocal relationships further empowered the movement through a shared and publicly performed anti-coal rhetoric.

Here's What Worked with Us: Rhetorics of Reciprocity and Trust among Rural Groups

Not only did local anti-coal organizations receive information from the NPOs, but they mobilized their members to support other groups' events and shared best practices with one another. During and after the Texas coal wars reached their peak in 2007, several rural activist groups called on TPOWER's Robert Cervenka to speak at their local gatherings and to help with their efforts, utilizing Cervenka's rhetoric of experience. Despite being in his eighties and exhausted from the years battling Governor Perry's fast-track permitting process, he got in his truck with his wife, Jo, and assisted whatever groups he could. According to Cervenka, the urgency to build numerous coal plants coincided with "a time when [the price of natural] gas was so high and everybody rushed in, thought they'd come get it built before lax environmental regulations"[44] were eliminated by the anticipated EPA limits on plant emissions. He considered these trips reciprocal arrangements, as he was still learning something new from each new encounter while teaching others what he had already learned.

One way that coal opposition groups showed support and solidarity for other groups was by attending and speaking out at one another's hearings, meetings, and functions. A large number of attendees contesting pro-coal policies at public hearings demonstrated to the hearing commissions that coal plant opposition was well represented in the community and that current rulings on coal plant issues were unacceptable to the locals. The rhetoric of opposition was often embodied and silent—the mere presence of numerous anti-coal citizens in the room signaled strength and unity within the resistance to coal plant–friendly regulations. Public hearing attendees also had the option to verbally express their opposition, usually within a limit of three minutes, in front of hearing boards; often individuals signed up to speak, then gave their allotted three minutes to a more impassioned or articulate speaker so that the speaker more fully developed a persuasive argument. Commissioners and hearing officers rarely reversed policy due to the arguments of attendees, but a solid presence by opposers in public fora created additional obstacles for the permitting process and pressured officials toward a reassessment of energy industry–friendly decisions.

Members of local opposition groups also attended other groups' functions, such as monthly meetings, retreats, and public anti-coal events. Members of the Fayette County Texas Pecan Growers Alliance (TPGA)[45] and the Corpus Christi Clean Air Coalition often drove to Bay City to attend NCC's monthly meetings, and vice versa. Eva Malina noted that NCC had "kind of an alliance with the pecan growers. We had them come and talk about what Fayette [Power Plant] has done to their pecan trees. It was very well attended. I was real surprised. Lot of people that we didn't consider members showed up."[46] In the Texas coal-opposition movement, farmers and ranchers served as symbolic legitimizers of the cause.[47] As a politically conservative pecan farmer, TPGA's Harvey Hayek legitimized the more current coal plant resistance movement as the "face" of the Texas movement.[48] Thus reciprocation was not only a means to rhetorically amplify the message but also an interdependent barter of resources—local groups gained credibility within their informal relationships with Hayek and the pecan farmers while TPGA received educational materials from Austin nonprofits and embodied support from local groups for their public contestations of the Fayette Power Plant. Among Sierra Club's ABC activists, Hayek was a folk hero and deeply respected for his public opposition of the plant, which is the largest employer in Fayette County.

Within their collaborative efforts, coal-opposition groups shared their best practices and successful strategies with one another. For Bay City's NCC, asking local physicians to endorse their position with letters to the editor of local newspapers was a very effective rhetorical strategy. Most Bay City residents knew one or more of the local physicians, physician assistants, and nurses who signed a coal plant opposition letter published in the *Bay City Tribune*. Malina discussed how a prominent local physician "was on board [with the anti-coal campaign] early on. He organized the physicians. He was a GP, but he was the doctor for many, many, many people. He wrote the letter and took it personally and visited with thirty-eight doctors and got thirty-four or thirty-five of them to sign it."[49]

NCC members also used e-mail and social media to network with groups in more distant parts of Texas, such as the Abilene-area organization Texans against Tenaska. Malina described how Facebook allowed coal-opposition group members to share successful approaches with one another, such as the idea to enlist the help of local medical professionals: "[Former NCC chairperson] Allison [Sliva] and I both got on their [Facebook] page and said, 'Here's what worked with us. Get your physicians. Talk to your physicians. Because if you can enlist their cooperation, you're gonna get a whole lot of credibility.'"[50] Just as Hayek legitimized the localness of the anti-coal movement, the physicians' collective opposition to coal plants legitimized anti–coal plant claims within the community, symbolically representing credibility and professional expertise to gain local support. While these trust-building and reciprocal efforts were successful in geographically dispersed coalitions, different approaches and strategies were implemented within co-located urban anti-coal coalitions.

Common Threads: Reciprocity within Urban Coalitions

East San Antonio NFA leader T. C. Calvert has been involved with social justice, civil rights, and environmental justice activism for over four decades and put together many coalitions to improve the quality of life in his economically and racially marginalized community. For years, these coalitions achieved numerous victories against environmental injustices that primarily affected residents living in East San Antonio. He shared with me a brief history of the environmental justice and social justice movements in San Antonio as a collective effort:

> Our environmental justice campaign started off fighting the BFI [waste management company] garbage dump. . . . [NFA] was an out-birth of those groups that were already dealing with environmental justice issues and so the coal power plant, it's just something that came naturally. . . . It became a growing big issue and it caught the eye of people from Austin and from around the country. That we, just a ragtag group of citizens, would get together. We started off very small but our coalition grew. We had a coalition of Anglos, Hispanics, as well as African Americans that fought this issue. I think that's one of the things that was very unique in San Antonio.[51]

Calvert used his rhetorical skills to "bring the troops together" for the fight against the nearby J. T. Deely plant. The quantity and heterogeneity of people gathered to publicly oppose the plant was a powerful persuasive strategy that local decision-makers and media could not ignore.[52] He explained that his success in getting all the organizations pointed in the same direction was to, first, determine the issue/s for which each group in the coalition sought resolution, and, second, discover what issue they jointly agreed on: "In the game of organizing, and in the whole institute of organizing, you organize based on people's self-interest. One of the things that would bring us together is that each one of these groups that dealt with, whether it's a coal power plant or contaminated dirt, they all had their self-interest. But we all had a common thread. And the common thread that brought us together is that the toxins and the pollution was a threat to our families and to our community."[53]

Anti-coal activists had different sets of motives for enacting their opposition to coal-fired power plants, advanced by their personal identities as concerned citizens, caring parents, agricultural "stewards of the earth," civil rights, social and/or environmental justice activists, and, sometimes, environmentalists. Their identities were frequently—but not always—transformed or altered through the process of collaborating with discrete entities with often-dissimilar personal experiences and political leanings, as seen within the alliances between environmental organizations and groups launched in conservative small towns and rural areas.

Sometimes groups, personalities, and organizing styles are incompatible with one another, organizations experience a change in leadership, or other circumstances occur to fracture organizational relationships. The success of coalitional efforts is hard to predict since "agency amplifies the element of risk inherent in any social interaction,"[54] but without trust, sustaining coalitional efforts was a challenge. Due to the diversity inherent within the Texas coal-opposition movement, not all alliances remained harmonious, as was the case for the NFA-SEED coalition against the Deely plant. The final section addresses discordant situations in which common ground remained elusive within the movement or tensions were left unresolved.

We Don't Operate Like That: Unsuccessful Coalitions

Successful coalitions within the anti-coal movement were built using the rhetorical constructs of trust and listening, while unsuccessful affiliations failed to adequately strengthen the bonds of trust and mutual dependency required for close interactions with different others. Despite a shared sense of purpose within combined efforts of multiple entities addressing a particular environmental issue, "stakeholders often find themselves in conflict over the actions to implement their shared agenda"; disputes must be reframed "in order to find an acceptable solution to the conflict."[55] Yet some tensions and dissonances remained irreconcilable. Certain groups had no interest in working with other organizations, or after a period of time they disengaged from these alliances. Individuals felt underappreciated by others in the group or clashed with others and ceased involvement with an organization, while some people chose to continue their efforts outside the coalition within newly formed organizations. In other words, the betrayal-trust dialectic remained unresolved and "unperfected"; the level of trust needed to enact coalitional activism became insurmountable when "partners whose diversity [had increased] in scope and complexity [exceeded] our capacity to understand the basis for their actions or their level of commitment to common goals."[56]

There are numerous environmental, social justice, and civil rights organizations in San Antonio and Austin, many of which have existed for decades. For certain issues these groups may work with one another, but these coalitions do not always lead to successful partnerships. SEED and NFA were partners in the anti-Deely coalition toward the end of a five-year campaign. The relationship between the two organizations initially was successful, and NFA's T. C. Calvert was hired by SEED to spearhead its anti-coal campaign in San Antonio. Karen Hadden praised Calvert as "a gifted organizer who's very well connected."[57] Calvert recalled, "It was a nickel-and-dime kind of thing. I wasn't getting rich off of it. They expected me to deliver the world to them. But it was a fun experience."[58] Eventually Calvert experienced problems with the coalition due to incompatible organizational styles; Calvert was trained in the social justice tradition of Saul Alinsky,[59] in which

> we like to get a victory for the people and we like to move on. That's what makes us different from the rest of them. I'm not going to work on an environmental issue for thirty or forty years. We gotta go in there and get and move on. Because guess what happens? What happens [if you don't], you lose the interest of your people. Your people are not going to come to the meetings. They're going to get burned out and they're going to say this is going nowhere. I can't put my people in that position and I'll never do that.[60]

The traditional environmental campaign enacted by SEED was too drawn out to be compatible with his Alinsky style of activism. In addition, Calvert surmised that he was being used by SEED for his ability to rally "warm bodies to draw a crowd" for SEED's "protest-press conferences."[61] He also felt left out of SEED's planning process and declared, "They would only just come in and say, 'Hey, we're having a press conference, can you guys show up? Can y'all bring a bunch of people?' And so our group had a problem with that. We don't operate like that."[62]

Concerning the tension between the two groups, Hadden offered a different viewpoint in which Calvert was dependent on the scientific data and literature SEED supplied to his group. In a study on a coalition between migrant rights and LGBT rights organizations in Arizona, Chávez discussed how the migrant rights organization that was less reliant on grant money had more "flexibility to do different kinds of work"[63] than did the LGBT group that was restricted by the conditions of its grantors. Similarly, the lesser-funded NFA felt exploited by SEED because it did more of the legwork and heavy lifting, according to

Calvert. Chávez's observations aptly describe the dissonance between NFA and SEED in which the "heightened awareness of, and attentiveness to, the need for constant work and reflexivity"[64] remained unresolved and did not "[produce] the necessity for movement."[65]

When dissimilar groups and individuals failed to arbitrate the differing perspectives inherent within a coalition, the result was an inability "to articulate conceptions that successfully negotiate the dilemmas of difference."[66] The unresolved dissonance between NFA and SEED was also due to identity differences that inform different types of publics and counterpublics. Calvert strongly identified with efforts rooted in civil rights, not environmentalism. He did not embrace an environmentalist identity once he and NFA moved on to confront other issues after the anti-Deely campaign. However, the knowledge he acquired from agitating against numerous polluting industrial sites in his community changed his behaviors and heightened his awareness about environmentalism and environmental justice issues. When asked about identities he connected with, Calvert defined himself as "a progressive, independent. I am for environmental justice. At one point in my life, yeah, I considered myself an environmentalist, because I did, I was very heavily, deeply involved in the environmental movement," yet he no longer included "environmentalist" as a defining identity. He claimed he was "multi-issue" and criticized single-purpose activists, such as those involved with the environmental movement, as being "stuck in a tunnel" and having "a one-track mind."[67]

In addition to conflicts arising due to some activists' entrenched, inflexible frames of what counts as properly enacted activism and identifications within shared efforts, unrealistic expectations of others engaged in coalitional efforts created additional tensions within the Texas coal-opposition movement. Social justice, civil rights, and environmental organizations in San Antonio often experienced successful coalitional efforts. Yet for the anti-Deely coalition under Calvert's leadership, NFA ultimately failed to build and sustain the rhetoric of trust needed to maintain a shared sense of purpose with non–social justice or non–community of color organizations. Under Hadden's leadership SEED similarly failed to foster trust with a non-environmental group. Calvert was unable to mesh the collective anti–coal plant activist/environmentalist identity with his established social justice / civil rights identity (and vice versa for Hadden). Organizational incompatibilities, unresolved dissonance, and unsuccessful collaborations demonstrated that the coal-opposition movement was not some ideal, utopian counterpublic free of internal struggle.

Conclusion

The study of Texas coal-opposition movement rhetoric demonstrated how environmental activism is an adaptive and changeable process through which public engagement is enacted through coalition-building. The diverse populations in the opposition movement served as an exemplar to support three theoretical claims. First, while many people who were engaged with the movement, such as white ranchers and small-town political conservatives, may not outwardly appear to compose a counterpublic, the anti-coal organizations were nonnormative within their socially conservative communities due to their indirect connection to the environmental movement, their subordinate status, and their lack of access to power and decision-making about coal-fired energy plants. Second, successful coalitions were created by building trust and strong reciprocal relationships to resolve previous betrayals by "protectors" and by using dissonances as the impetus for a continued and mindful effort. Not only did members of local groups agitate against the plant closest to them, they joined in solidarity with the struggles of other coal-opposition groups, forging a new collective identity within their shared efforts and creating a dispersed counterpublic. Third, certain organizational relationships in the anti-coal movement were unsuccessful because they failed to resolve dissonances and establish solid foundations of trust, primarily through incompatible organizational styles and alliances limited by a multiplicity of core goals and purposes.

For the most part, the individuals and groups within the movement performed activism using established vernacular identities and value systems to normalize their activism within their respective communities. While each maintained their original identities, the process of integrating new approaches and attitudes learned by association with environmentalist organizations resulted in a unique combination of identities that are often at odds with one another in U.S. culture, such as conservative rancher / environmental activist. The emergence of anti-coal environmental activism in nonurban localities and urban communities of color indicates a new and innovative type of environmentalist identity that defies the long-standing derogatory "tree-hugger" stereotype as primarily situated within the domain of liberal urban whites.

Coalitions between mainstream environmental groups, localized "concerned citizens," and urban social justice organizations may lead to innovative problem-solving when members mindfully strengthen the bonds of trust through reciprocal actions. Faber argued that this model of activism is on the rise, and my field research on Texas anti–coal plant activism backs up this claim. The expansion of environmental activism into sparsely populated areas and within communities of color revitalizes the movement in two ways: first, it broadens membership and involvement in environmentally related groups, and second, it educates those who have never identified as environmentalists (and still may avoid identifying themselves with this term) on "traditional understandings of ecological impacts, particularly in terms of linking issues to larger structures of state and corporate power"[68] through which new organizational models are created.

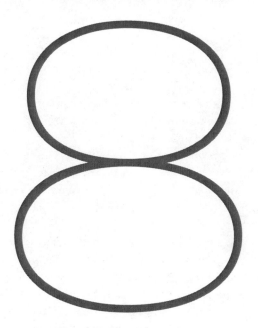

Being, Evoking, and Reflecting from the Field

A Case for Critical Ethnography in Audience-Centered Rhetorical Criticism

Alina Haliliuc

In 2001 Carole Blair asked a question with which we still grapple today: how do "we, as critics, make the object 'real'? How do we make it matter to our readers? The term 'matter' has an important double edge here, as a noun that suggests substance and presence, but also as a verb that implies the rendering of significance."[1] Blair came to these questions when she noted her students' deeper critical-analytical engagement with rhetorical criticism of artifacts they witnessed in person. Somehow, "being there" meant knowing differently and raised expectations for academic writing that matched one's experience as an audience member. In many ways, our discipline has taken a decisive turn toward examining the materiality of rhetoric and the experience of audiences, but we still wrestle with how best to do this work.

*In addition to the editors, the author would like to thank Jesse Schlotterbeck for his suggestions on drafts of this essay and Amanda Gunn for stimulating conversations in the early stages of this project.

In this essay I take on Blair's challenge and address my own experience as a critic and an audience member, an "audiencing critic," to coin a term. I propose that the intertwined practices of participant observation, self-reflection, and performative writing borrowed from critical ethnography bring the critic into a culturally situated and dynamic treatment of rhetorical experience that impresses on our readers rhetoric's significance and presence. Just like a critical ethnographer, an audiencing critic positions herself as an audience member, observes compassionately and reflects critically on one's verbal, embodied, and affective interaction with rhetorical texts and other audience members. She also evokes creatively the interpersonal, institutional, and cultural fields of the rhetorical event. In doing so, the audiencing critic is better able to account for the temporality, materiality, and cultural specificity of rhetoric, veering away from static analyses of audiences, whether positivist-empiricist studies of actual audience members or ideological-critical studies of audiences invoked by rhetorical texts.[2] Under critical ethnography's post-structuralist reluctance to reify the studied field, the audiencing critic approaches rhetorical processes as they happen within the self, in inter-subjectivity, temporality, within and across cultural and ideological fields.

I model the epistemological virtues of a critical ethnographic approach to rhetorical discourse through the case study of a rhetorical phenomenon from post-socialist Romania. In the case of Eastern and Central Europe, existing studies of post-socialist rhetoric have mapped how nationalist narratives of victimization,[3] nostalgic remembering of the communist past,[4] and neoliberal rhetorics,[5] among other forms of discourse, have constituted subjects for a new era. With the notable exception of Zala Volcic's ethnographic analysis of young Serbian intellectuals, these otherwise significant studies have not foregrounded audiences, the new post-socialist subjects.[6] When political regimes change, people must negotiate their senses of themselves in a changing symbolic order. As Serguei Oushakine reminds us in Foucaultian terms, "Becoming a new political, cultural, economic or social subject is accompanied by the establishment of a 'verbally constituted consciousness,' which is framed by historically specific 'limits and forms of the sayable.'"[7] Self-constituting subjects find themselves in a process that is both existentially necessary and disorienting. They face the possibility of failure in assuming future-oriented subject positions, and encounter the potential pitfalls of embodying regressive ones.[8] If all subjects' orientation in the world is "laced with contradictions," as Maurice Charland famously put it, post-socialist subjects experience sharp fragmentation and exhibit a need to negotiate public discourse that would give them subject coherence.[9]

I examine such dynamic co-constitution of self in relation to public address in post-socialist Romania, the country from which I emigrated to the United States. In my former home, ethnic nationalist rhetoric takes various guises despite the country's accession to the European Union in 2007. Nationalism is not new, having been ideologically aligned with right-wing movements and parties popular in the interwar period and with the socialist regime of Nicolae Ceaușescu (1965–89). Indeed, what distinguishes Romanian political culture, historian Maria Bucur notes, is the prominence of ethnic nationalist radicalism in the twentieth and twenty-first centuries, whether right or left wing, in a political culture that "still dwells much further to the right of that in Western Europe[,] lacks a strong liberal center and has, at best, a relatively weak social-democratic left."[10]

In this nationalist culture, actor and theater director Dan Puric has found celebrity through a religious ethno-nationalist discourse. His ideologically representative rhetoric has drawn my critical interest as both a Romanian post-socialist subject and a U.S.-based rhetorical scholar. Born in a small town, Puric left at fourteen to attend a competitive visual arts high school in the capital, Bucharest. While talented in drawing, he was interested in drama and, after high school and military service, joined Bucharest's main theater school. A successful career in pantomime followed, interrupted shortly in his forties by a divorce and health problems that forced him to give up the stage for three years. These events also precipitated his spiritual awakening to Orthodox Christianity, Romania's dominant religious denomination. In his late forties Puric started speaking publicly about Orthodoxy and the "Romanian spirit," becoming in the span of a few years a "prophet-mime" personality.[11] In addition to working full-time as an actor and director, performing at the National Theater and with his own company, Passe-Partout, Puric is also a public lecturer. He often appears as a guest on TV talk shows, he stars in advertisements promoting religious education courses in public schools,[12] and his collections of essays and stories are best sellers.[13] He gives public lectures throughout the country that, as the titles of his books suggest, discuss what it means to be Romanian. According to a reputed poll, Puric is now the most popular director in the country, known primarily for his public lectures that gather audiences as diverse as former Romanian royalty, celebrities, pensioners, and students.[14]

Listening to Puric's rhetoric from the comfortable distance of U.S. academia, I have worried about his espousal of nationalist and Orthodox Christian values at a key time of discursive changes. Unlike other nationalist figures, Puric performs his ideas with the intimacy of a storyteller and the talent of an actor. In the summer of 2012 I traveled back to Romania to witness his rhetorical performance in person and, through direct observation and self-reflection, to account for the polyphony of voices making up this persuasive field. My own critical positioning, situated in the West but still connected to Eastern Europe and its history, resonates with the position of Puric's audiences at the rhetorical event I attended: a lecture for white-collar workers with Western professional ties. Like them, I lived through the last years of a dictatorial communism and through the uncertain transition to both democracy and capitalism. While I left the country for graduate education in the United States, where I currently reside, my fellow audience members made a life in Romania, where they have been working in Western corporations.

I account for the vagaries, pleasures, and traps of identification that Dan Puric's rhetoric elicits by becoming an audience member among Romanian participants at this rhetorical event. Narrative, analytical, and self-reflexive writing will illuminate the audiencing selves, including myself, as permeable and changeable in the embodied process of persuasion. My intra- and inter-personally attuned writing aims to capture the polyvocality of the rhetorical process as a negotiated interaction with the rhetor, with other bodies sharing the same space and time, and with one's own inner voices. As a critic immersed in Puric's rhetorical field, I experience rhetoric's complex and subtle modulations in inner dialogue with my post-socialist and transnational selves and in outer dialogue with other post-socialist subjects. I navigate affectivity and analysis, move between aesthetic delight and repulsion, emotional comfort and discomfort, between analytical suspicion and edification. I dance with the rhetor as a laywoman and take the lead in critical appraisal of that audiencing position, and in the process I offer an embodied account of how rhetoric matters.

Critical Ethnography for Persuasive Discourse:
Becoming an Audiencing Critic

In my exploration of rhetoric's materiality and affectivity through an embodied dialogic immersion, I draw on efforts by both rhetoricians and critical ethnographers to speak from the field. Rhetoricians have drawn on ethnographic methods to write into rhetorical criticism the force of rhetoric, as audiences may experience it. Gerard Hauser has integrated such methods to study vernacular rhetoric in communities of dissent and to grasp how argumentation "depends on local knowledge, concerns, meanings, modes of arguments, value schemes, logics, traditions, and the like shared among ordinary people."[15] Phaedra Pezzullo's investigations of toxic tours use participant observation to notice how subaltern rhetoric challenges established environmentalist public discourse.[16] Samantha Senda-Cook has similarly become a participant observer in rhetorical communities to grasp their understanding of "authentic outdoor recreation experiences."[17] I stand with Hauser, Pezzullo, and Senda-Cook in aiming to foreground "the non-verbal activities that are involved in negotiating public life, including physical, visual, emotional, and aural dimensions" and in hoping to "expose sense-making processes in more raw and revealing ways" through direct observation and interviews.[18] This line of scholarship has offered insight into the embodied experience of persuasion. It has foregrounded the audience in a disciplinary context that, as Sara McKinnon notes, has otherwise "tended to pay more attention to the audience's showy sisters—rhetor and text."[19]

Yet while I converge with these and other scholars' immersive sensibilities—and, like them, treat the researcher's presence in the field as key to deciphering the embodied and affective dimensions of persuasion for audiences—I hold that such criticism has still more to yield. Our subdiscipline is notorious for its non-evocative writing about rhetorical artifacts and processes, which we usually engage as interesting puzzles to be solved even when the researcher is a participant observer. The "raw" "physical, visual, emotional, and aural dimensions" of which Hauser and Pezzullo speak above and which make rhetoric matter are yet to be evoked. This may be due, in part, to our habits of regarding rigor as a function of analytical detachment and not so much a function of thick description, creative writing, and self-reflection. We have still to lose face and recover, at least partially, the naïve experiences of persuasive processes that make rhetoric matter, as we and others may have lived them. If what is at stake is capturing the affective, embodied, temporal, and polyvocal dimensions of rhetorical discourse, then we need to learn how to engage in the intertwined practices of observation, creative nonfiction writing, and self-reflection.

Our colleagues in postmodern ethnography have already taken up this task. Having placed in "crisis" processes of representation taken for granted in "objective" ethnography, critical ethnographers have developed forms of investigation and writing that position the researcher self-reflectively in the field and try to do justice to the multiplicity of voices that make up social life and social selves.[20] They have asserted "the need for more dialogic and reflexive approaches" to writing that recognize the porous boundaries between researcher and the fields researched, and have explored the polyvocal "complexity of social forms, experiences and biographies," aware of "the politics and poetics of research writing."[21] Creative and performative genres, ranging from thick description to ethnographic poems, ethnodrama, and autoethnography, are part of a methodological toolbox mindful of the rhetoricity of social scientific research.[22] Such writing attends to the researcher and the researched as dynamically immersed in cultural, social, and political fields. The sense of presence conferred by critical ethnography gives both researcher and reader access to modes of knowledge that make the object of study "matter" in the senses that Blair wished for rhetoricians.

Critical ethnographic writing is worth pursuing especially for rhetoricians dealing with rhetorical situations in culturally changing, liminal, or transnational settings, like my own. If reflective ethnography captures the inter- and intra-subjective movement of the "I" in culture, as the researcher narrates, evokes, and remakes experience reflectively, such methodology can attune critics to the processes of one's co-constitution during and after persuasive discourse. As such, the reflexivity, time-sensitivity, and evocative abilities of critical ethnography may very well make the difference between audience-centered rhetorical criticism that reifies the rhetorical field by trying to extract some stable truth about audiences, on the one hand, and scholarship that treats persuasion as the continuous, polyvocal, temporally fluid process that it is, on the other.

The task of accounting for how one's subjectivity, as audience, is cocreated in the rhetorical exchange is not an easy one, requiring us to enter into dialogue with our bodies, with our subjects, with our readers, and to turn writing into a methodology of discovery. Christopher Tindale intimates that it is the nature of identity-related questions that makes audience-centered research such a difficult task, arguing that "the individual complexity of our identity . . . only serve[s] to compound the difficulty of pinning down" actual diverse audiences.[23] As poststructuralist theorists have shown, our subjectivity is a complicated dialectic between change and embeddedness in groups, where agency is "promiscuous and protean."[24] My audience-centered criticism aims to attend to the interaction between "text," rhetor, and audiences in a way that honors the fluidity of that relation and the multiplicity of voices present in the persuasive field. In doing so, I continue what Dilip Gaonkar has called "the fragmentation of the rhetorical object" into its context, a movement of our analyses away from close readings of text "into the orbit of critical social theory."[25] In this "orbit" the assumption articulated since Samuel Becker is that persuasion is a process that happens in "'longer chains' and complex loops rather than in discrete encounters."[26] I follow the "complex loop" of Puric's persuasive process by starting with my arrival at his lecture in Bucharest in the summer of 2012. My evocative narration is interrupted by voices from the audience, by the rhetor's own, and by my own empathetic or analytical reflections about the Romanian post-socialist "field" at large. My analysis will dramatize the polyvocal complexity of the rhetorical encounter and the movement of my own self-constitution in the rhetorical process.

Being There

I pay the driver and step out of the cab, recognizing this neighborhood at Bucharest's periphery. I used to live around here. I'd take the tram that passed the flower market and the run-down buildings with young Roma men glued to front stoops eating sunflower seeds and throwing banter at one another and the passersby. I'd walk its uneven streets of patched-up asphalt and cobblestone. Only a couple of new tall glass buildings on the horizon now challenge my memory of this post-socialist home. The graceless concrete construction that hosts Puric's lecture is not one of them. Sheltered behind a tall cement fence and heavy metal gates, it finds itself at odds with my expectations of a handsome conference center, which had been raised by the $350 registration fee. I take a breath and remind myself that this won't be the first time I'll feel puzzled back home in Romania.

As I enter the building, organizers greet participants with a relaxed smile characteristic of American performances of public selves. Romanian professionals in their thirties and forties are slowly finding their way to the tables, talking with acquaintances or using food and cell phones to occupy themselves. I take a seat and strike up a conversation with the two women already chatting. I learn that they are heads of human resources in their companies, and I share that I'm writing an academic piece about Puric, hoping to hear what they may be expecting to learn in this workshop. "I don't expect to learn anything in particular," says one of them. "I've come for the experience," she adds in a thoughtful, almost meditative tone. Like the other attendees who've joined our table, she has already attended some of Puric's other public lectures. "Why?" I repeat the question differently for neighbors who have joined our table in the meantime. They squint pensively and take a while to answer, as if trying to figure it out for the first time. It gets them out of the professional world, a man offers, gives them access to something else. This "something else" remains a mystery they won't or can't name, but which they all seem to need.

There's an air of reverence in my peers' answers, hinting that "the experience" they're anticipating is of a different kind than one of mastery and networking normally expected from a "professional development" workshop. Our gathering has a ceremonial feel, a tinge of piousness that draws us, the participants around the table, into a circle of expectant silences. People share their answers to my few questions, but don't ask back. They are friendly and open, but they seem more willing to listen than speak. The organizers don't keep us waiting for too long. Puric appears and, during our applause, steps on a slightly elevated stage. After playing down humorously his assigned status as the intellectual star of the event, Puric suggests an interactive meeting. But this will remain a one-man performance.

There's no glamour to Puric's fame, and he bears no hint of awareness of his power. He's a middle-aged man with a tired smile. His earth-toned clothes and slightly grayed hair complement his overall dusty physique. If you tried, you couldn't tell him from the crowds of rushed people with deep worry lines, sad smiles, and self-protective gazes in the streets of Bucharest. People who try to make sense and a living out of the fast-changing world around them. Middle-aged men, too old and unskilled to find another job after being laid off from their socialist posts, who numb their shame with daytime drinking or dilute it by becoming jacks-of-all-trades for their extended families. Schoolteachers who tutor to supplement their $300 monthly salary and occasionally treat themselves with a visit to the secondhand store in the neighborhood or a ticket to an independent theater show downtown. Students who still live with their parents, work part-time jobs on paper, full-time in reality, dreaming to secure a position, a recommendation letter, or at least add a little to the family's income. People without savings, without annual doctor's appointments, without regular visits to the dentist. People who spend all their salary on bills and inexpensive food from local markets where impoverished small farmers also scrape by a living, and try to patch together signs of a more dignified existence. People whose systemic poverty is not contained by their clean clothes and the occasional pair of trophy shoes or pants, but shows itself in their worn-out hands and thinned-out nails, in their missing teeth, or a poorly done hair dye. Small people, nimble in their efforts at continuous adaptation, yet tired, scared, and carrying an underlying pride and shame for not living up to the consumerist standards they've been seeing on TV, in movies, and advertisements. People of post-socialist neoliberalism. People who die slowly, people who float sideways. My people.

Lauren Berlant proposes the concept of "slow death" and "floating sideways" to make sense of life experienced as survival by groups caught in systemic conditions of limited agency, such as poverty.[27] For them, temporality is anchored in the near present, where the paying of bills and the management of kids take up one's imaginative and material energies. Worn out in the daily activities of reproducing life, one's agency is "an activity of maintenance, not making; fantasy, without grandiosity; sentience, without full intentionality; inconsistency, without shattering."[28] While rhetorics of crisis may occasionally ring loudly enough to present this state as exceptional, the scene of slow death is "neither a state of exception nor the opposite, mere banality," but a regime of "crisis ordinariness," a "structurally motivated attrition of persons notably because of their membership in certain populations."[29] Agency here comprises small gestures, not big projects; it is aimed at managing the present because there is little control over the distant future.

Berlant captures the affect under a regime of crisis ordinariness when she writes, "Life feels truncated—more like doggy paddling than swimming out to the magnificent horizon."[30] If life-building, future-oriented acts in which the default liberal subject of our imagination is supposed to engage are not available, small pleasures are. Eating, smoking, or watching TV produce experiences of self-suspension, of relief from the liberal and capitalist call to "intentionality and effective will."[31] They are forms of self-stabilization against the wearing out of life through "small vacations from the will itself."[32] And while Berlant knows better than to celebrate these forms of agency as liberating, she also gives them due credit for making bearable a life that erodes the person.

Walking in the streets of Romania, slow death is everywhere, whether in the crumply facades of buildings or in the worn-out faces of people. Erosion,[33] Berlant's favorite adjective for the slow-dying, is a fitting descriptor: it captures the slowness and gradual diminution that people experience in post-socialism, its banality when courageous, concerted, and creative political will is missing.

Dan Puric dramatizes such experience of systemic powerlessness, reading in its manifestations remnants of ingenuity, and relying on a compassionate rhetoric to make sense of it. He calls for a renewal out of post-socialist erosion through reclaiming a spiritually attuned, nationally proud, and Western-skeptic subjectivity.

In his lecture he acknowledges the diminution of the self humorously. "Romanians have the brain of stray dogs, they are on the lookout for threats," he announces, before dramatizing through an anecdote this allegedly canine suspicion. "An old man, Gheorghe, was taking his cows to the pasture each morning," Puric starts. "One day he sees a beautiful wooden bridge, newly built over the mountain river he'd been crossing by foot all his life. Gheorghe scratches his head and voices the obvious: 'Well, they've built a bridge. . . .'" Following the imaginary line of the new bridge with raised eyebrows, Puric in Gheorghe's character steps through the river, going around the new construction. "Around seven in the evening, here comes Vasile, another peasant, happily herding his sheep to the river. Gheorghe sees the neighbor and warns him loudly from the other side of the pasture: 'They built a bridge!'"

People in the audience snicker and giggle as Puric performs Gheorghe yelling out the notice with an expression that condenses both deep curiosity and fear toward his neighbor's decision whether to walk the bridge. Vasile, we're reassured, also carefully crosses the river through the water. Ion, a third peasant, goes by insouciantly later that same evening. The two neighbors see him and yell in unison, "'They built a bridge!' Ion looks at the water, then at the bridge, then walks the bridge nonchalantly, just like we're invited these days to step on all sorts of bridges." Puric imitates Ion's confident walk, as he delivers the quick allusion to Romania's EU and NATO accession. "And when he gets midway, the bridge crumbles and Ion finds himself struggling in the middle of the river, while the neighbors utter to each other, with knowing eyes, 'We told him that they built a bridge!'" This story, Puric explains didactically, would reflect a Romanian attitude of healthy suspicion that does not come from ignorance or fear, but rather from a prudence learned over generations.

The figure of the Romanian peasant as an exemplar of both healthy suspicion and transhistorical serenity is recurring. Another of his anecdotes, for instance, features an old peasant woman who flew to the United States to visit her daughter. Stopped at customs to have her luggage checked, the peasant perplexes the officers with a rock she'd picked from the river in which her daughter bathed as a child. The woman's desire for permanence, taking the form of a stone from the river, is cast as characteristic of what Puric calls a beautiful Romanian. Puric's own father, a village doctor, often appears as another example of a serene, transhistorical perspective. The father lost his land to the communization of property yet remained unruffled by it, continuing his life in the communist system with dignity. The serene acceptance of historical fate

Puric casts as inspired by Orthodox Christianity, a faith that would uniquely equip Romanians to handle post-socialist transformations.

This aestheticization of the Orthodox, ethnically Romanian peasant as the exemplar of the "beautiful human" stages a nostalgic rhetoric of return to a pre–European Union past that is not without history and ideological significance. The figure of the beset, yet dignified, peasant was central to the early twentieth-century homegrown fascist movement, the Iron Guard. Its pro-peasant rhetoric rallied the support of the newly urbanized Romanian ethnics making up the majority population, against the entrepreneurial middle class dominated by Armenian, Greek, and especially Jewish ethnics.[34] The movement's leader, Corneliu Zelea Codreanu, aestheticized the peasant by wearing traditional attire and riding a white horse to impress on the recently urbanized youth that he was one of the people, "a true Romanian."[35] Public intellectuals and politicians at the time also supported the ideology of revitalizing Romania through a return to a premodern simplicity and Orthodox spirituality, with tragic consequences manifested in local measures of "purifying" the nation's ethnic and religious Others: domestic Jewish pogroms and affiliation with Hitler's Germany during most of World War II.[36] During socialism, the figure of the poor Romanian peasant was co-opted as an anti-bourgeois symbol: communist subjects with "healthy origins" in the poor peasantry were rewarded by the new regime, and the patriarchal peasant family with numerous children was used as the demographic model for forced reproduction starting in 1966.[37] After the fall of socialism, the figure of the Romanian-ethnic peasant has become a recurrent signifier found in nation branding campaigns, the public memory of communism, the emergence of "ethno-" television stations playing Romanian folk music, and the popularity of ethnographic museums.

In Puric's rhetoric, this figure carries and reinforces traces of its discursive articulation with anti-Western, antimodernist, and nationalist ideals from the past. The possibility of interpellation into a moral community populated by peasant figures gains force from Puric's vivid and humorously performed narratives. He becomes the very embodiment of Walter Benjamin's premodern storyteller: his stories and characters stir up our past lives, dust off the spilled beads of our fragmented selves, and string them up into a rosary, turning us into a "community of listeners" to his "wise counsel."[38] They revive my own memories of a distant past, of a grandfather I barely knew, of people from the village where I spent many early years and summers. What I remember about my grandfather is his unruffled demeanor. I was six when he died of cancer, a diagnosis he had received a couple of years earlier, so I may have known him when he'd already made peace with his fate. Even in his last months, when he was already very sick yet traveled from the countryside to the city to see his grandchildren, he'd carry the same serene expression: his big eyes curious and alert, his whole face soft with a handsome smile. By then parts of his esophagus had been removed and he'd feed himself by pushing mashed food into a funnel attached to a short elastic hose that ended up in his stomach. "Back to baby food," he'd joke. "Does it hurt?" I'd inquire. "Nah, just some pressure. Saves me the chewing." He was the first dead man I saw, lying down in his bed, candles by his side, his expression just as peaceful as always. They moved him into a coffin and carried him to the cemetery by cart, accompanied by grandma's mourning cries and the loud ceremonial wailing of other women. "Why have you gone, Traiane? Why have you left us?" they'd weep, as if trying to wake him up from his death. But he kept unruffled in his coffin, his stillness a reassurance that everything was just as it was supposed to be.

Puric's construction of the peasant glides smoothly over my imagination and, it seems, that of my captivated peers. After all, most people in the room, a group in their thirties and older, have been partly raised by rural grandparents or moved out of villages. They were first- or second-generation urbanites due to communist planned urbanization and industrialization that took place in the 1950s yet was inefficient enough to return folks to villages for family reunions, for help with raising children, and for material support from small-scale agriculture.[39] His nostalgic stories of the serene peasant connect us affectively with significant times, geographies, and people in our past and give narrative coherence to our currently complex urban, post-socialist, and internationalized liminal identities. By storying the figure of the peasant, Puric performs tradition for and with the audience in the room. Tradition so performed is not, as Robert Glenn Howard writes, "the empirical quality of an act as having been handed down" but a "vernacular authorizing force perceived by those participating in an act."[40] What Puric authorizes are selective childhood memories of family relations and their accompanying sense of freedom and connection, emotions hard to come by in adulthood, especially neoliberal, transitional, and transnational adulthood. His vernacular discourse authorizes him as an authentic rhetor, counter-hegemonic to the neoliberal ideologies of work and success in which we audiences are usually immersed. At the same time his rhetoric forges an ideological narrative coherence of us, audiences, "suppressing the fact that, in a very real sense, no person is the same as he or she was a decade ago, or last year, or indeed yesterday."[41]

Yet, while Puric's stories carve affective ties with the past, he also lets the needle of his ideology scratch over the complex album I have become, showing the shadow side of his "beautiful human." He steadily constructs a world of binaries. The government, big transnational corporations, and their respective bureaucracies lead to "incredible forms of pollution" and alienation, while the world of children, wise old men and women, and peasants is there to save us. There are left-wing "intellectual traitors who create doubts instead of certainties" and intellectuals like himself who help us to live better. Finally, there are "corporate women" and "women." In this dichotomous world of the inauthentic and the authentic I'd belong to the caricaturized former. I am the intellectual who has more doubts than certainties. I recognize some of my assertiveness in the "corporate women" dominating his examples. I am the American who comes off as too formal in interpersonal encounters, shaking hands and keeping my distance. I remain, therefore, an outsider and wonder what keeps my peers enthralled. After all, they're also split subjects, navigating between East and West on a daily basis. In management literature they even have a name, "host-country nationals," people who work in their own country but spend most of their time in Western organizational cultures, "making at least their work life similar to living abroad."[42] And that is when Puric surprises me.

"The truth is that Romania is a place with people full of potential; that's the truth. The reality is that Romania is a work ghetto," he says matter-of-factly, pausing for a moment, looking around the room to see how his statement sinks. Puric's distinction between "truth" and "reality" somehow renders me more familiar to myself. I can see the spark of recognition in other people's eyes as well. I know all too well their working lives through friends and relatives: 7:00 A.M. until 8:00 P.M., maybe weekends, maximum flexibility required by international corporations. They are the internationalized corporate worker, trained by socialism to submit to institutional authority, lured by capitalism with higher salaries and professional development accounts, yet exhausted in the rhythm of the job and lost in the logic of the commodity. They lean forward, eager for the possibility of transcendence.

For a moment, Puric's words take me out of the camp of the Other (the doubtful intellectual, etc.) and turn me into one of the Romanian ghetto workers whose truth and reality clash affectively yet coexist. The incongruence between my "real" status in the configuration of capital and national boundaries, on the one hand, and my multiple national and personal belongings, on the other, finds recognition in his words. My "reality" is spelled out in the documents I had just submitted days earlier for my U.S. visa application: "temporary worker." Having just gathered immigration paperwork, meticulously looking for all the dates when I was in and out of the country, retracing my journey through the past ten years, I had become painstakingly aware of my outsider status in the United States and of my dependence on "institutions of sponsorship." The limit of my belonging was captured by my legal position as a "temporary worker," someone who passes through and can stay only as long as she can work. The political "reality" of my status resonated with the overworked corporate professionals in the room, and I experienced the instantaneous mutual understanding that Victor Turner calls a *communitas*—the feeling that I was part of the transnational neoliberal Romanian workforce Puric addressed. Turner speaks of the "flash of lucid mutual understanding on an existential level" that sometimes overtakes a group and affectively connects people across differences.[43] I recognized myself in the others' tiredness, their desire for (Western) status, our lost opportunities to be more connected with our families of origin in our search for professional success. In the moment, guilt toward my Romanian roots washed over me and suspicion toward my American communities arose: Who was I for them? Who are they for me? What is the foundation of our relation when I'm, by law, just a worker from the Romanian "work ghetto," whose illusion of belonging will be exposed by the visa's expiration date? Out of disparate, idiosyncratic subjects, differently positioned along class, age, gender, sexuality, and spirituality, Puric's words seemed to have energized a spontaneous homogeneous *communitas* through emotional identification with the figure of the patient, overworked, and full-of-potential Romanian neoliberal worker carrying traces of the patient, overworked, yet resourceful peasant.

It was not until days later, with some temporal and physical distance as well as purposeful reflection, that Puric's words got distilled into an acute awareness of my multiple belonging. My "reality" was my job, its fragility, the outsider status it conferred, and the potential barren existence to which it could confine me as a "temporary worker" sacrificing relations to job stability. My "truth," however, was not my "potential," as Puric put it, another individualist and mercantilist way of understanding oneself. It was my deep multiple belonging, the richness of my relations in a state of liminality. Puric reminded me of belonging to and with my family of origin, my Romanian friends and mentors from whom I had grown apart. Like the "foreign locals" in the conference room and throughout Romania, I was also mourning the loss or diminishment of relations with people who have been part of my life for more than twenty years.

But Puric's stories did not account for my belonging to the country's public space and its counterpublic feminist spaces. Nor did it account for my affective ties to my American Midwestern partner and friends, colleagues, mentors, and students—the affective and intellectual communities in which I have grown for the past ten years. While Puric's simple dichotomy between "reality" and "truth" exposed the fragility of my "reality," and reminded me of what I shared with many of my co-nationals, it was critical self-reflection that gradually anchored me back into the ineffable "truth" of my multiple belonging. While Puric's "truth" and "reality" were meant to give a nostalgic nudge toward a more stable identification with an aestheticized and victimized national community, self-reflection turned the familiar "truth" of my multiple national, institutional, and personal belonging into a conscious anchor.

"Be longing": I borrow the term from Aimee Carrillo Rowe, who casts subjectivity as an affective process. We long to be with others by default and unreflectively, by virtue of having bodies that are placed in history and in the care of others. The subjects that we become are "an effect of belonging—of the affective, passionate, and political ties that bind us to others."[44] Subjectivity is always already intersubjective, and while our affective ties exist by default,

Carrillo Rowe invites us to engage them reflectively and critically. Puric throws his overworked neoliberal subjects, as well as his systemically impoverished slow-dying ones attending this and other of his "lectures," into a fantasy of belonging to a redemptive ethnic community, whose affective boundaries are drawn by suspicion to the foreign and care for one another. Belonging to the ethnically "beautiful" community is a solution to dying slowly, to cultural uprootedness, and to the guilt of ideological and physical migration. It is the "something else" for which his audiences are searching: a narratively coherent affective experience of belonging.

Puric's nostalgic narrativized rhetoric created for us a powerful moment of slippage into a soothing fantasy of coherent national subjectivity. Experiencing this rhetorical performance in the presence of other audience members and that of the rhetor made palpable the fluidity of even my academically and critically trained subjectivity, its potential for rhetorical destabilization by ideologically regressive rhetorics. It is not a proud realization, but one reached through embodied presence and critical reflection during and after the rhetorical event.

Writing from the Field

Writing self-reflexively from the perspective of audiences assumes the risks of losing face. The audiencing critic has to step out of the known of disembodied inquiry into the thick of the rhetorical situation experienced as a liminal space where subjectivity is set on the fire of intersubjective affective molding. If "we are always already being hailed by our various (be)longings," critical ethnography teaches us *how* this constitutive rhetorical interpellation is lived and negotiated.[45] My critical ethnographic rhetorical analysis of Puric's discourse has shown rhetorical experience as a complex articulation between older ideologies (ethnic nationalism, Orthodox Christianity), memory (of my own past, of a collective past), exemplary figures (the Romanian peasant, the neoliberal slow-dying subject, the corporate worker), stories performed and witnessed with others, and post-socialist neoliberal affective searches for differentiated subject-positions during sociopolitical transition.

By positioning myself amid the cultural, political, emotional, and physical fields in which Puric matters, reflective ethnography impressed on me the porous constitution of audiences in the affectively negotiated symbolic order. Attending to my interrupted resonance with Puric's *communitas* meant tracking the network of affect and reflection linking my experience of Puric's words with other people's words and emotions, with surges of memory from my early village upbringing, with the materiality of Romania's spaces and bodies, and with my Western relations and responsibilities. As such, critical ethnography moves beyond the "audience invoked" and "existing audience" divide to analyze the unpredictable and polyvocal process of persuasion as it happens in time and in between people, places, emotions, and inner voices. By placing the critic in the audience, critical ethnography for rhetorical purposes reveals the audience as neither a positivist static object nor an ideological position in a rhetor's text, but as going through affective, self-reflexive, contextually, and materially bound becoming.

Furthermore, a critical ethnography for rhetoric positions our discipline to attend to the temporality of self-constitution in relation to persuasive discourse. What does it mean to be moved by rhetoric? Are we moved in the rhetorical moment? After? How does the subject negotiate oneself and "the text" when jolted, stirred, or rocked by rhetoric? Critical ethnographic rhetorical analyses magnify the moments that move us, translate them through evocative writing, watch them change under the curious attention of the self-observer, and let writing further change that early experience of being moved. This process is unpredictable: the critic risks losing self and losing face; s/he cannot know the "thesis" in advance, having to let it "arise" in the course of "being there" and during self-reflective writing.

But it is such unpredictability that shows, rather than tells, how rhetoric matters. The audiencing critic can offer access to a different way of knowing rhetorical processes that illuminates their temporality and the risks of embodiment. It would have been emotionally easy to read Puric's rhetoric in its many mediated forms.[46] It would have been analytically and formally faster to approach his nationalist and anti-Western rhetoric through ideological criticism of his "texts." It would have been as easy as it was for him to criticize (me as a) Westernized subject(s): a disembodied exercise, one without risks. In the critical rhetorical project undertaken from the field, I would not have received the gift of understanding my own and others' permeable selves through dialogue, self-listening, and writing.

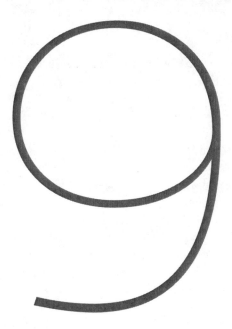

Holographic Rhetoric

De/Colonizing Public Memory
at Pueblo Grande

Roberta Chevrette

"What is the common narrative of the American Indian or the Native American?
We have to rethink that. We have to think about it differently. . . . We have over
twenty-one reservations in this state alone, in the state of Arizona. Did you know
that 'Arizona' is an O'Otham word? *'Ali ṣona-g.'* 'The place where there is a lot of
little rivers.' Did you know that, Roberta?"

"No," I say. "I didn't."

"Did anybody know that?"

There is silence.

"Right. So what I want you to do is open your mind a little."

—SHANNON RIVERS, "THE PEOPLE'S HISTORY: AN O'OTHAM
PERSPECTIVE" (LECTURE IN THE CIVIL DIALOGUE SERIES)

*I would like to thank the editors for insightful feedback that has helped shape the arguments in this essay. The conceptualizations offered here have also been influenced by Marie-Louise Paulesc, Karen J. Leong, Daniel Brouwer, Sarah Amira de la Garza, and Aaron Hess.

From street signs to place names to souvenir shops to staged "Old West" towns to the patterns and images that appear on billboards, buildings, and freeway overpasses, residents and visitors to the U.S. Southwest encounter a landscape saturated with Native American symbols. Designated places of public memory including museums, ruins, and other historical sites further infuse the region with symbolic importance. This rhetorical landscape propels a particular kind of remembering in which Native American nations and peoples are frequently imagined as existing in "some 'other worlds,' some other place" outside the present.[1] More a "haunting" than a "forgetting," Native Americans serve as the spectral figures against which dominant settler colonial narratives are re/enacted.[2]

Connecting the historical expansion of tourism in the Southwest with portrayals of the area's peoples as disappearing relics, Leah Dilworth argues that popular renderings of "Southwest Indians"[3] played a central role in the imaginaries of the American West and the greater United States, producing the Southwest as a symbolic and material "national playground" for American (self) discovery.[4] In contrast to the stereotype of "wild" Indians, Native Americans in the Southwest were romanticized as "noble savages" who, existing "in the imagined purity of the primitive,"[5] offered a window onto the childhood of Anglo-European civilization. Many contemporary memory places in the U.S. Southwest continue to reproduce such portrayals, depicting a "vanished" Native American past evidenced only by its material traces. And yet, within present Southwest landscapes, Native American peoples endure, negotiating the commodification of their cultures, working to retain (or re/acquire) rights to land, water, and sacred places, and individually and collectively narrating their own histories. The Southwest is thus an important location for engaging contestations of public memory as they relate to place, visibility, materiality, and belonging.

This essay explores struggles over memory as they unfold within and in relation to Phoenix's Pueblo Grande Museum, the site of an excavated platform mound once occupied by the region's Indigenous peoples. Like numerous other area sites such as the Deer Valley Rock Art Center and Casa Grande Ruins National Monument, Pueblo Grande materially attests to the area's long inhabitance by Indigenous peoples preceding the establishment of the U.S. nation-state. As such, the land on which the museum resides and the artifacts contained within are an important part of the cultural history of the local Akimel O'Otham (also spelled O'Odham) (Pima) nation and other area peoples, the descendants of the people who have come to be known as the Hohokam (Huhugam). However, by emphasizing Indigenous disappearance and valorizing scientific knowledge, Pueblo Grande is also a site where settler narratives, and the forms of empire with which they are associated, are preserved and reproduced.

Utilizing examples from fieldwork in the museum, this essay engages Pueblo Grande as a site where colonial identities are re/enacted through symbolic, material, and social encounters. At the same time, I seek to also address decolonizing possibilities residing within, and beyond, the museum site. I argue that approaching rhetoric as *holographic* enables attention to contested memories as they unfold within the imaginative and material geographies of U.S. settler colonialism. My argument is rooted in the holographic metaphor deployed by qualitative scholars, which is based on the lensless photographic method of creating a hologram: a three-dimensional "likeness" of an object. Yvonna Lincoln and Egon Guba utilize this metaphor to describe interconnected and "dynamic process[es] of interaction" by which information is distributed throughout systems, "rather than concentrated at specific points."[6] From this perspective rhetorical fragments can be seen to contain information about systems, or "wholes."

The holographic analytic productively connects rhetorical inquiry in specific places to larger symbolic, material, and social landscapes to attend to multiplicity and difference without attempting to flatten it into a "definite image-repertoire."[7] Such a perspective engages rhetorical fragments taken from multiple places and perspectives while also calling attention to critics' positionalities in relation to their object(s) of study. In its emphasis on fragmented knowledges, multidimensionality, temporal emergences, and connectivities within places of remembering, this analytic offers a means by which to "address [the] epistemic coloniality" of our field as well as our methods of critique.[8] In particular I draw attention to how public memory scholars have approached their objects of analysis and how recent expansions in both our sites and methods of inquiry present opportunities as well as new challenges for decolonizing our approaches. This essay thus places the concerns broadly taken up by this volume in relation to Darrel Wanzer's call for rethinking critical rhetoric "from a global perspective attentive to coloniality."[9] Such a rethinking requires interrogating the received knowledges and "guiding ideals" that manifest as "taken-for-granted realit[ies]."[10]

I begin by discussing rhetorical approaches to public memory places. I argue that even as scholars deploy qualitative methods as "tools" they nonetheless focus on the symbolic and material inducements of *memory place as text*. The holographic analytic shifts our attention to other sources/fragments of information and is thus useful in addressing multiple and emergent meanings in the field. Through this framework I turn to a discussion of Pueblo Grande, attending to the symbolic, material, and social encounters through which settler colonialism is re/enacted against the absent presence of Native Others.[11] In the subsequent section I expand my discussion of the holographic analytic by offering a counter-analysis of the memories present in the site. I argue that viewing rhetoric as holographic brings dimensions into focus that might otherwise be elided. In the case of Pueblo Grande the holographic analytic challenges critics to understand the site's absences through the lens of Indigenous presence. In conclusion, I discuss the theoretical and methodological implications of the holographic analytic for engaging multiplicities in sites of contested memory, for deepening self-reflexivity in relation to our sites, and for broadening the scope of our fields of inquiry.

Three-Dimensional Memories: Colonial Re/enactments at Pueblo Grande

Given their "self-nomination" as sites "of significant memory of and for a collective,"[12] and their role in re/presenting the past for present purposes, rhetorical scholars have frequently approached public memory places with attention to their symbolicity: "Collective memory, after all, is publicly shared and negotiated through symbols, a process that lies at the heart of what constitutes rhetorical theory."[13] However, as three-dimensional, emplaced objects, public memory places exhibit characteristics that are distinct from many traditional rhetorical "texts." A key distinction concerns the difficulty of engaging them from a distance. As such, they have propelled rhetorical scholars into the field where, increasingly, arguments have been made to move beyond analyzing symbols and representations to also attend to rhetoric's materiality and the rhetoricity of place.[14] This has further required a reconsideration of critics' relationships to their sites of study.[15] Public memory places are thus opportune for engaging broader conversations propelled by rhetorical scholars' turn toward "the field" to examine "live" and "*in situ*" rhetorics.[16]

As argued by Carole Blair, Greg Dickinson, Brian Ott, Eric Aoki, and numerous others, public memory places exert influence on—or quite literally *move*—visitors through their sheer physicality, including their materials, design, and organization, and their placement within larger landscapes.[17] Acting directly on visitors' bodies, they prescribe particular pathways that influence reception and engage the "full sensorium."[18] While theorizations of rhetoric's materiality emerging from public memory places have profoundly influenced the field, much of this scholarship continues to view *memory places as texts*—as material rather than symbolic texts, or as "diffuse" rather than "discrete" texts, but as texts nonetheless.[19] In other words, even as the emplaced nature of their objects of analysis pushes public memory scholars into the field where they engage in participant observation to the extent of "being there," they still primarily treat material forms and embodiments as texts that can be read through the critic's experiences *in situ*. Even claims made about visitors are frequently extrapolated from what has been referred to as the "rhetorical pilgrimage"[20] or "interpretive tour,"[21] in which the critic reads the site "from the perspective of the scholar-as-visitor" without really engaging other visitors.[22] As a consequence we risk reifying what Richard Handler and Eric Gable describe as approaching museums as static cultural texts, whereby researchers have "*proceeded by ignoring most of what happens in them*."[23]

Public memory places are fundamentally social encounters through which identities, relationships, and belongings are forged. Not only do they narrate important community histories, they enable visitors to become part of a collective with others. Furthermore, as people engage with these sites they do so less as spectators or audience members than as active participants involved in intersubjective meaning-making. While public memory places serve as symbolic and material locales where "official" pasts are represented and interpreted, they are also places where the past is negotiated and reworked by the members of society. In this manner, memory places "are inevitably multivocal" not only through the polysemy of the rhetorical artifacts they include, but also through visitors' multiple and embodied interactions within.[24] The movement of public memory scholars into the field thus raises questions about how we might engage memory places as "sites where individual members of the remembering collectives experience—and interact with—the rhetorical representations of the past."[25]

In suggesting a holographic approach, I argue that incorporating methods not readily perceived as rhetorical enables further attention to social dimensions of remembering as they intertwine with symbolic and material enactments. A holographic approach to rhetoric emphasizes the three-dimensionality of our objects of study while also implicating critics in relation to their analyses. In addition, this approach highlights the relationship of micro events to macro structures.[26] While the hologram is of course a metaphor, metaphors are consequential; they "render events and contexts intelligible and commit us to particular values and beliefs."[27] In deploying the holographic metaphor I wish to draw attention to how various rhetorical fragments from different locations and dimensions together operate as "parts imaging the whole."[28]

The notion of "imaging" is crucial in order to avoid a reductive reading of the metaphor in which "parts" are sometimes argued to *contain* "wholes." Emphasizing the hologram's imagistic properties subverts the presumption of reflections containing material realities, turning our attention instead to the ways reflections are encoded on matter. The holographic analytic is therefore apt for illuminating the "'flicker' of presence/absence, or of difference/sameness,"[29] making it useful for engaging Pueblo Grande, a place shaped around the dual absent presences of Native American persons and epistemologies.

Symbolicity at Pueblo Grande: Absent Presences

In its very existence Pueblo Grande demonstrates the long inhabitance of the region by Indigenous peoples. The Akimel O'Odham (Pima), Tohono O'Odham (Papago), and Mexican Pima are all direct descendants of the represented culture, which archaeologists call the "Hohokam." While this naming itself— a derivative of the O'Odham "Huhughkam"—attests to connections between the peoples represented and contemporary area peoples, museum displays largely elide these connections, instead presenting the "vanished" civilization of the Hohokam as an intriguing mystery that can be solved through archaeological evidence.

The museum's emphasis on archaeology is consequential for its (in)ability to incorporate Indigenous subjectivities. In the "Dig It!" gallery, various exhibits describe "the tools of the trade" and invite visitors to test their archaeological knowledge. The only picture of a Native American person in this room is a photograph of a contemporary pottery-maker situated between an oversized pot replica and a display of animal bones. Its caption reads, "Clues from Tradition." As Aaron Hess and I discuss elsewhere, this juxtaposition renders the woman "not as a contemporary subject but as a historical object or living fossil, a 'clue' to be studied by archaeologists as well as the larger public for whom the display is intended."[30]

Indigenous knowledges are positioned in subordinate relationships to science throughout the museum. The first sign atop the platform mound commemorates Dr. Joshua Miller, the man who excavated the site in 1901 at a time when academics and tourists alike were flocking to the Southwest to collect relics of the past while experiencing and documenting its "disappearing" cultures. One museum sign asks, "Did They Disappear?" before offering three scientific interpretations regarding the site's "abandonment." In various exhibits, maps and models further present reconstructions of the past as scientific "facts." In this manner the museum both perpetuates the long-standing fascination with the "vanishing Indian" and the related anthropological impulse to excavate, collect, and "preserve" this history for white settlers. In contrast, in the rare instances where they are included, Native accounts are described as "stories," or even as "legends." The museum's official discourses thus decentralize Native peoples' narrations of their own "living relationships with the past"[31] and, in doing so, performatively deny Indigenous peoples authorship over their own histories.

The description placed at the entrance to the outdoor interpretive trail offers further insight into the museum's re/production of Native alterity. Stepping through a doorway flanked by Kokopelli and other petroglyph-style designs, visitors encounter a sign that reads, "A Special Place: Welcome to Pueblo Grande, a prehistoric Hohokam Indian village. For the next half hour your walk along this trail will take you back in time when this place was very different." The naming of Indigenous material history as "prehistoric" enables the aforementioned distinction between stories/legends and science, while the notion of "going back in time"—a phrase that appears throughout Pueblo Grande and in numerous other Southwestern memory places—is closely intertwined with the historical and contemporary production of the Southwest as tourist spectacle. Conceptualized as a place where settler visitors could learn about "foreign people, with foreign speech and foreign ways,"[32] tourists to the Southwest have long imagined themselves as not only traveling to a physical destination but as traveling to a different era, as evidenced in numerous visitor comments about life "back then." Johannes Fabian describes the construction of temporal distance, in which difference becomes time and time becomes difference, as the means by which anthropological Others are denied coevalness.[33] Excluded as subjects from the shared time of the (settler) present, Native Americans become its objects.

Materiality at Pueblo Grande: Exploring the Ancient

Attending to the museum's material dimensions offers further insight into how Native absence is temporally constructed in relation to the larger landscapes in which the museum resides. As a destination, Pueblo Grande "demand[s] physical labor of a would-be audience member," including the travel required to get there.[34] On that journey, vacationing visitors experience the physical surroundings within which the museum is embedded; moreover, they frequently travel to other related memory places, the meanings of which "spill over" into their experiences of Pueblo Grande.[35] Many visitors were on larger Southwest tours; when asked what her favorite place she had visited was, one woman said, "I can't even remember its name! We've been a lot of places." Public memory within Pueblo Grande is thus enfolded within a constellation of places and meanings.

In terms of its immediate surroundings, one of Pueblo Grande's most remarked-on attributes is its proximity to downtown Phoenix. Against the freeway overpasses and light rail tracks that mark the "modern" urban present, the entrance sign calls visitors to "Explore the Ancient." Within the site, visitors stroll through "ancient" grounds while planes descend into neighboring Phoenix Sky Harbor International Airport. These juxtapositions influence how visitors experience the site: "It's pretty phenomenal that all this is still here after all these years, and we see it's in . . . downtown Phoenix," one noted in awe. Another, descending from the platform mound, told me, "Pretty neat stuff up there! . . . Pretty amazing that it exists in the middle of a city." One sign proclaims Pueblo Grande to be "a prehistoric island in a sea of urban development," situating the museum in a different place/time from the surrounding cityscape.

Other sensory experiences help construct "the past" as tied closely to nature. Birds chirp as visitors tour the mound under the heat of the Arizona sun. The temperature shifts upon entering the re-created living structures. Painted lizards point down a path teeming with real lizards, jackrabbits, and other animals. Small placards identify various plants and animals while dynamic tour guides and static signs describe how Native Americans lived off the earth. As the represented Native past is connected with embodied experiences of the natural environment against the sights and sounds of the city, time transforms into difference through visitors' experiences in relation to the museum's material landscape and surroundings.

Playing Indian: Social Encounters at Pueblo Grande

While the discussion above largely focuses on the museum's symbolic and material inducements—or what I have referred to as the reading of *memory places as texts*—engaging rhetoric as holographic moves us toward other sources of data. My engagement with Pueblo Grande included over thirty hours of participant observation spread out across a two-year period during which I took extensive field notes, recorded fragments of visitor conversation, went on guided tours, and conducted interviews. My data also included experiences at additional area sites, mediated communications, and other sought-out or chance encounters. I utilized analytic methods, including open coding and thematic clustering, to make connections between collected fragments, a process that offered further insights into the juxtaposition of past and present within Pueblo Grande and into the production of Native "difference" in relation to settler identities.

During interviews visitors expressed great admiration for the "ancient" culture represented. Some noted their amazement at how people survived without access to modern consumer goods, while others emphasized the cooperation required by living in a past where individuals had to rely on one another and on nature. One university student stated that "back then" you were "busy living with a purpose." In this romanticized narrative—one that closely aligns with Southwest imaginaries but did not emerge from a "reading" of the museum itself—Native peoples of the past are imagined to have lived more "authentic" lives than those allowed by contemporary civilization.

The desire to experience "authenticity" has been theorized in relation to ethnic tourism, in which people seek out "exotic" experiences with members of other racial and cultural groups. Dean MacCannell noted that tourists desire an "original" and unadulterated cultural experience;[36] one couple, leafing through pamphlets for other area sites as they decided whether to enter Pueblo Grande, asked a staff member how it compared to the nearby Heard Museum, renowned for its large collection of Native American art. "We're different. They're an art museum and we are an archaeological site," she explained. "Good," they responded. They had come from the Heard but it was not what they were looking for—they wanted to see relics from a different era. The search to experience an "authentic" Native past can be connected with what Renato Rosaldo has described as "imperialist nostalgia," in which "people mourn the passing of what they themselves have transformed."[37] Framing this loss as an inevitable outcome of progress, the Native past becomes "a defiled grave" on which settler colonial identities can be continually rebuilt.[38]

The long-standing infatuation with "going Native"[39] or "playing Indian"[40]—performative practices in which white U.S. settlers attempt to take on Native identities as their own—is also connected to the production of settler identities in the United States. Pueblo Grande itself can be seen as, at least in part, a reproduction of the desire to "play Indian" through voyeuristic consumption of Native culture. White visitors and docents frequently arrived bedecked in turquoise and silver, wearing beaded belts and hatbands, or adorned in cowboy hats, denim, and leather fringe. Children played with mortar and pestle replicas near the mound trail entrance or with blocks in the child-friendly "Build Your Own Adobe Compound" exhibit. On one visit I encountered an anthropology undergraduate constructing an atlatl, a "prehistoric" hunting device. Dressed in earth tones, he wore bone jewelry and handmade leather sandals, with his dark hair falling past his shoulders from underneath a plaited hat. As he worked with his hands, he removed a wadded-up bunch of sinew from his mouth and placed it on his knee. He explained to the small audience that while we probably thought he was crazy, he liked the taste. An almost too-perfect enactment of the trope of anthropologist "gone Native," he consumed Native culture in his dress, his work, and—quite literally—in his mouth.

Such performances highlight how contests of memory are inscribed through words, places, and embodied performances. During my observations, Indigenous persons were markedly absent despite being the subjects on display. Other nonwhite persons were sometimes present but often surrounded by larger groups through which their bodily "difference" was subdued. On one visit, however, three Latina women entered the museum, one of whom wore a traditional-style blouse with brightly embroidered flowers around the neckline. Moving through the galleries they spoke to one another and played each video in Spanish; these mediated voices resonated in the otherwise quiet space. Visibly and verbally out of place amid the other Anglo-American visitors, their embodied "difference" seemed to subtly challenge the museum's emphasis on disappearance. Their bodily presence called forth colonial histories in the U.S. Southwest and neighboring Mexico, temporarily interrupting dominant narratives of white settlers arriving in unoccupied lands while simultaneously rendering the absence of other racialized bodies more visible.

What rhetorical significance arises from this temporary reconfiguration of the space? May we regard this reconfiguration as a fleeting, if unplanned, resistance? Nothing suggested that these women were deliberately engaging in "resistant" practices. Yet by adopting the holographic analytic we may consider the ways in which parts, or fragments, image the "whole." This approach encourages critics to attend not only to the ways in which memory places influence, or move, visitors through their inducements but also to the transient moments and performances that emerge within.[41] We often focus on more "permanent" elements of memory: monuments etched in stone and displays designed with the intention to persuade. But observing how visitors interact with and in the presence of public memory places offers a different layer of interpretation, encouraging critics not to move away from the "text" or "object" of analysis, but to consider it as always already intertwined with other practices and processes.

In outlining how symbolic, material, and social practices together shape meaning-making in Pueblo Grande, I have attempted to show how each dimension builds on the others. "Reading" fragments of data acquired in various ways and from various places, including rhetorical analysis of "texts" encountered within and in relation to the museum, offers a strong foundation for engaging its symbolic entailments. Participant observation and immersion enables further attention to rhetoric's material dimensions as well as to emergent meanings unfolding in the field. Conducting visitor interviews and utilizing grounded-theory coding to identify themes further attends to public memory as a participatory act. Through these various methods I have approached the museum through a holographic perspective that "suggests the interrelationship of the whole not only to its parts, but also to the larger whole—the relationship of the [artifact] to the *techne* in which it emerges."[42] By "whole" I do not mean to suggest that through a holographic approach critics may suddenly and transparently know the totality of a rhetorical artifact. Despite their three-dimensional properties, holograms are representations. However, by drawing our attention to connections and "intra-active"[43] interactions between various fragments and by emphasizing rhetorical processes rather than products,[44] a view of rhetoric as holographic promotes attention not only to various topoi, but also to relationships between them.

To summarize the relationships discussed above, whether consumed for touristic pleasure or studied for the advancement of scientific knowledge, Native Americans largely appear in the museum as absent presences against which settler colonial identities are re/enacted. As in the greater Southwest, the infusion of Native American symbolic and material culture into the Arizona landscape does not require visitors to engage the present presences of the twenty-two federally recognized tribes living within the state. Instead, it naturalizes white settler presence as the consequence of passing time. As Scott Lauria Morgensen has argued, "Native people's seeming 'disappearance' from a modern, settled landscape" is in fact constituted by "indigeneity's recurrent appearance."[45] Invoked as relics of an always-already-before "our" time, Native American histories become the collective past of (white) visitors while Indigenous cultures are located elsewhere, beyond the shared time of contemporary civilization's imagined geographies.

While the preceding discussion has primarily centered on Pueblo Grande itself and, specifically, on the settler colonial memories enacted within, the next section discusses how the holographic analytic might further move beyond such a reading toward a more decolonial engagement with the museum and surrounding con/texts. While engaging the symbolic, material, and social dimensions of public memory through field methods at Pueblo Grande offers three-dimensional insights into how the museum and practices within elide Native subjectivities, I wish to suggest that the discussion above still elides a fourth, and crucial, dimension of public memory: the meaning of memory places for different publics. In the next section I reflect on my own interpretive practices in relation to Pueblo Grande to address the necessity of reflexivity for attending to absence and multiplicity.

A Fourth Dimension: Engaging the "Fourth World" of Indigenous Memories

An important dimension of the holographic analytic not yet taken up is its positioning of rhetorical critics in relation to their objects of analysis. Holograms imply "the viewer's active participation as [s]he shifts positions to discover the different views and colors that may be obtained from different angles."[46] As it relates to the study of public memory places, this analytic draws our attention to the partiality of any perspective, including the critic's. In attending to the interrelationship between different meanings residing within memory places and viewers' positionalities, the holographic analytic thus urges critics toward the "ethic of reflexivity" called for by the editors of this volume.[47]

While rhetorical scholars have increasingly drawn attention to how texts mean differently for different audiences, and while calls for critics' reflexivity have also been prominent, published scholarship at times continues to overlook these dimensions and their interrelationships. Instead, the critic is still presented as the expert who holds the tools, or knowledge, by which to access these different meanings. Reflexivity is thus often conceptualized as an act of voicing. However, in unsettling the presumption of the omniscient and disembodied critic, reflexivity performs a methodological function beyond that of a written accounting of oneself. As a methodological practice, reflexivity suggests that by engaging in the ongoing process of accounting for ourselves we might arrive at absences in our analyses, or dimensions of our con/texts that would otherwise be overlooked.

As it relates to Pueblo Grande, my own subject position as a white middle-class U.S. citizen from Northern California's "Gold Rush" area, who grew up immersed in "cowboys and Indians" mythologies, closely parallels that of many museum visitors. Reflecting on my relationship to the site thus led me to consider how critiquing the museum as (only) a place where settler colonial identities are enacted was an interpretive act that in many ways reproduced the very absences I sought to problematize. In other words, Pueblo Grande—while certainly a site in which dominant settler colonial narratives and memories are reproduced—is, at the same time, still a part of the cultural history of Indigenous peoples in the area, for whom the site offers different forms of remembering than the ones discussed above. However, these counter-memories—existing in the sphere of the subaltern—may not be readily or easily accessible to non-Native visitors or critics. Engaging with competing memories that reside within and in relation to such places thus presents a methodological quandary: if Native American presence is frequently defined—and rhetorically enacted—as *absence*, how might rhetorical scholars critically engage U.S. memory places without reproducing these absences?

While the issue of absence has been central to the development of critical rhetoric, engaging such absences presents challenges. If "absence is not presence's opposite," but rather "presence's barred Other,"[48] how can we, as critics, know what this Other is? And what absences (read: colonial and epistemic violences) do we re/enact in this attempted knowing? Put simply, we don't *know* what we don't know—an assertion that leads Amira de la Garza to argue against the "guiding ideals" of ethnographic inquiry, which bely the "Western," positivist epistemologies from which they emerge.[49] So, too, is the discipline of rhetoric rooted in and informed by Anglo-European epistemologies. In relation to Pueblo Grande, understanding significant absences within the site thus requires engaging precisely that which is absented: Indigenous perspectives.

Returning to the narrative with which I opened this essay, drawn from a recent public lecture, "The People's History: An O'Otham Perspective" offers a means by which to begin to approach Pueblo Grande's significance for local Indigenous peoples. At this talk, Shannon Rivers (Akimel O'Otham), a delegate for the United Nations Permanent Forum on Indigenous Issues, called the thirty-odd individuals present—both members of Arizona Native communities and non-Native Arizona residents—to rethink the ways in which we remember. In his reference to the O'Otham word *Ali ṣona-g*, from which the state name was derived, Rivers tied the history of his people to the state of Arizona while also drawing attention to the present absence of "little rivers"—they have been diverted for the aims of the settler colonial nation. A holographic approach engages Rivers's lecture as another fragment from which to draw meaning; moreover, it calls attention to meaningful absences shaping my own engagement with the site. Having introduced myself to Rivers as a researcher prior to his presentation, he addressed me by name, asking whether I knew of the connection between the state's name and his people's language. Like the other audience members, I did not. While, of course, no critic can assume to know all there is to know about a particular subject, the holographic analytic is useful in its emphasis on how various fragments, sources of information, and perspectives shape the contours of our analyses.

Indigenous perspectives deepen our engagements with relationships between place and memories as they circulate within, and beyond, the site of

Pueblo Grande. Mishuana Goeman (Seneca) observes that Indigenous "politics are often conceived, represented, and determined as geographically and historically situated and bound to a particular community."[50] This geographic and historical rootedness provides a sense of identity. Native Hawaiian Hannah Kihalani Springer states, "I am shaped by my geography."[51] In other words, the grounding offered by the land, "even while considered abject space by the settler state, is of utmost importance to the imaginative geographies that create the material consequences of everyday existence for Native people."[52]

From such a perspective the museum must be seen as a place where Native peoples stake claims to their own identities in various ways, one of which is the celebration of their cultural histories. While Pueblo Grande hosts a yearly Indian Market that we may see as linked to the settler colonial consumption of Native cultures and material objects, Kevin Stevens (Pee Posh) describes the museum as providing "a home-like atmosphere"[53] during its annual event, while Yolanda Hart Stevens (Pee Posh) states, "It's a good feeling to be able to get out and share our culture."[54] Incorporating Native voices into our analyses thus reenvisions public memory places like Pueblo Grande as not only places where settler colonial histories and identities are re/presented and re/produced, but also as places that exist as "intercultural performative contexts" where Native peoples participate in their own rememberings.[55] Engaging these voices, however, necessitates looking beyond the *memory place as text* to engage other rhetorical fragments.

While the land offers grounding for Native identity and material belonging, Indigenous concepts of land and place are not fully encompassed by the notion of geographically bounded and demarcated spaces. The "bounding" of Native places and identities is instead directly tied to the process of "colonial spatializing" in which nationalist discourses "ensconce a social and cultural sphere, stake a claim to people, and territorialize the physical landscape by manufacturing categories and separating land from people."[56] As Dr. David Martinez (Gila River Pima) notes in a videotaped lecture filmed at Pueblo Grande, "When we contemplate the boundaries of our historical homeland, the boundaries aren't limited to the reservation. . . . For us the boundaries are much more vast and encompassing."[57] For the numerous Indigenous communities in the Phoenix area and beyond, the sprawling city and its surrounding suburbs are all part of their homelands. Though mapped and populated by the settler nation-state, the land is still storied by their oral traditions. As the camera pans out, revealing the vast stretches of settled land visible from the mound, Martinez notes that Native peoples don't have to visit the mound to remember their past. Moreover, he states, "The remains, the ruins of our ancestors are places that you really don't want to visit. They're sacred enough where you have to respect that boundary around that location 'cause these things, this place, belongs to them."[58] Seen in this light, *not* visiting the mound is itself an act of remembrance.

From Indigenous perspectives, the land "represents the interconnected physical, symbolic, spiritual and social aspects" of being.[59] Manulani Aluli Meyer, an Indigenous scholar in Hawai'i, describes the notion of 'aina, or land, as difficult to define or encapsulate. Identifying the multiplicity of meanings present in "land," she describes "'aina as origin, 'aina as mother, 'aina as inspiration."[60] Land—as tied to but not reduced to geographical place—is the wellspring from which all things emerge. Martinez echoes this sentiment:

> As so many people from the outside world have settled this land, it's not that we've lost respect for these places, you know, on the contrary. I think persons like myself, speaking for myself, are willing to come here and talk about this place . . . precisely because I want others to learn about why this place is special to us and about how they can approach this location, you know, from a point of humbleness, from a point of wanting to learn, to understand, to appreciate this place as being a part of their sacred geography too. It's not just a tourist attraction.[61]

While tourists may engage the site as "just a museum," where they can "learn about the Indians who vanished long ago,"[62] Indigenous perspectives suggest a different approach in which Pueblo Grande is not a ruin or a site for commercial entertainment, but a spiritual, sacred, and living site. While it may not be readily visible, this "part" is also present in the "whole." Employing a holographic analytic, we may attend to the ways in which memories are encoded onto matter. The land itself contains the "flicker" of Native presence.

In/Conclusions

Through an analysis of the symbolic, material, and social encounters through which settler colonial identities are re/produced at Pueblo Grande, I have argued that white visitors enact "modern" belongings against the reflection of a generalized Native Other cast outside the sphere of the present.[63] I have further suggested that the holographic analytic offers an ethical imperative to engage what is absented from view. Such an endeavor suggests that, like the museum visitors whom Martinez encourages to approach the site in a spirit of "humbleness," so, too, is humility required from rhetorical critics who might be inclined to read Pueblo Grande and other similar sites as "just tourist attractions." As Goeman argues, "Beyond examining the discursive frameworks located in specific historical, political, and cultural moments, we must also think critically about 'sets of choices, omissions, uncertainties, and intentions' that are 'critical to, yet obscured within' the mapping of the body polity and nation-state."[64] Taking seriously such an argument requires self-reflexively engaging our own positionalities in relation to our texts. In other words, just as we train a careful eye toward what is elided within the artifacts we engage, it is necessary to turn that same gaze toward what is elided by our ways of looking.

In directing attention to the various fragments from which critics might draw meaning, the holographic perspective encourages attention to the de/colonizing force of our choices, prompting questions such as: How do we select and analyze our objects of inquiry and to what ends? How should the field of our rhetorical fieldwork be defined? The city of Phoenix, like the greater United States, is written over Native lands in ways that are not only symbolic but fundamentally material and embedded in social relationships. Pueblo Grande, rather than being a discrete rhetorical object, is deeply implicated in and connected to a larger "ecology of memory,"[65] one that recalls and enacts the colonial past and present of U.S. settler society while containing fragments that reflect other potentialities. If museums and other public memory sites are not just individual entities, but rather places where meanings constellate within larger imaginative geographies, expanding the scope of our inquiries beyond their borders may be necessary, especially if we want to engage voices harder to hear within. Offering one means by which to disrupt the characterization of "settlement or place . . . as bounded, as enclosure, and as directly counterposed to spaces as flows,"[66] a view of rhetoric as holographic directs our attention to memories as moving through multiple dimensions, mapping onto both geographical landscapes and spatial imaginaries.

What other potentialities might a view of rhetoric as holographic yield for the field of rhetoric? In opening, I suggested that such a perspective might be especially apt for examining sites of contested memory. My analysis of Pueblo Grande pushes this point further: attending to practices, processes, and emergences, a view of rhetoric as holographic might reveal contestations that might otherwise be missed. Approaching rhetoric as holographic thus urges us to think through what we, as critics, center and what specters haunt our analyses. In doing so, we may move a step closer to Barbara Biesecker's provocation: "It is possible to remember otherwise."[67] Moreover, it offers a necessary correlative to our disciplinary predispositions to "read" memory places as "texts" that can be interpreted through the critic's trained gaze. Such tendencies may flatten our engagements with contested memories circulating within places of memory and fail to fully engage the effects of our positionalities on the shape of our "texts." Finally, the holographic analytic challenges the ways our modes of inquiry may inadvertently re/produce notions of cultural homogeneity or wholeness through which "geo-spatial and bio-graphic understandings of knowledge and culture are 'hidden in the transparency and universality of the zero point' of Western power knowledge."[68] By drawing attention to the different meanings, and levels of meaning, that reside within public memory places and exceed their borders, reframing rhetoric as holographic allows us to attend to rhetorical "wholes" in a way that better emphasizes multiplicity, difference, and fragmentation.

Context Drives Method

*Studying Social Media
Use in a War Zone*

Lisa Silvestri

One story may be an anecdote, but a collection of them is data.
—PETER SINGER, *WIRED FOR WAR*

Social network sites allow participants to publicize their affections. Take a U.S. marine in desert camouflage who stands in front of a sand-colored wall holding a yellow legal pad that reads in all capital letters, "Happy 4 year anniversary [wife's first name]. I love you." The marine made this image his profile photograph to send an anniversary message to his wife. Within the context of Facebook, using a profile photo to communicate a specific message to a particular audience is unconventional and, therefore, compelling to communication scholars like myself. The profile photo is the first image visible on a Facebook page. Regardless of friendship status or privacy settings, the profile photo is generally visible to anyone. Practically speaking, the profile image represents *you*.[1]

In this particular case, the marine changed his profile photo instead of updating his status, a move that can be read as a more potent declaration of his affection because the image is accessible to more than just those on his "friends" list. Moreover it is inherently linked to his online identity. According to subsequent time stamps, his wife responded within hours by posting a photo of their son to her husband's Facebook wall. Read within the context of Facebook culture, the phatic style of this exchange is relatively typical and serves as a charming example of the morale-boosting benefits of social network sites for U.S. troops and their families. The ability to send quick, frequent personal messages across fronts creates a previously unmatched feeling of closeness or "digital intimacy" for deployed personnel and their loved ones.[2] Although both service members and civilians value "connected presence," its ubiquity in daily life at home causes it to go relatively unnoticed.[3] For service members in a theater of war, however, Facebook presents the impression of casual civilian conversation, a form of communication previously excluded from the war zone. Thus, when considered outside the context of social network site communication, this exchange takes on new meaning.

Digital discourses highlight the fact that meaning is situated; it resides in human experience. The rhetorical nature of social media communication suggests that people might say one thing on Facebook but report that it means something quite different to them when interviewed out of that context. The post- 9/11 service members I spoke with, for example, describe that with technological capabilities for increased connection across fronts comes a compulsion to rhetorically perform their connectedness through mundane interactions on social media. Contextualized within this frame, the Facebook exchange between husband and wife looks different. Another reason the marine would change his profile picture beyond declaring his love for his wife would be to *automate* his affection in a more permanent and prominent way so that he can direct fuller attention to combat operations. Cultural and contextual location of online participants is an important consideration for the rhetorical analysis of digital culture. Field methods are a useful way to understand and access those contexts.[4]

The extreme setting of a war zone dramatizes the need for a more comprehensive interpretive framework, one that emphasizes the significance of *context* when studying communication attitudes, values, and practices. Historically, troops in a war zone were exempt from home front relational commitments. In previous U.S. conflicts, and even earlier in the conflicts being studied here, a lack of communication with the home front kept the troops focused on their immediate well-being, the health and safety of their comrades, and the goal of the mission. In her piece "The Democratization of Intimacy," Stefana Broadbent argues that until recently, places like the battlefield were settings in which people were removed for long periods of time from their closest ties. War activity "meant leaving behind the family and its concerns," and "going on a mission meant limiting contacts to a few letters."[5] Geography wasn't the only reason for this isolation; the social expectations were just as binding. But today the widespread use of personal computers, Internet accessibility, and the proliferation of social network sites pose fundamental challenges to the maintenance of dualities between work and leisure. This is true for all of us. When communication takes place over nonphysical networks, it complicates distinctions between work and home as well as the social roles that go along with them.

At issue is the fact that social network sites present the impression of a single shared social space. Yet, as the example of the communicative exchange between the marine and his wife demonstrates, social network site members occupy multiple social contexts simultaneously. For rhetorical critics, social media exacerbate the process of situating discourse because people can talk to multiple network members across a variety of contexts.[6] In this way participatory media access presents a tension for researchers between online participant observation and direct interviews. In my research, for example, listening to service members describe how they interacted with social media was markedly different from seeing it unfold in real time. Interviews helped situate texts, and online observations invited close reading, a technique familiar to most rhetorical critics. Paying attention to textual indicators of an imagined audience offered clues about which contexts were being privileged, or which were informing communication practices.[7] In what follows I describe how rhetorical analyses of digital culture can benefit from various field methods.

Rhetorical Scholarship 2.0

The proliferation of global communication technologies and the consequent digital diffusion of discourse demands that rhetoricians pay careful attention to the contexts that generate online exchanges. Internet texts are both digitally diffuse *and* culturally specific, prompting critics to immerse themselves in the emergent habits and practices of online populations. Facebook, for example, is not a "text" in the traditional sense. Rather, it is a polymediated social space.[8] The digital discourses occurring therein are multiple, contingent, and dynamic.

The in-the-field nature of Facebook discourse requires methodologies beyond primary textual analysis because it highlights the fact that what motivates human behavior derives from personal experience with colloquial social worlds, or what Gerard Hauser calls "street-level" discourse—the quotidian ideas, values, and attitudes that prompt action. "You can't understand a people without understanding the culture of their language use," argues Hauser, "because that's where you discover their social world."[9] The vast social space of the Internet, however, involves complex relationships between local practices and global implications.[10] In other words, although the Internet connects us globally, we still make meaning locally. Thus the rhetorical critic must be adept at tacking back and forth between broad, context-based and specific, text-based perspectives.

The persistent expansion of digital communication as a mode of expression warrants more studies exploring the rhetorical aspects of digital culture. This is not to say that recent scholarship has not begun doing this work. In fact, some rhetorical treatments of digital culture have already started tapping into the benefits of various field methods to understand why people do what they do online. Robert Glenn Howard's work on digital evangelism, for example, supplements close textual analysis with direct interviews and participant observation about Christian fundamentalist websites.[11] Other work, such as Daniel Brouwer and Aaron Hess's examination of milblogs, or my scholarship on the rhetorical practices of YouTube commentary, adds dimension to traditional orator-text-audience relationships by considering digital texts as alive and malleable, with complex audiences and modes of address.[12] These new iterations of rhetorical scholarship demonstrate progress toward a more supple treatment of digital discourse. Moving forward, rhetoricians should continue to resist the urge to treat online communication as relatively fixed within a single digital space. As the opening vignette demonstrates, it is important to consider the cultural location of online participants, including the contexts (imagined and otherwise) in which they are operating.[13]

The expansive context of our digital world underscores the role of the critic in delineating one that is worthy of study. In other words, the digital vernacular fragments of text existing in our online spaces only emerge as meaningful through contextualization. Through this method, rhetorical critics assemble textual fragments into a coherent logic. The process of contextualization is recursive, beginning with the types of questions being asked and often continuing throughout the project as the critic answers, throws out, adds to, or refines her initial questions. Broad, unbound contexts yield limitless methodological choices. Different fragments reveal themselves through alternative methods. As such, the critic must be creative and draw from a variety of methods to gain access to new fragments. Methods are responsive—they serve the ends of contextualization. Rhetoric, after all, is the study of *situated* discourse. Deciphering the dynamics of the situation is paramount. This is especially true for rhetoricians who want to study digital discourse. Therefore, the orienting framework for rhetorical scholars must be *context* rather than method. Context drives method.

Generally speaking, my current research plumbs the intersection across two primary contexts—war and Facebook.[14] Through direct interviews and online participation, I examined how U.S. troops interacted with social media during their deployments in Iraq and Afghanistan. The direct interviews helped me identify the *kairos* of the Facebook exchanges. The process of conducting this research affirmed my belief that we need to continue exploring more holistic approaches to treat the study of digital communication. How can we, as rhetorical critics, immerse ourselves in the particular human realities that give rise to certain digital discourses? Or put differently, if we accept that meaning resides in human experience then we should exhaust methodological opportunities to understand those experiences.[15]

Field methods help parse the sociocultural dimensions of meaning-making. I used a combination of methods concurrently, pulling from a variety of techniques and tools to study a mix of practices, representations, structures, rhetorics, and technologies. As Christine Hine argues, "The key to insight is immersion, not necessarily through being in a particular field site, but by engaging in relevant practices wherever they might be found."[16] Within the limitations conferred by context, I found a mixture of methods to be the best way to access some of the details of digitally mediated social behavior across fronts. My methods included conducting in-person interviews, observing various text-based practices online (including wall posts, photo posts, video posts, commentaries, and "liking" activities), and taking extensive field notes and jottings.

Conducting in-person interviews on active bases offered two key benefits to my research. First, the information I gleaned from the interviews helped me establish a lay of the land by identifying recurrent topics, themes, and ways of speaking about particular subjects. Second, in-person interviews on an active base allowed me to get a sense, in a very real and embodied way, for the military as an institution and as a culture. An appreciation of culture requires close attention to repeatable habits and practices shared by a group.[17] As critical cultural scholar Lawrence Grossberg eloquently describes, it's about appreciating "the texture of life as it is lived."[18] It is an important step in the process of contextualization. Following Grossberg, my methodological perspective represents the symbiosis between rhetorical studies and critical cultural studies. These camps tend to adopt a performance lens as an outlook and a method with the common goal of apprehending culture through the perspectives of those who live or have lived it.

Paying attention to practices illuminates a culture's "politics of *doxa*"—the backdrop of shared values and beliefs, or the vaguely held notion of common sense that motivates action.[19] Often the best way to access a group's shared practices is to observe them operating locally in their respective social fields. For example, after each interview on base in Okinawa, a designated lieutenant marine "escort" accompanied me to the next location. We entered barracks and office buildings bustling with junior marines in camouflage uniforms who immediately stopped what they were doing, snapped to attention, and saluted the lieutenant every time we entered a room. Conducting interviews on bases in Okinawa, Japan, and Camp Pendleton, California, helped me better appreciate the military's cultural milieu. But because I was also interested in *digital* life worlds, I had to broaden my outlook on community to include both geographically contained communities as well as those constituted by the circulation of discourse in a variety of mediated forms. Just like any speech community, membership in an online community is performative, relying on members' ability to call up intelligible discourses.[20]

Accessing service members' participation in social media required online fieldwork. I followed the Facebook pages of nine service members over the course of their deployments in Iraq or Afghanistan. The consent process involved a personal message to existing marine "friends," explaining the purpose and goals for the study; this communication stated, "Taking part in this research study is completely voluntary. If you decide not to be in this study, or if you stop participating at any time, you won't be penalized or lose any benefits for which you otherwise qualify. If you do not wish to participate in this study or if you decide to leave the study early, we will ask you to send the PI [principal investigator] a message indicating your decision to withdraw. You may also 'de-friend' the PI through the Facebook option."[21] As to be expected, I lost a handful of "friends," but nine of them agreed to participate.

I scrutinized their wall posts, video posts, photo posts, and all the accompanying sidebar commentary, making field notes and taking screen grabs. These methods drew my attention to circulation patterns and processes of text production. When I first began online observations I didn't know what I was looking for; I simply took it all in. But as I began to transcribe my interviews, some of the Facebook activities I was observing (e.g., time stamps and photo genres) began to take on relevance. Interview responses and online observations informed one another throughout the interpretive process.

Without the on-site interviews, which gave me a fuller understanding of the constraints of military culture and the demands of a combat deployment, I could not have sufficiently situated the marines' Facebook activities. If I had strictly adhered to a text-based approach, for example, I might have contextualized the exchange between a husband and wife differently. I might have read the online exchanges as nothing more than a remediation of the war letter. The following section presents a case study to expand on the need for more dynamic methods of contextualization in contemporary rhetorical scholarship. I tried to write transparently about the situating process as it unfolded in my research, in order to help readers better appreciate the creativity and reflexivity needed to pursue methods that will best serve particular contexts. First I situate myself in relationship to the context of war. Next I give a brief overview of contemporary wartime communication and then, finally, I offer an interpretive analysis of social media use in a war zone.

Situating Digital Discourses

The culture of combat has compelled my curiosity since childhood. My grandfather, father, and brother are all combat veterans. In my eyes, the three of them were reluctant heroes, members of a burden-laden boys' club of which I could never be a part. I always wanted to understand the culture they shared. But I knew I could never access it directly or understand it in a meaningful way by studying war in its mythic sense, or as it exists in mass-mediated tropological form. All cultures, including combat culture, are made up of ideas realized and materialized in practice.[22] If I wanted to understand "boots on the ground," I needed access to their daily practices.

As it turned out, the university would not sponsor my proposal to embed in Afghanistan with the International Security Assistance Force. Thus I scaled my interests back to include combat's *communication* culture, rather than combat culture in its entirety. In the spring of 2010 I began conducting on-base interviews with service members who had recently returned from Iraq and Afghanistan to learn about their communication norms, habits, and rituals while at war. After a pilot study with the Iowa Army National Guard, I decided to focus exclusively on U.S. marines because, of all the branches, they are the unit most frequently deployed to combat environments. Also, our collective imagination holds the Marine Corps to be the most rigid and inflexible institution. For these reasons, I felt the Marine Corps would serve as a useful point of juxtaposition against which to study a constantly shifting, messy, and undefined social media culture.

Before the interviews, I anticipated that my research would center on advancements in digital photography. I based my assumption on my brother's enormous photographic archive documenting almost every aspect of his deployment in Iraq. The extent of his digital documentary efforts stood in stark contrast to my father's handful of black-and-white photos depicting his thirteen-month tour of duty in Vietnam. Around the same time as my brother's return from Iraq in 2006, and on the heels of the infamous Abu Ghraib photos, both popular and academic sources were paying close attention to U.S. troops' "snapshots of war."[23] Like those authors, I found myself compelled by service members' propensity to document war and continued to assume that digital photography would be the crux of my research. I even framed many of my early interview questions around the subject of digital photography. But the service members I interviewed did not want to talk about advancements in digital photography, or at least they only wanted to talk about them in relationship to social network sites. In the words of a lance corporal at Okinawa, "It's Facebook today, ma'am. Facebook is everything." Until then I never considered the significance of Facebook at the front. I didn't even have an active Facebook account. I hadn't realized how much the communication landscape had changed in terms of Internet access since my brother's 2006 deployment.

Contemporary Wartime Communication

Since 2006 Internet access has become much more widely available to U.S. troops on deployment. Today, although some of the most remote outposts

FIG. 10.1 Military personnel accessing the Internet while in the combat field. Photo courtesy of U.S. Department of Defense.

in the mountains of Afghanistan do not have access to running water, many of them do have access to "Internet cafés," portable satellite units equipped with a router and up to eight laptops to provide service personnel with free Internet access and phone calls home.[24]

Because U.S. military personnel in Iraq and Afghanistan gained Internet access around the same time Facebook emerged as a public sensation, the majority of our fighting forces adopted the multimodal platform as their chief means of communication with loved ones back home.[25] In fact, they bypassed e-mail in favor of Facebook altogether. As one marine said, "I only e-mailed one person one time and that was like a high school football coach."[26] What is more, during interviews many personnel bracket experiences with "pre-Facebook" and "post-Facebook" deployments as qualitatively different, often referring to them as two distinct "types" of deployment. For example, during a pilot study I conducted with the Iowa Army National Guard, a soldier described the difference between his first 2006 "pre-Facebook" deployment and his most recent 2010 "post-Facebook" deployment as follows: "It's definitely a change from the first [deployment] 'til now. There's a lot more connection, I mean, it's, you can even as a unit, AKO [Army Knowledge Online] can be a real pain. AKO is our military e-mail.[27] And unfortunately to say, it's much easier to get a hold of a deployed soldier on Facebook than it is on AKO. As sad as it sounds it's the truth. That's been a big deal." The soldier's comment references improvements in terms of efficiency. But speed and access are not the only ways technological advancements affect communication. The soldier initially makes an ontological distinction, sensing a definite "change" between deployments resulting from "a lot more connection." Surely this sense of connection is more than just the idea that it's "easier to get a hold of people" or that access is faster. What other conditions contribute to connection? What are the broader implications of this increased sense? Is it correlated to what individuals choose to disclose, how often they make contact, or with whom they are interacting?

To be sure, the present moment operates by a new set of values and ideas about what it means to communicate in an era of globally connected, perpetual contact.[28] Some communication researchers have begun to examine the emergent relational practices and "mobile maintenance expectations" unique to this era.[29] Jeffrey Hall and Nancy Baym argue, for example, that "while being able to contact others is one of the most liked qualities . . . being continuously available for others' contact is also one of its disliked qualities."[30] The results of Hall and Baym's survey data reveal a tension between the ability to stay in touch through technology and feeling *entrapped* by technology. My research builds on these observations and raises the stakes on emergent social pressures by examining how they operate among U.S. troops in the context of the wars in Iraq and Afghanistan.

Constant and immediate access to home marks a revolutionary change from how we once imagined combat deployment—namely, a lonely soldier suffering through months of desperate isolation. Today individual service members can chat with their mothers from a forward operating base and receive the dreaded "Dear John" instantly via status update. During interviews with older personnel who experienced multiple deployments, they tended to flag the years 2007 to 2009 as a critical threshold of change in combat's communication culture. This may have been the point where Internet access became more widely available in the field, depending on a service member's location and military occupational specialty (MOS). Like the service member I referenced earlier who identified "a definite change," others described "increased access" or the fact that they "didn't feel as behind" as they had in earlier deployments. Another indication of the recent, dramatic shift in combat's communication culture was how rare it was for personnel to write letters from the field. While at Camp Pendleton I spoke to a nineteen-year-old lance corporal who had just returned from his first deployment to Afghanistan a few months before our 2012 interview.

SILVESTRI: Did you write any snail mail letters?
MARINE: I don't even know what that is.
SILVESTRI: Like old-fashioned letters. They're called "snail" because snails are slow.

MARINE: ooOOooh, I got it.

SILVESTRI: [laughs] Sooo did you send any?

MARINE: Uhm. No.

I do not suggest that this young man's inexperience with traditional mail represents the experiences of all our currently deployed personnel. Nevertheless, the conversation was illuminating with regard to generational norms. According to a 2012 demographics update released by the U.S. Marine Corps, roughly two-thirds of marines are twenty-five and under.[31] This means they were born in 1987 or after. They were in elementary school when the wars began and were not eligible to serve until 2006 or after. And most notably for my interests, they grew up as fluent natives in the digital age. This is the generation shaping war's communicative culture today.

Considering all these factors, I focused my research on social media use among marines deployed between 2008 and 2012 because those years seem to mark a critical flashpoint for the use of real-time social media software in Iraq and Afghanistan.[32] Noticeable changes in doxa point to moments of social transformation.

Field research and direct interviews were vital to establishing a contextual frame and situating digital discourses therein. In what follows I present an example from my research to demonstrate the application process—the relationship between various methods and my close reading. In other words, this is the meaning I derived from interfacing texts and contexts.

Social Media Use in a War Zone

At first glance social media appear to be a morale boost for the troops, because they can stay in touch and receive emotional support from loved ones back home. That perspective is not incorrect, but, if fully contextualized through field methods, it becomes clear that things are a little more complicated than that. Internet access and the prevalence of social media in Iraq and Afghanistan enable U.S. troops to import civilian norms of casual conversation into a war zone.[33] Participation in social media culture facilitates a constant tacking back and forth between war and home. When I asked a marine how his deployment would have been different if he didn't have Facebook, he laughed and said, "I would have gotten more work done." This is a sentiment that resonates with many of us. Social media can pull us out of our immediate context—filling out Excel sheets one minute and chatting about weekend plans the next. But in the context of a war zone, "work" can be a matter of life and death.

The pressure to remain in constant contact appears to create a moral dilemma unique to the social media age. At Camp Pendleton I sat across from a young lance corporal (L.Cpl.) who had just returned from Afghanistan one month prior. His 3531 MOS designated him as a motor vehicle operator. When I asked about his interactions with Facebook during deployment, he said,

> **L.CPL.:** At first I thought [Facebook] was kinda cool because you know you're . . . you kinda get homesick right away and you wanna talk to your family and friends and stuff. But like after a month went by, I kinda got tired of it because your head kinda . . . you have one foot over there and one foot here. You just wanna focus on things that are going on over there. So I kinda stepped away from it a little bit . . . I was constantly busy like . . . I left the wire a lot.[34] I just wanted to be more focused. People would actually get mad at me 'cause I wouldn't be on as much.
>
> **SILVESTRI:** OK. So who would get mad at you?
>
> **L.CPL.:** Uh, family, friends. And then, uh, at the time, I had a girlfriend, you know, of three years. But we ended up breaking up when I was over there and that was one of the reasons why, is 'cause talking and things like that.

The lance corporal shifted in his chair. His eyes were down. As he spoke, I could hear a lump forming in his throat. I didn't press him on the breakup. It was hard to tell whether he considered talking or *not* talking to be the reason for the relationship's end. In either case, the level of connectivity between fronts was an issue. And as painful as it was, his story was not unique. It did, however, capture an emerging dichotomy with regard to social media at the front. The handwritten letter, formerly the most dominant mode of wartime communication, has gone virtually extinct. Social media platforms like Facebook have taken over, causing a (re)negotiation of what it means to "keep in touch" during wartime. The lance corporal described a pressure to maintain a dual "footing" and how that pressure affected his relationships. His girlfriend assumed that since it is *possible* to be on Facebook, he *should* be on Facebook.

The prevailing logic of perpetual contact resulting from our incessant engagement with mobile communication technologies fosters an anxiety-provoking relational dependence, or what Sherry Turkle calls a social "tethering" and Christian Licoppe calls "connected presence."[35] James Katz and Mark Aakhus refer to a similar phenomenon, "hyper-coordination," a mode of "friendship" that ritualizes constant contact and produces an obligation to be responsive, available, and connected.[36]

The context of war emphasizes how egregious our demands have become. One marine told me that he got in "big trouble" with his wife after he lost contact with her following a serious accident in Afghanistan. An eighteen-wheeler struck his Humvee, throwing him from the vehicle, knocking him unconscious and causing serious injuries. As he tells it, "I wasn't able to contact her for the better part of a week while in the hospital and when I finally did, she was more a wreck from wondering why I hadn't mentioned anything than from me actually being injured." This marine's wife was operating by a new set of communication norms ushered in by social media. For the most part, because it is possible, we have come to expect frequent and regular "status updates" from everyone in our social network, including deployed service members. During my online observation, for example, two marines wrote posts to reassure their family and friends of their safety after word got out of an attack near where they were stationed.[37] The taken-for-granted sense of entitlement to be informed about others' "status" is more noticeable in the context of war, a situation where previously lack of contact was not only accepted but was to be expected.

In this way, the contemporary war zone represents a collision of cultures—the civilian culture of perpetual contact collides with combat culture, which is quintessentially associated with a lack of contact. Advancements in drone technology have done much to draw public attention to this point as psychologists, technology researchers, and legal experts concern themselves with the emotional disturbances drone pilots experience as they shoot at targets seven thousand miles away and then return home to eat lasagna dinner with their families.[38] In the case of drones, the context of war bleeds into everyday life. But for troops on deployment it's the inverse. Aspects of everyday life (via social media) bleed into the context of war.

A communication climate of constant contact introduces a new set of emotional challenges for troops, as a growing dependency on outward communication begins to affect the way they feel about themselves. One marine described how social network messaging made him feel "loved."

SILVESTRI: How often did you send and receive messages via Facebook while you were away?
MARINE: Um, I'd have four or five different people like popped up sending messages and I'd be talking to all of them at once. A lot.
SILVESTRI: Did you access Facebook every day?
MARINE: Every day that I could. Yeah.
SILVESTRI: What was that like?
MARINE: The day that I didn't it was nice 'cause I'd come back and have seventeen notifications and I'd be like "Woo-hoo, people love me!"

What strikes me about this conversation is the marine's fractured attention structure—the fact that he could be "chatting" with four or five people at once. With his attention split across five Facebook chats, it is safe to assume that the depth of conversation was at a minimum. But what I found most compelling about our conversation was the way he attached his sense of self-worth to how many notifications he received. And therein lies the greatest concern—that this culture of constant contact gives way to a generation of people, even beyond the context of war, who experience solitude as loneliness. If "love" is equated with "notifications," it can be a devastating blow to your emotional psyche when your inbox is empty.

Because of this new equation, some marines seek opportunities to feel a connection with someone, and sometimes anyone. "You can tell if somebody's on," says one marine, "and you wanna tell them something really quick." The difference is that *whom* you connect with matters less and less. Facebook multiplies opportunities to talk to "somebody" or "someone" about "something." As the marine went on to say, "Just to be able see if they're on you know even though most the time they weren't because of the time difference but you'd always have that small hope that someone was on and you could talk to 'em even if it was just for five minutes."

In fact, one marine told me that when the United States was sleeping, he and his comrades would Facebook chat one another from the same forward operating base or across bases. In his words, "Like uh, me and like my roommate would be messing around and messaging like 'ha ha ha you're gay,' you know . . . like a little chat would pop up real quick 'ha ha you're next to me,' 'oh hey how's it goin'?'" At its most basic, this form of exchange (beyond its participation in the ritual of gendered insult redolent of hypermasculine military culture) tests the line of communication. Is it open? Is this person available to me? Even if you do not necessarily have anything to say, there is something comforting about knowing the line is open. You are not alone. It seems to fulfill a social utility similar to the familiar sleepover question, "Are you awake?" When you are alone in the dark, in a strange place, it is comforting to know someone else is there.

To be sure, social media present opportunities to create digital intimacy, but doing so requires a great deal of time and attention. Platforms like Facebook are built on architectures of active participation. Users are the content. Having a presence on Facebook requires a person to post many pictures, have active conversations with friends, and share personal interests and information. Social media's potential to be a distraction caused a senior enlisted noncommissioned officer to make a seemingly counterintuitive claim. He said he felt happiest and most secure on a small patrol base outside the wire because his men did not have access to the Internet. "As bad as it may sound," he said, "there are a lot of issues that arise when young guys have unlimited communication access to their loved ones. . . . I needed the marines to remain focused on their mission and not left wondering what their young, newly married wife may be doing." One could imagine that the troops always wondered what was going on back home, but now social media access from the battlefield provides a tempting opportunity to find out. And beyond the opportunity, there is an underlying social pressure from the civilian side to remain in constant contact. For the most part, it seems marines have adopted civilian norms of conversation, even from their posts in Iraq and Afghanistan.

Concluding Remarks

This chapter offered one example of how new communication environments complicate matters of situating discourse. Digital life worlds expand and exponentially increase communication contexts, demanding that rhetoricians rely on their expertise as close readers as well as develop new tools to approach a fuller appreciation of multivalent contexts. One way to do this is to go into "the field," wherever that may be, talk with and observe the people there, and closely read the "texts" they produce.[39] The goal is to understand more completely the conditions under which communicators act. Fortunately, rhetorical scholars are uniquely equipped to handle such a pursuit, as their scholarship reflects a strong history in reading particular texts for how they vibrate against institutional, social, political, historical, and technological structures. The only thing rhetoricians need to do, now, is expand their methodological horizons to include more person-centered and context-driven approaches. By and large, good rhetorical research methods should reflect a humanitarian effort, the recognition that participants are meaning-making actors with their own reasons for doing what they do. An important outcome of rhetorical scholarship, especially in an era of rapid growth in our ability to communicate, is to temporarily slow down the present unfolding of communicative dynamics to critically examine their moral implications before we continue barreling ahead into the future. To my knowledge there is no singular way to grasp the present. As our canon goes digital, rhetorical critics should meet consequent challenges with enthusiasm and ingenuity. No one does situated discourse better than we do. Thus we need to be proactive about broadening our methodological tool kits to meet discourses where they exist on the ground.

Afterword

Decentralizing and
Regenerating the Field

Phaedra C. Pezzullo

Opening and interpreting lives is very different from opening and closing books.

—DWIGHT CONQUERGOOD, "PERFORMING AS A MORAL ACT: ETHICAL
DIMENSIONS OF THE ETHNOGRAPHY OF PERFORMANCE"

It is perhaps when all these critical forces come together, as well as draw resources from each other, that rhetoric as a discipline will undergo its next paradigmatic shift where it is able to sensitively listen to all those diverse groups of people who . . . have been relegated to places "out there."

—RAKA SHOME, "POSTCOLONIAL INTERVENTIONS: AN 'OTHER' VIEW"

We need to continue to refine our ways of capturing the full range of symbolic, social, material, and political economic realities that animate places where rhetoric emerges, circulates, and is experienced by real people.

—PETER SIMONSON, "OUR PLACES IN A RHETORICAL CENTURY"

*In addition to the insightful feedback of Sara McKinnon and Robert Asen, as well as editing by E. Cram as I moved across country, the author wishes to thank Kathleen de Onís for responses to this work and our ongoing conversations about what it means to work as rhetoricians in and out of "the field."

Some might consider it ironic that academics dedicated to studying public address and public culture need to reflect on why some of us conduct research in public spaces and/or with publics. Given that ancient rhetorical scholars commonly moved between their roles as teachers, advocates, consultants, poets, and more, it should be uncontroversial to affirm rhetorical analysis that draws on critical ethnographic practices and sensibilities.[1] Yet, too often, introductions to rhetoric exclude these approaches or include them at the end of a course or edited book collection as something new, experimental, or fringe.[2] In these instances, the field of rhetoric is portrayed as established, marked off with high walls around the borders, and somehow impermeable. More like a root cellar than a field.

Nevertheless, the editors of *Text + Field* suggest that there is a surge of interest among rhetorical scholars wanting to conduct fieldwork, or as Conquergood calls it (above), "opening and interpreting lives." I tend to agree, given the packed academic convention rooms I have seen when sessions are offered on this topic, as well as the excited buzz I hear when students and faculty have questions about the pragmatics, ethics, and value of these research approaches to rhetorical studies. Raka Shome has argued that a paradigmatic shift of the field is required to listen to more diverse voices, too often relegated to occupying the simultaneous state and space of "out there." This collection offers a timely pulse check on a growing body of work in communication studies analyzing a fuller range of, as Simonson notes, "where rhetoric emerges, circulates, and is experienced." Notably, the editors of this volume claim in the introduction, "These critics have not abandoned the field; rather, they have reconceptualized what it means to be in the field and to do fieldwork."

In addition to marking a watershed moment in the discipline for the popularity and establishment of such approaches as vital to the work of rhetorical studies, *Text + Field* seeks to illustrate what difference it makes for rhetorical scholars to gather firsthand evidence for our archives, to record observations about the immediate context, to interview people, and/or to share one's autoethnographic perspective. This volume includes emerging voices as well as those who are more established. Throughout the book the contributing authors are moved by some public affair or conceptual conundrum and then draw on their research to illuminate, nuance, extend, and challenge rhetorical norms.

While I do not believe that writing something exhaustive in response to this collection is possible or desirable, I do want to offer three topoi that I found while reading the preceding essays: space, immediacy, and documentation. These are not discrete, but rather connected categories. I also ask questions throughout these pages in an attempt to help generate further conversations about the choices we face as researchers, the stakes of fieldwork, and the broader professional contexts in which this research might be produced today.

On Space

Since ancient times, rhetoricians' stories about inventing symbols, articulating discourses, policing or challenging boundaries, making judgments, negotiating shared understandings, and moving people often have involved examples from our travels, classrooms, advocacy, consulting work, public service, and other modes of living. In other words, "public engagement" and "civic scholarship" are not merely new buzzwords to rhetorical studies. Most of us, regardless of whether we draw on critical ethnographic practices, find that the field exceeds our involvements with the pages or images of a book or an archive. Our bodies as rhetoricians in the world were and are constitutive of our rhetorical practices and theories, as well as our possibilities and our restrictions. We live in dynamic systems. Nevertheless, the editors of this volume suggest in the introduction that it may be timely for us to reflect on what "the field" means to norms of rhetorical culture. Whatever our answers are, our perceptions are entangled in part with questions of location, which reflect intertwined geographic and cultural hierarchies.

Prior to this work, rhetorical scholars in communication studies have built a compelling case not only for embodied experiences and expressions, but also for the ways that space and place constitute oppressive power relations. Expanding rhetoric's geopolitical imaginary, Shome emphasizes the significance of space as a technology or power that constitutes colonial identities and cultures globally, disciplining bodies and boundaries of the field.[3] Likewise, Lisa Flores notes the value of speech as a way for Chicana feminists to open discursive spaces to reflect on their experiences of living in border cultures.[4] Also writing about racial hierarchy, Kirt Wilson subsequently describes place as a rhetorical condensation symbol through which racial patterns of segregation have been determined and enforced, dictating how people and things should or should not interact spatially in order to uphold particular social orders.[5] Further, I argue that toxic pollution patterns are predicated on alienated sacrifice zones in which waste and certain populations (raced, classed, gendered, and stigmatized through illness) are deemed appropriately in their place.[6] Each one of us—in addition to more—has argued that while embodied rhetorics oppress in these specific historical moments through disciplining spatial relations, they also help constitute the spatiotemporal conditions of possibility for tactics of resistance and transgression, such as listening and touring.[7]

Building on these arguments, this volume refuses to privilege dominant and residual conventional styles and instead engages emergent, oppressed, and marginalized voices, as well as unconventional, embodied, spatial social practices and nonhuman elements. In particular, each essay illustrates how rhetorical address, acts, and artifacts are discovered and coproduced in a wide range of spaces, including in school board meetings, through social movement coalitions, at art events, standing on bridges, through the rhetoric of the streets, on colonized islands of the United States (such as Guåhan and Puerto Rico), in nations beyond the United States, on Native American reservations, near oceans, witnessing corpses, through tours, at public hearings, in professional development workshops, during public lectures, in our homes, while traveling (on boats or in cabs, etc.), walking through museums, and online. In each instance, "the field" of research once again is shown not as a binary in tension with rhetorical archives and repertoires, but as co-constitutive of rhetorical promise and limits within particular cultural spaces.

Given the aforementioned colonial, racist, and unjust patterns of segregation that persist globally, it is not a coincidence that many who draw on fieldwork lived, worked, and/or played in the communities they are writing about prior to their lives in academia. As Alina Haliliuc invokes Lauren Berlant's words at the end of a poetic paragraph about the people she witnesses in the streets of Bucharest, "People of post-socialist neoliberalism. People who die slowly, people who float sideways. *My people*" (emphasis added). Here, Haliliuc performatively links the people she is studying with herself, shrinking the space we might otherwise imagine between authors and interlocutors. In doing so, she publicizes not only the place she is writing about, but also how she imagines her scholarship as bridging "There" with "Here" and as resisting slow death as unspeakable or inevitable.

Sometimes the distance and connections between "the field" and the field of rhetoric are most palpable in narratives of return. A compelling deconstruction of this fraught tension may be found in Tiara R. Na'puti's conclusion: "At the end of the summer, I have to leave Guåhan and travel back to the continental United States. Leaving home is difficult for me. The long airplane ride over the Pacific Ocean provides an unavoidable physical reminder of the distance I will have to travel when I return. I will experience the back and forth, and complex articulations of self, place, and texts (created, collected, and performed)."

Similarly, in attempting to link "There" with "Here," Kathleen de Onís closes her essay by noting how "the field" is neither spatially nor temporally fixed for her: "Anticipating this essay's inclusion in the *Text + Field* volume, I e-mailed an early draft to several community members. Those who replied were pleased overall with what they read. Santiago, mentioned earlier in this essay, shared the following: 'I think the article is very good. Thanks for sending it and your solidarity.' Hernández, whose rhetoric animates this essay's epigraph, offered helpful feedback on a footnote and assured me that I was 'boricua de pura cepa' / 'pureblood Puerto Rican.'"

These passages and more throughout this volume and beyond poignantly remind us that many are drawn to critical ethnographic practices because we identify with and believe we can learn from those too often relegated to "the field." For us, such voices, things, and places are not expendable or easily ignored. To do so would erase ourselves. Making space for their bodies and those places is a way to make space for us. We listen so that we can find new ways to speak. We speak in the hopes that someone will listen.[8]

As such, we may want to discuss further: What are the historical conjunctures that open up and/or constrict rhetorical scholars from reflecting on one's relationship with those spaces one is writing about? What do we consider our best practices for sharing fieldwork with other academics, as well as our own academic work with those we've written about? How do digital technologies and circulation of one's publications transform or reify the distance between the worlds we write about and the spaces where those writings circulate? When do rhetoricians imagine scholarship drawing on critical ethnographic research as capable of empirical value not only as a democratizing endeavor for oppressed people, but also as contributing to the ongoing development of rhetorical theory? As we translate our research into emerging assessment models of higher education, when do we claim our work as "public" or "civic engagement"? And with the rising influence of corporate logics of branding and efficiency at universities, how can we resist challenges to dwelling in a place, engaging people and practices that challenge the status quo, or studying nonsystematic particularity? While we live in an age of information abundance, when and how do ethnographic methods offer an opportunity to expand not just the quantity of public discourse, but the quality of rhetorical theory?

On Immediacy

What occurs in the immediate moment shapes us—it is not all that shapes us, but it is part of what shapes our processes of becoming. When foregrounding interactions with people, places, and elements, the authors in this volume share a vulnerable disposition indebted to the palpable topos of *immediacy*. Giving credence to immediacy tends to be not an act of displaying arrogant mastery but an attunement to interdependence, cultural differences, and embodied epistemologies. Our goal is not to romanticize a monolithic public sphere with a homogeneous reaction. We seek out contradictions, failures, senses of loss, anger, love, and much more. Critical ethnographic research promises the possibility of rhetorical studies valuing greater attention to embodied facets of particular situations, including our physical, emotional, aural, olfactory, and proxemic sensual relations in everyday life and heightened moments of moral dramas.

In this volume, for example, some observe the ways grain elevators and other ephemeral objects in our landscapes and communities can signify a great deal about cultural norms and changes (see chapters 1 and 6, in particular). Jamie Landau explores her own unexpected feelings toward a museum exhibit of a bottle labeled as "ectopic pregnancy" and its contents, as well as significant choices of display, participant navigation, and verbalized affective reactions within the museum space. "Co-presence," as de Onís writes, "alters the ways we communicate about and experience our environments and interactions with human beings, animals, structures, and landscapes."

In addition to participant observation, many authors in this collection conduct informal and semi-structured interviews. Some focus on disagreements among organizers and everyday people negotiating social change (see, for example, chapters 1 and 2). Some reflect on whether audiences adhere to the values of the organizers (as in chapters 1 and 2). One considers when word choice does or does not resonate within a specific cultural group, like "grassroots" in Puerto Rico (chapter 6).[9] Yet another interviews U.S. troops to discover what she could learn from their reflections on how social media use shaped their experiences at home and abroad, which could not be determined by looking only at their posts online (chapter 10). As these essays attest, an investment in public affairs should not be one solely concerned with what already is established as public, but also the processes of publicity that fail or succeed to garner attention.

Many also include critical autoethnographic writing. Aaron Hess shares that, in order to more fully appreciate embodied and interactive judgments and choices of drug users and DanceSafe volunteers, he didn't merely observe, but "joined DanceSafe and traveled to desert raves across Arizona, enacting the localized judgments regarding drugs by interacting with volunteers and users alike within arenas of active drug use." Haliliuc claims that the charismatic nostalgia invoked by a Romanian political leader reminds her of an intimate food scene with her grandfather when he was dying of cancer, giving insight into the speech's enthymematic work of invoking personal feelings of memory, intimacy, and loss. Lisa Silvestri recalls her father's experiences fighting in Vietnam.

In "Interrogating the 'Field,'" Samantha Senda-Cook, Michael Middleton, and Danielle Endres offer an engagement with ethnographic evidence that illustrates compellingly the difference critical ethnographic practices can make to one's research. Offering vivid accounts of the immediacy of a dinner party on a two-lane bridge, they share Senda-Cook's detailed field notes and images of a revival of an artisan culture that values craft and ecological sensibility with smells of hay and the feel of eating out of a mason jar. They observe that sharing the ephemeral and multisensory experience of immediacy is challenging, but that doing so discloses significant values and acts that become part of their study. On the mason jars, for example, they elaborate: "The group's canning efforts communicate the themes of small batches, slow preparation, and local-mindedness privileged by the event. Likewise, this food station linked its food with the nostalgia of homegrown, family-style cooking implied by the food canning process and the informal presentation of the food. In addition to photographing the station and taking notes about the reactions of the guests, the mingling sounds of conversations and highway traffic, and the heat of the sun on the exposed bridge, Samantha . . . also interviewed people present."[10] This reflexive, embodied retelling of the event on the bridge reminds us of the rich environments in which we consume food and navigate politics. If one is invested in changing food cultures, this essay might remind us that the first questions many ask when choosing a restaurant include judgments about taste, as well as material objects and places: What are you in the mood to eat? How much will it cost? Do you want to go to somewhere noisy or quiet? Inside or outside? Family-friendly or romantic? Are we expected to dress up or not? How far do you want to travel for your meal? And so forth.

The research shared by Senda-Cook, Middleton, and Endres, therefore, can help local organizers gather information about how their event is experienced by participants, inspire communities elsewhere to organize similar events, and move us as readers to do a double-take the next time we eat out, feed a crowd, or see a mason jar. Their essay reflects on and encourages critical thinking about how everyday objects and landscapes may constitute judgments (such as local value creation); when organizing social events for political purposes can build communities (through scaled payment and events); and the ethics of eating (in ways that reduce one's carbon footprint and support a local economy or not). Ideally, creating such a forum for praxis—and analyzing it through scholarship—could generate debate, change practices, and foster new ideas.

Immediacy, therefore, is a topos worth discussing further in terms of what we learn from physical co-presence, as well as how traveling to a scene or interviewing someone can change one's perspective. Additional questions might include the following: By imagining rhetorical scholarship as part of the ongoing process of social drama, when do we decide to stop researching and to start writing or publicizing our work? When is sharing criticism an act of solidarity or another way to marginalize particular people, elements, and ideas? How do ongoing trends of the nonhuman (crops, toxic pollution, climate disruption, digital media practices, drug use, etc.) challenge rhetorical concepts of agency or not? Are there different expectations in the field of rhetoric when we write about spectacular events versus everyday life? What genealogies of emotion and affect can rhetoricians identify to open up our ways of thinking about embodied experiences? How can studying life beyond what we find in headline news be articulated in such a way that we still contribute to arguments exceeding the particular context? While we can (and should) draw from performance studies, anthropology, folklore, and other disciplines, what does the rhetorical tradition offer us in terms of exemplars of "fieldwork"?

On Documentation

When I conduct interviews, start writing notes on participant observation, or decide to share autoethnographic accounts as part of my research, it usually is because either there is no existing archive that can answer my research questions more compellingly or it is a result of the fact that my body was "in the field" prior to writing and discovered new research questions worth bringing back to the field of rhetoric. Likewise, the authors here turn to critical ethnographic practices when the stories they believe or know to exist cannot be found through already established *documents* at the library, online, or through other archives. Simply put, then, if we limit ourselves by privileging official records, we lose the opportunity to learn from the undocumented.[11] That is, we risk excluding people and elements that are not shown, heard, or otherwise exist in texts, often—though certainly not always—created, collected, and displayed by those already in dominant or mainstream social positions.

In doing so, contemporary rhetorical scholars fall prey to the logic that everything that matters to public culture has been—or will be—documented.[12] As the volume editors note in the introduction, however, performance ethnographer Dwight Conquergood powerfully critiques textualist ethnocentrism; he notes "the ocular politics that links the powers to see, to search, and to seize."[13] A compulsion for documentation as the primary or preferred source of testimony too often reinforces oppressive norms in ways that are damaging to a discipline that values orality, particular situations, hidden transcripts, tricksters, emotion, and a broader range of relevant inventional cultural performances.[14] That is, if we reduce rhetorical studies to analyzing existing records, we risk radically narrowing the relevance of our field by ignoring many practices of everyday life, as well as agents and acts that are not yet widely accepted, known, or deemed legal. It also cuts the field off from a richer exploration of the generative topoi that can be discovered through politics of embodied proxemics and intersubjectivity.

As rhetoricians long have argued, democratic imaginaries are nurtured and stifled in spaces not simply involving great speeches by great men or even at great events with great photojournalists on hand. This volume provides evidence that public values are negotiated in meaningful ways by a wide range of people, including food justice activists, Occupy protesters in and out of costume, people who have been colonized, artists, the deceased, ravers, climate justice advocates, environmentalists, social networks, those who elect politicians, those who are ill, indigenous people, soldiers, and more. It is worth noting that this diversity of identities signifies not only relevant actors for public address but also groups that might matter to us, at least in part, because we find them under-addressed. That is, for some of us, fieldwork helps contribute more to our understanding of marginalized and emergent figures or elements by not only studying acts but also reflecting on the power relations that contribute to misrecognition or nascent popularity.

Although important, we should not limit ourselves to writing about people and events everyone already has heard about. To be clear: in some instances, public address should focus on an established rhetor (e.g., the U.S. president's State of the Union speech and campaign debates remain attention-worthy). Yet part of what rhetoricians, like those gathered in this book, also want to explore is why certain cultural performances in particular situations have not garnered conventional audiences and why emergent and marginalized rhetorical practices might become—or should become—attractive to broader audiences in the future. My own fieldwork on Warren County, North Carolina, troubled an established story of origin of the environmental justice movement with the goal, at least in part, to garner the governor's attention to clean up a landfill.[15] Likewise, my ethnographic research in southern Louisiana allowed me to make an argument about why we should pay attention to environmental injustice in the region—before Hurricane Katrina made landfall.[16] Although the government and the nation generally were ignoring these communities at the time I began my research, I hope hindsight will help validate the value of helping publicize injustices such as these against people who are not (yet) famous and in places many cannot (yet) find on a map. This volume, likewise, might be drawing attention toward people and communities less frequently discussed in the field and in headlines today; however, their marginalization is not inevitable for all time. Further, we can learn from those who remain in the margins of history books if publicity remains deferred.

Fieldwork is not the only way one can attend to vernacular, outlaw, or colonized voices. Roberta Chevrette, for example, draws on videos and arguments in print to make indigenous critiques of colonization more present. Nevertheless, critical ethnographic practices should be recognized and taught as a valid approach.

A scriptocentric and ocularcentric bias tends to marginalize the embodied rhetorics of communities constituted by people who are like most of us, assuming we have never held an elected office, worked for a mainstream media outlet, or had the luxury of legibility to those in dominant positions. Excluding "fieldwork" as viable sources of knowledge creates false binaries between us and them, objectivity and subjectivity, symbols and cultures. Perhaps most dangerously, this prejudice reinforces—under the guise of intellectual norms—the violent (colonial, racist, sexist, heterosexist, ableist, etc.) notion that convictions, strategies, situations, and effects do not matter until those occupying relative positions of power claim they do.

Even as rhetorical scholarship has disciplined fieldwork at times, rhetorical scholars in communication studies consistently have issued calls over the past few decades for critical ethnographic fieldwork through interviews, participant observation, autoethnography, and more.[17] We are not solely interpreters of the archives of others. We can and do take photographs, conduct interviews, walk through memorials and museums, participate in and observe social movements, provide consultations for politicians, write blogs, and so on. Sometimes we coproduce rhetorical appeals with those we engage in our research because we choose to do so or because we never had a choice to not be speaking as the Other. Sometimes our published work shapes the world about which we are writing.

Valerie Thatcher, for example, provides a compelling account of anti-coal advocacy in Texas based on participant observation and interviews. As she concludes, Thatcher reminds us that part of the motivation of her research is that the ways publics were being mobilized in this social movement previously were undocumented; her work also runs counter to fossil fuel ads many of us have seen in the United States, which often portray a narrowly elitist view of the figure of the "environmentalist." She writes, "The emergence of anti-coal environmental activism in nonurban localities and urban communities of color indicates a new and innovative type of environmentalist identity that defies the long-standing derogatory 'tree-hugger' stereotype as primarily situated within the domain of liberal urban whites." By studying how these publics work together, perform solidarity, face challenges, and distinguish themselves, Thatcher helps us think through the possibilities and limitations of rural politics, collaboration, and political critique. Given the overwhelming financial advantage of fossil fuel corporations to buy publicity and silence politicians, more rhetoricians would do well to study dominant, well-documented frames of the industry and more marginalized, undocumented voices of those who are resisting their stranglehold on our planet and people.

Becoming more reflexive about the politics of documentation and labels of "undocumented" raises additional questions for the field: In what ways does co-presence with the energy, material, species, or information shape one's approach to one's research? How should we balance expertise among communities we teach, write about, and/or identify with? How can immediacy reveal norms of rhetorical culture? Do rhetoricians have an ethical duty to articulate our research interests in multimodal ways (such as radio, documentary films, photographs, blogs, protests, public comments, etc.)? Is there an obligation for rhetoricians to seek out or at least make space for the undocumented or perspectives that run counter to dominant frames? At what cost do we fetishize the familiar or corporate media outlets as our criterion for scholarship?[18] Can one draw on critical ethnographic sensibilities without doing ethnography?[19] How is the logic of documentation influencing the labor of academics today? What acts of resistance to compulsory documentation are most compelling and/or futile?

Conclusion

This volume reminds rhetorical scholars that critical ethnographic work can help broaden our knowledge about topics we long have studied, no matter which research approaches we engage. Many of the essays contribute to ongoing conversations about enduring concepts engaged in rhetorical studies, including but not limited to *imitatio* (chapter 2); feelings (chapter 4); *phronesis* (chapter 5); judgment or *krisis* (chapters 5 and 6); presence (chapter 6); counterpublics (chapter 7); audience (chapter 8); and memory (chapters 1, 2, 5, 8, and 9).

Contributors to this volume also theorize alternative imaginations for public life by traveling to a range of places, listening to voices less heard, acting attuned to scenic elements, and reflexively accounting for the experiences sought out. Although I won't name them all here, the authors notably offer us alternative ways to imagine living lives that resist and trouble the existing order: detailed observations about a playful event to help denaturalize our taken-for-granted or alienated assumptions about where food comes from, how it travels, and ways we might consume it differently (chapter 1); a performative chant that a healthy democracy should involve large public protests in the streets rather than be narrowly defined by counting votes (chapter 2); an examination of a successful coalition in building trust through the number of bodies in a room as an act of solidarity that can trouble singular issue assumptions about social change (chapter 7); and anticolonial imaginaries of justice, which publicize possibilities for decolonizing relations between people, the planet, and profits (chapters 6 and 9).

Overall these essays also suggest timely scholarly trends and dilemmas that should be of interest to scholars who do or do not engage in critical ethnographic research. Joshua P. Ewalt, Jessy J. Ohl, and Damien Smith Pfister, for example, note that the emerging digital humanities could include sharing field notes online and/or cowriting work with those one is studying. Na'puti emphasizes how we might become more reflexive about our relationships with the communities from which we come and/or do research about. Posed as an ethical challenge for advocates, de Onís goads us to consider the limitations of English monolingualism. In many essays throughout this volume the authors emphasize the need to pay more attention to the perspectives of people who are colonized, as well as to how critical ethnographic practices can serve as one significant way students and faculty from marginalized communities may negotiate what it means to become part of and survive working in the academy. This call feels even more pressing as our institutions of higher education are increasing recruitment globally and struggling to do more than give insincere lip service to racial/ethnic diversity.

Hopefully the insights offered regarding space, immediacy, documentation, and more will excite rhetorical scholars who already are committed to drawing on critical ethnographic research. Perhaps this volume will help establish critical ethnographic practices—once again—as valuable to rhetorical studies and encourage more to try it. Ideally, rhetorical scholars might be moved by research such as this to give greater attention to our bodies, nonhuman elements, technologies we use in everyday life, and oppressed voices in our classrooms, books, conventions, and public advocacy. As this book illustrates, drawing on critical ethnographic practices can offer the potential to *decentralize*—decolonize, diversify, deanthropomorphize—and to *regenerate*—rebuild, reimagine, rejuvenate—what rhetoric is becoming. Rather than compulsively reproducing the status quo, isolating ourselves from one another, or allowing conditions to become fallow, we should encourage passion about and commitments to rhetorical labor that nourishes the health of the field.

CONTRIBUTORS

Robert Asen is Professor of Rhetoric, Politics, and Culture in the Department of Communication Arts at the University of Wisconsin–Madison. He conducts research in the areas of public policy debate, public sphere studies, and rhetoric and critical theory. In addition to his two coedited volumes, he is the author of *Visions of Poverty: Welfare Policy and Political Imagination*, *Invoking the Invisible Hand: Social Security and the Privatization Debates*, and *Democracy, Deliberation, and Education* (Penn State, 2015).

Karma R. Chávez is Associate Professor of Rhetoric, Politics, and Culture in the Department of Communication Arts at the University of Wisconsin–Madison. Her work examines social-movement building, activist rhetoric, and coalitional politics, highlighting the rhetorical practices of groups marginalized within existing power structures. She is the author of *Queer Migration Politics: Activist Rhetoric and Coalitional Possibilities* and the coeditor of *Standing in the Intersection: Feminist Voices, Feminist Practices in Communication Studies*.

Roberta Chevrette is a doctoral candidate in the Hugh Downs School of Human Communication at Arizona State University. Utilizing rhetorical and qualitative methodologies, her research explores the gendered, racialized assemblages through which bodies are abjected from or interpellated into national imaginaries and/or other publics.

Kathleen M. de Onís is a Ph.D. student in the Department of Communication and Culture at Indiana University. Her research explores climate, environmental, and reproductive (in)justice in Latin and Caribbean communities. Her scholarship has appeared in *Environmental Communication: A Journal of Nature and Culture*, *Women's Studies in Communication*, and *Women and Language*.

Danielle Endres is Associate Professor of Communication and a faculty member in the Environmental Humanities Masters Program at the University of Utah. She is a rhetorical theorist and critic with expertise in environmental communication, science communication, social movements, and field-based methods.

Joshua P. Ewalt is Assistant Professor in the School of Communication Studies at James Madison University. His scholarship attends to the relationship among rhetoric, place, and social struggle by examining places of public memory, regional rhetorics, activist cartographies, and the relationship among rhetoric, mobility, and matter.

Alina Haliliuc is Assistant Professor of Communication at Denison University, where she researches and teaches in the areas of rhetorical theory and criticism. Her work may be found in such venues as *Communication, Culture, and Critique*, *Journal of Popular Culture*, *Aspasia: The International Yearbook of Central, Eastern, and Southeastern European Women's and Gender History*, and *Text and Performance Quarterly*.

Aaron Hess is Assistant Professor of Communication in the College of Letters and Sciences at Arizona State University, Downtown Phoenix. His primary research focuses on public advocacy, the intersection between rhetorical and qualitative methods, the use of social media for deliberation and protest, and public memory.

Robert Glenn Howard is Director of Digital Studies and Professor of Communication, Religious Studies, and Folklore in the Department of Communication Arts at the University of Wisconsin–Madison. His research addresses the possibilities and limits of empowerment through everyday expression on the Internet by focusing on the intersection of individual human agency and participatory performance. He is the author of *Digital Jesus: The Making of a New Christian Fundamentalist Community on the Internet* and *Network Apocalypse: Visions of the End in an Age of Internet Media*.

Jamie Landau is Associate Professor in the Department of Communication and Philosophy at Keene State College. Her research explores how rhetoric influences social change related to gender/sexuality and health/medicine. Rethinking scholarly methodologies and taking seriously the role of emotion/affect in politics are central to her scholarship.

Sara L. McKinnon is Assistant Professor of Rhetoric, Politics, and Culture in the Department of Communication Arts at the University of Wisconsin–Madison.

Her research and teaching are in the areas of intercultural rhetoric, transnational studies, and legal rhetoric. Her essays have appeared in *Women's Studies in Communication, Text and Performance Quarterly,* and the *Quarterly Journal of Speech.* She is the author of the book *Gendered Asylum: Race and Violence in U.S. Law and Politics.*

Michael K. Middleton is Assistant Professor of Argumentation and Public Discourse and Director of the John R. Park Debate Society in the Department of Communication at the University of Utah. His research focuses on rhetoric, argumentation, public discourse, and cultural studies in the contexts of political advocacy and social movements. His current research examines how homeless populations in Sacramento, California, have carved out spaces of democratic participation within their surrounding communities.

Tiara R. Na'puti is a member of the Chamoru diaspora from Guåhan (familian Kaderon and Robat) and Assistant Professor of Communication at the University of Colorado–Boulder. Her scholarship and activism address militarization, colonization, social movements, and indigenous cultural discourses— particularly among Chamorus and throughout Oceania.

Jessy J. Ohl is Assistant Professor of Communication and Digital Studies at the University of Mary Washington. He teaches and conducts research in the areas of rhetorical theory, political communication, public deliberation, and the rhetoric of war.

Phaedra C. Pezzullo is Associate Professor in the Department of Communication at the University of Colorado–Boulder. In addition to her award-winning book *Toxic Tourism: Rhetorics of Travel, Pollution, and Environmental Justice,* she has edited *Cultural Studies and the Environment, Revisited;* coedited *Environmental Justice and Environmentalism: The Social Justice Challenge to the Environmental Movement* and *Readings on Rhetoric and Performance;* and coauthored the fourth edition of *Environmental Communication and the Public Sphere.*

Damien Smith Pfister is Assistant Professor in the Department of Communication Studies at the University of Nebraska–Lincoln. His research interests are at the intersection of networked rhetorics, public deliberation, and visual culture. He is the author of *Networked Media, Networked Rhetorics: Attention and Deliberation in the Early Blogosphere* (Penn State, 2014) and numerous journal articles.

Samantha Senda-Cook is Assistant Professor in Communication Studies and a faculty member in Environmental Science at Creighton University. She studies rhetoric, environmental communication, materiality, authenticity, and place.

Lisa Silvestri is Assistant Professor of Communication Studies at Gonzaga University. Her research interests focus on American politics and popular culture, with a special focus on war and social media. Some of her recent publications have appeared in *Media, War, and Conflict*, *Review of Communication*, and *Visual Communication Quarterly*.

Valerie Thatcher holds a Ph.D. from the Department of Communication Studies in the Moody College of Communication at the University of Texas at Austin and currently teaches at St. Edward's University. Her work explores the relationship among environmental communication, social movements, and community and/or nonprofit organizing.

NOTES

Introduction

1. Edwin Black, *Rhetorical Criticism: A Study in Method*, 2nd ed. (Madison: University of Wisconsin Press, 1978), xi.

2. Ibid., x.

3. Ibid., xiv.

4. Ibid., xiii.

5. Charles E. Morris III, "(Self-)Portrait of Prof. R.C.: A Retrospective," *Western Journal of Communication* 74, no. 1 (2010): 12.

6. Ibid.

7. Thomas W. Benson, "Another Shooting in Cowtown," *Quarterly Journal of Speech* 67, no. 4 (1981): 347–406; Richard B. Gregg and A. Jackson McCormack, "'Whitey' Goes to the Ghetto: A Personal Chronicle of a Communication Experience with Black Youths," *Today's Speech* 16, no. 3 (1968): 25–30; Richard B. Gregg, A. Jackson McCormack, and Douglas J. Pedersen, "The Rhetoric of Black Power: A Street-Level Interpretation," *Quarterly Journal of Speech* 55, no. 2 (1969): 151–60.

8. Kent A. Ono and John M. Sloop, "The Critique of Vernacular Discourse," *Communication Monographs* 62, no. 1 (1995): 19–46.

9. Clifford Geertz, *The Interpretation of Cultures: Selected Essays* (New York: Basic Books, 1973), 20.

10. Dell Hymes, "Models of the Interaction of Language and Social Setting," *Journal of Social Issues* 23, no. 2 (1967): 12.

11. Jack Daniel and Geneva Smitherman, "How I Got Over: Communication Dynamics in the Black Community," *Quarterly Journal of Speech* 62, no. 1 (1976): 26–39; Joseph J. Hayes, "Gayspeak," *Quarterly Journal of Speech* 62, no. 1 (1976): 256–66; Gerry Philipsen, "Speaking 'Like a Man' in Teamsterville: Culture Patterns of Role Enactment in an Urban Neighborhood," *Quarterly Journal of Speech* 61, no. 1 (1975): 13–22; Gerry Philipsen, "Places for Speaking in Teamsterville," *Quarterly Journal of Speech* 62, no. 1 (1976): 15–25; Marsha Houston Stanback and W. Barnett Pearce, "Talking to 'the Man': Some Communication Strategies Used by Members of 'Subordinate' Social Groups," *Quarterly Journal of Speech* 67, no. 1 (1981): 21–30.

12. William G. Kirkwood, "Shiva's Dance at Sundown: Implications of Indian Aesthetics for Poetics and Rhetoric," *Text and Performance Quarterly* 10, no. 2 (1990): 93–110; Joni L. Jones, "Performing Osun without Bodies: Documenting the Osun Festival in Print," *Text and Performance Quarterly* 17, no. 1 (1997): 69–93; Shannon Jackson, "Ethnography and the Audition: Performance as Ideological Critique," *Text and Performance Quarterly* 13, no. 1 (1993): 21–43; Dwight

Conquergood, "Poetics, Play, Process, and Power: The Performative Turn in Anthropology," *Text and Performance Quarterly* 9, no. 1 (1989): 82; Dwight Conquergood, "Ethnography, Rhetoric, and Performance," *Quarterly Journal of Speech* 78, no. 1 (1992): 80–97; Dwight Conquergood, "Performance Theory, Hmong, Shamans, and Cultural Politics," in *Critical Theory and Performance*, ed. G. Reinelt and J. R. Roach (Ann Arbor: University of Michigan Press, 1992), 41–64; Dwight Conquergood, "Rethinking Ethnography: Towards a Critical Cultural Politics," *Communication Monographs* 58, no. 2 (1991): 179–94; Richard Bauman, "American Folklore Studies and Social Transformation: A Performance-Centered Perspective," *Text and Performance Quarterly* 9, no. 3 (1989): 175–84; Ronald J. Pelias and James VanOosting, "A Paradigm for Performance Studies," *Quarterly Journal of Speech* 73 (1987): 219–31.

13. Norman K. Denzin and Yvonna S. Lincoln, introduction to *Handbook of Qualitative Research* (Thousand Oaks, CA: Sage, 2000), 1.

14. James Clifford, *The Predicament of Culture: Twentieth-Century Ethnography, Literature, and Art* (Cambridge, MA: Harvard University Press, 1988); James Clifford and George E. Marcus, *Writing Culture: The Poetics and Politics of Ethnography* (Berkeley: University of California Press, 1986); Judith Stacey, "Can There Be a Feminist Ethnography?" in *Women's Words: The Practice of Feminist Oral History*, ed. S. B. Gluck and D. Patai (New York: Routledge, 1991), 112–20; Kamala Visweswaran, *Fictions of Feminist Ethnography* (Minneapolis: University of Minnesota Press, 1994); Elizabeth E. Wheatley, "How Can We Engender Ethnography with a Feminist Imagination? A Rejoinder to Judith Stacey," *Women's Studies International Forum* 17, no. 4 (1994): 403–16; Ruth Behar, *Translated Woman: Crossing the Border with Esperanza's Story* (Boston: Beacon Press, 1993); Lila Abu-Lughod, "Can There Be a Feminist Ethnography?" *Women and Performance: Journal of Feminist Theory* 5, no. 1 (1990): 7–27; Margery Wolf, *A Thrice-Told Tale: Feminism, Postmodernism, and Ethnographic Responsibility* (Stanford, CA: Stanford University Press, 1992).

15. Marwan M. Kraidy, "The Global, the Local, and the Hybrid: A Native Ethnography of Glocalization," *Critical Studies in Mass Communication* 16, no. 4 (1999): 456–76; George E. Marcus, "Ethnography in/of the World System: The Emergence of Multi-Sited Ethnography," *Annual Review of Anthropology* 24, no. 1 (1995): 95–117; Aihwa Ong, *Flexible Citizenship: The Cultural Logics of Transnationality* (Durham, NC: Duke University Press, 1999).

16. Linda Tuhiwai Smith, *Decolonizing Methodologies: Research and Indigenous Peoples* (New York: Palgrave, 2006); Sarah Amira de la Garza (published as Maria Cristina González), "The Four Seasons of Ethnography: A Creation-Centered Ontology for Ethnography," *International Journal of Intercultural Relations* 24, no. 5 (2000): 623–50; D. Soyini Madison, *Critical Ethnography: Method, Ethics, and Performance* (Thousand Oaks, CA: Sage, 2005).

17. Michael K. Middleton, Samantha Senda-Cook, and Danielle Endres, "Articulating Rhetorical Field Methods: Challenges and Tensions," *Western Journal of Communication* 75, no. 4 (2011): 386–406.

18. Herbert A. Wichelns, "The Literary Criticism of Oratory," in *Landmark Essays on American Public Address*, ed. Martin J. Medhurst (Davis, CA: Hermagoras Press, 1993), 1–32; Dilip Parameshwar Gaonkar, "The Oratorical Text: The Enigma of Arrival," in *Texts in Context: Critical Dialogues on Significant Episodes in American Political Rhetoric*, ed. Michael C. Leff and Fred J. Kauffeld (Davis, CA: Hermagoras Press, 1989), 255–75.

19. James Jasinski, *Sourcebook on Rhetoric: Key Concepts in Contemporary Rhetorical Studies* (Thousand Oaks, CA: Sage, 2001), 571–72.

20. Ibid., 574.

21. Leah Ceccarelli, "Polysemy: Multiple Meanings in Rhetorical Criticism," *Quarterly Journal of Speech* 84, no. 4 (1998): 395–415.

22. See, e.g., Martha Solomon, "The Things We Study: Texts and Their Interactions," *Communication Monographs* 60, no. 1 (1993): 62–68; Lisa Glebatis Perks, "Polysemic Scaffolding: Exploring Discursive Clashes in *Chappelle's Show*," *Communication, Culture, and Critique* 3, no. 2 (2010): 270–89.

23. Phaedra C. Pezzullo, "Resisting 'National Breast Cancer Awareness Month': The Rhetoric of Counterpublics and Their Cultural Performances," *Quarterly Journal of Speech* 89, no. 4 (2003): 350.

24. Robert Asen, *Democracy, Deliberation, and Education* (University Park: Penn State University Press, 2015).

25. Black, *Rhetorical Criticism*, 14.

26. Kenneth Burke, *Language as Symbolic Action: Essays on Life, Literature, and Method* (Berkeley: University of California Press, 1966), 45.

27. Kelly Jakes, "*La France En Chantant*: The Rhetorical Construction of French Identity in Songs of the Resistance Movement," *Quarterly Journal of Speech* 99, no. 3 (2013): 317–40.

28. Daniel C. Brouwer and Aaron Hess, "Making Sense of 'God Hates Fags' and 'Thank God for 9/11': A Thematic Analysis of Milbloggers' Responses to Reverend Fred Phelps and the Westboro Baptist Church," *Western Journal of Communication* 71, no. 1 (2007): 69–90.

29. Cara A. Finnegan, "FSA Photography and New Deal Visual Culture," in *American Rhetoric in the New Deal Era, 1932–1945*, ed. Thomas W. Benson (East Lansing: Michigan State University Press, 2006), 115–55.

30. A. Cheree Carlson and John E. Hocking, "Strategies of Redemption at the Vietnam Veterans Memorial," *Western Journal of Speech Communication* 52, no. 3 (1988): 203–15; Greg Dickinson, Brian L. Ott, and Eric Aoki, "Spaces of Remembering and Forgetting: The Reverent Eye/I at the Plains Indian Museum," *Communication and Critical/Cultural Studies* 3, no. 1 (2006): 27–47.

31. Phaedra C. Pezzullo, *Toxic Tourism: Rhetorics of Pollution, Travel, and Environmental Justice* (Tuscaloosa: University of Alabama Press, 2007).

32. This example also illustrates some of the logistical issues that may attend fieldwork. In Asen's case, the number of meetings attended during the period of fieldwork totaled over two hundred, which required the efforts of a team of researchers. For an example of collaborative scholarship resulting from this extensive effort of data collection, see Robert Asen, Deb Gurke, Pamela Conners, Ryan Solomon, and Elsa Gumm, "Research Evidence and School Board Deliberations: Lessons from Three Wisconsin School Districts," *Educational Policy* 27, no. 1 (2013): 33–63.

33. Carole Blair, Marsha S. Jeppeson, and Enrico Pucci, Jr., "Public Memorializing in Postmodernity: The Vietnam Veterans Memorial as Prototype," *Quarterly Journal of Speech* 77, no. 3 (1991): 272.

34. Carlson and Hocking, "Strategies of Redemption," 203.

35. Blair, Jeppeson, and Pucci, "Public Memorializing," 272.

36. Dwight Conquergood, "Performance Studies: Interventions and Radical Research," *Drama Review* 46, no. 2 (2002): 147.

37. Ibid., 146.

38. For key examples see Robert J. Branham and W. Barnett Pearce, "Between Text and Context: Toward a Rhetoric of Contextual Reconstruction," *Quarterly Journal of Speech* 71, no. 1 (1985): 19–36; Lloyd F. Bitzer, "The Rhetorical Situation," *Philosophy and Rhetoric* 1, no. 1 (1968): 1–14; Michael Calvin McGee, "Text, Context, and the Fragmentation of Contemporary Culture," *Western Journal of Speech Communication* 54, no. 3 (1990): 274–90.

39. Michael C. Leff, "Textual Criticism: The Legacy of G. P. Morhmann," *Quarterly Journal of Speech* 72, no. 4 (1986): 382.

40. John M. Murphy, "Presidential Debates and Campaign Rhetoric: Text within Context," *Southern Journal of Communication* 57, no. 3 (1992): 227.

41. John Louis Lucaites, "Burke's 'Speech on Conciliation' as Oppositional Discourse," in *Texts in Context: Critical Dialogues on Significant Episodes in American Political Rhetoric*, ed. Michael C. Leff and Fred J. Kauffeld (Davis, CA: Hermagoras Press, 1989), 86.

42. Branham and Pearce, "Between Text and Context."

43. Leff, "Textual Criticism," 382.

44. Carole Blair, "Reflections on Criticism and Bodies: Parables from Public Places," *Western Journal of Communication* 65, no. 3 (2001): 275.

45. Ibid., 275–76.

46. Ibid., 276.

47. Karma R. Chávez, "Counter-Public Enclaves and Understanding the Function of Rhetoric in Social Movement Coalition-Building," *Communication Quarterly* 59, no. 1 (2011): 1–18.

48. Greg Dickinson, Carol Blair, and Brian L. Ott, eds., *Places of Public Memory: The Rhetoric of Museums and Memorials* (Tuscaloosa: University of Alabama Press, 2010).

49. Maegan Parker Brooks, *A Voice That Could Stir an Army: Fannie Lou Hamer and the Rhetoric of the Black Freedom Movement* (Jackson: University Press of Mississippi, 2014).

50. Jasinski, *Sourcebook*, 68–69.

51. Bitzer, "Rhetorical Situation," 7.

52. Ibid., 11–12.

53. For critiques of Bitzer's objectivity, see Barbara Biesecker, "Rethinking the Rhetorical Situation from within the Thematic of *Différance*," *Philosophy and Rhetoric* 22, no. 2 (1989): 110–30; Alan Brinton, "Situation in the Theory of Rhetoric," *Philosophy and Rhetoric* 14, no. 4 (1981): 234–48.

54. Edwin Black, "The Second Persona," *Quarterly Journal of Speech* 56, no. 2 (1970): 113.

55. Ibid., 112–13.

56. Maurice Charland, "Constitutive Rhetoric: The Case of the 'Peuple Quebecois,'" *Quarterly Journal of Speech* 73, no. 2 (1987): 133–50.

57. Celeste Michelle Condit, "The Rhetorical Limits of Polysemy," *Critical Studies in Mass Communication* 6, no. 2 (1989): 103–4.

58. Ceccarelli, "Polysemy," 400, 402.

59. Stuart Hall, "Encoding, Decoding," in *The Cultural Studies Reader*, ed. Simon During (New York: Routledge, 1993), 101.

60. Ibid., 103.

61. David Morley, *Television, Audiences, and Cultural Studies* (New York: Routledge, 1992), 57.

62. Jonathan Gray and Amanda D. Lotz, *Television Studies* (Malden, MA: Polity, 2012), 85.

63. Sara L. McKinnon, "Essentialism, Intersectionality, and Recognition: A Feminist Rhetorical Approach to the Audience," in *Standing in the Intersection: Feminist Voices, Feminist Practices in Communication Studies*, ed. Karma R. Chávez and Cindy L. Griffin (Albany: State University of New York Press, 2012), 189–210.

64. Black, *Rhetorical Criticism*; McGee, "Text, Context."

65. John M. Sloop and Kent A. Ono, "Out-Law Discourse: The Critical Politics of Material Judgment," *Philosophy and Rhetoric* 30, no. 1 (1997): 54.

66. See Sonja K. Foss and Cindy L. Griffin, "Beyond Persuasion: A Proposal for an Invitational Rhetoric," *Communication Monographs* 62, no. 1 (1995): 2–18; Karen A. Foss and Sonja K. Foss, "Personal Experience as Evidence in Feminist Scholarship," *Western Journal of Communication* 58, no. 1 (1994): 39–43.

67. Aaron Hess, "Critical-Rhetorical Ethnography: Rethinking the Place and Process of Rhetoric," *Communication Studies* 62, no. 2 (2011): 127–52.

68. Robert Glenn Howard, *Digital Jesus: The Making of a New Christian Fundamentalist Community* (New York: New York University Press, 2011).

69. Ibid., 150–56; Robert Glenn Howard, "Crusading on the Vernacular Web: The Folk Beliefs and Practices of Online Spiritual Warfare," in *Folklore and the Internet: Vernacular Expression in a Digital World*, ed. Trevor J. Blank (Logan: Utah State University Press, 2009), 191–218.

70. Yvonne S. Lincoln and Egon G. Guba, *Naturalistic Inquiry* (Newbury Park, CA: Sage, 1985).

71. Olga Idriss Davis, "A Black Woman as Rhetorical Critic: Validating Self and Violating the Space of Otherness," *Women's Studies in Communication* 21, no. 1 (1998): 77–89.

72. Morris, "(Self-)Portrait," 19.

73. Ibid.

74. Megan Foley, "Of Violence and Rhetoric: An Ethical Aporia," *Quarterly Journal of Speech* 99, no. 2 (2013): 191–99; Robert C. Rowland and Deanna F. Womack, "Aristotle's View of Ethical Rhetoric," *RSQ: Rhetoric Society Quarterly* 15, no. 1 (1985): 13–31; Kenneth R. Chase, "Constructing Ethics through Rhetoric: Isocrates and Piety," *Quarterly Journal of Speech* 95, no. 3 (2009): 239–62; Robert J. Olian, "The Intended Uses of Aristotle's Rhetoric," *Speech Monographs* 35, no. 2 (1968): 137–48; Lawrence Flynn, "The Aristolelian Basis for the Ethics of Speaking," *Speech Teacher* 6, no. 3 (1957): 179–87; Lisbeth Lipari, "Rhetoric's Other: Levinas, Listening, and the Ethical Response," *Philosophy and Rhetoric* 45, no. 3 (2012): 227–45; Raymie E. McKerrow, "The Ethical Implications of a Whatelian Rhetoric," *RSQ: Rhetoric Society Quarterly* 17, no. 3 (1987): 321–27; Janice Norton, "Rhetorical Criticism as Ethical Action: Cherchez la Femme," *Southern Communication Journal* 61, no. 1 (1995): 29–45; Scott R. Stroud, "Rhetoric and Moral Progress in Kant's Ethical Community," *Philosophy and Rhetoric* 38, no. 4 (2005): 328–54; Steve Schwarze, "Performing *Phronesis*: The Case of Isocrates' *Helen*," *Philosophy and Rhetoric* 32, no. 1 (1999): 78–95; Christopher Lyle Johnstone, "Dewey, Ethics, and Rhetoric: Toward

a Contemporary Conception of Practical Wisdom," *Philosophy and Rhetoric* 16, no. 3 (1983): 185–207; Krista Ratcliffe, *Rhetorical Listening: Identification, Gender, Whiteness* (Carbondale: Southern Illinois University Press, 2005).

75. Christopher Lyle Johnstone, "An Aristotelian Trilogy: Ethics, Rhetoric, Politics, and the Search for Moral Truth," *Philosophy and Rhetoric* 13, no. 1 (1980): 1.

76. Wayne C. Booth, *The Company We Keep: An Ethics of Fiction* (Berkeley: University of California Press, 1988). Others, including Gerard Hauser, Erik Doxtader, and Michael J. Hyde, have also considered ethics in the practice of criticism. It seems fair to say, however, that the ethics of criticism and all that it entails—collecting/creating texts, analyzing and evaluating them, and writing about them—has not been a central preoccupation among rhetorical critics, at least in their published writing.

77. Ibid., 10.

78. Ibid., 134–36.

79. Sarah Amira de la Garza (published as Maria Cristina González), "An Ethics for Postcolonial Ethnography," in *Expressions of Ethnography: Novel Approaches to Qualitative Methods*, ed. Robin P. Clair (Albany: State University of New York Press, 2003), 77–86; Yvonna S. Lincoln and Egon G. Guba, "Paradigmatic Controversies, Contradictions, and Emerging Confluences," in *Handbook of Qualitative Research*, ed. Norman K. Denzin and Yvonna S. Lincoln (Thousand Oaks, CA: Sage, 2000), 97–128; Thomas R. Lindlof and Bryan C. Taylor, *Qualitative Communication Research Methods* (Thousand Oaks, CA: Sage, 2002); Laurel Richardson, "Evaluating Ethnography," *Qualitative Inquiry* 6, no. 2 (2000): 253–56; Angharad N. Valdivia, "bell hooks: Ethics from the Margins," *Qualitative Inquiry* 8, no. 4 (2002): 429–47; Judith N. Martin and R. L. W. Butler, "Toward an Ethic of Intercultural Communication Research," in *Transcultural Realities: Interdisciplinary Perspectives on Cross-Cultural Relations*, ed. Virginia H. Milhouse, Molefi K. Asante, and Peter O. Nwosu (Thousand Oaks, CA: Sage, 2001), 283–98; Paula Saukko, *Doing Research in Cultural Studies: An Introduction to Classical and New Methodological Approaches* (Thousand Oaks, CA: Sage, 2003); Anselm Strauss and Juliet Corbin, *Basics of Qualitative Research: Techniques and Procedures for Developing Grounded Theory*, 2nd ed. (Thousand Oaks, CA: Sage, 1998); Smith, *Decolonizing Methodologies*.

80. Martin Hammersley and Anna Traianou, *Ethics in Qualitative Research: Controversies and Contexts* (Thousand Oaks, CA: Sage, 2012), 3.

81. Madison, *Critical Ethnography*, 111.

82. González, "Ethics for Postcolonial Ethnography," 84.

83. Ibid.

84. John Waite Bowers, "Pre-scientific Function of Rhetorical Criticism," in *Essays on Rhetorical Criticism*, ed. Thomas R. Nilsen (New York: Random House, 1968), 126–45.

85. Wen Shu Lee, "In the Names of Chinese Women," *Quarterly Journal of Speech* 84, no. 3 (1998): 297.

Chapter 1

1. "I-80 50th Anniversary Page," Nebraska Department of Roads, http://www.transportation.nebraska.gov/i-80-anniv/.

2. Michael K. Middleton, Samantha Senda-Cook, and Danielle Endres, "Articulating Rhetorical Field Methods: Challenges and Tensions," *Western Journal of Communication* 75, no. 4 (2011): 386–406; Michael K. Middleton, Aaron Hess, Danielle Endres, and Samantha Senda-Cook, *Participatory Critical Rhetoric: Theoretical and Methodological Foundations for Studying Rhetoric In Situ* (Lanham, MD: Lexington Books, 2015).

3. We use the word "place" to imply a localized and particularized space of rhetorical action. Place cannot be talked about without reference to space. We follow Blair, Dickinson, and Ott's suggestion that while space and place are mutually constitutive, space is more abstract and general than place. Particular places are manifestations of or challenges to more general spatial practices. Place is not only a physical location but also a set of normative and discursive practices. In this regard place and space are interrelated concepts that refer to meaningful areas that are both particular and general, respectively. And both place and space are social constructions with material consequences and manifestations. For more on the relationship between space and place see Danielle Endres and Samantha Senda-Cook, "Location Matters:

The Rhetoric of Place in Protest," *Quarterly Journal of Speech* 97, no. 3 (2011): 257–82; Carole Blair, Greg Dickinson, and Brian L. Ott, "Introduction: Rhetoric/Memory/Place," in *Places of Public Memory: The Rhetoric of Museums and Memorials*, ed. Greg Dickinson, Carole Blair, and Brian L. Ott (Tuscaloosa: University of Alabama Press, 2010), 1–54.

4. Endres and Senda-Cook, "Location Matters," 277.

5. Samantha Senda-Cook, "Rugged Practices: Embodying Authenticity in Outdoor Recreation," *Quarterly Journal of Speech* 98, no. 2 (2012): 129–52. For a discussion of this see Samantha Senda-Cook, "Practicing Rhetoric," in *Purpose, Practice, and Pedagogy in Rhetorical Criticism*, ed. Jim Kuypers (Lanham, MD: Lexington Books, 2014), 149–61.

6. Raka Shome, "Space Matters: The Power and Practice of Space," *Communication Theory* 13, no. 1 (2003): 39–56; Tim Cresswell, *Place: A Short Introduction* (Malden, MA: Blackwell, 2004); Gerard Kyle and Gary Chick, "The Social Construction of a Sense of Place," *Leisure Sciences* 29, no. 3 (2007): 209–25; Isaac West, "PISSAR's Critically Queer and Disabled Politics," *Communication and Critical/Cultural Studies* 7, no. 2 (2010): 156–75.

7. Numerous essays address conversations in the field of rhetoric about the definition of and role of context in rhetorical theory and criticism. Some notable engagements with context include Lloyd Bitzer, "The Rhetorical Situation," *Philosophy and Rhetoric* 1, no. 1 (1968): 1–14; Raymie E. McKerrow, "Critical Rhetoric: Theory and Praxis," *Communication Monographs* 56, no. 2 (1989): 91–111; Michael Calvin McGee, "Text, Context, and the Fragmentation of Contemporary Culture," *Western Journal of Speech Communication* 54, no. 3 (1990): 274–89.

8. Bitzer, "Rhetorical Situation."

9. Carole Blair, "Contemporary U.S. Memorial Sites as Exemplars of Rhetoric's Materiality," in *Rhetorical Bodies*, ed. Jack Selzer and Sharon Crowley (Madison: University of Wisconsin Press, 1999), 16–57; Carole Blair, "Reflections on Criticism and Bodies: Parables from Public Places," *Western Journal of Communication* 65, no. 3 (2001): 271–94; Blair, Dickinson, and Ott, "Introduction: Rhetoric/Memory/Place"; Greg Dickinson, "Memories for Sale: Nostalgia and the Construction of Identity in Old Pasadena," *Quarterly Journal of Speech* 83, no. 1 (1997): 1–27; Greg Dickinson, "Joe's Rhetoric: Finding Authenticity at Starbucks," *Rhetoric Society Quarterly* 32, no. 4 (2002): 1–27.

10. See, e.g., Blair, "Reflections on Criticism and Bodies"; Phaedra C. Pezzullo, *Toxic Tourism: Rhetorics of Pollution, Travel, and Environmental Justice* (Tuscaloosa: University of Alabama Press, 2007).

11. Kenneth Burke, *On Symbols and Society* (Chicago: University of Chicago Press, 1989).

12. Ibid., 135.

13. David Fleming, *City of Rhetoric: Revitalizing the Public Sphere in Metropolitan America* (Albany: State University of New York Press, 2008), 23.

14. Kevin Michael DeLuca, "Unruly Arguments: The Body Rhetoric of Earth First!, ACT UP, and Queer Nation," *Argumentation and Advocacy* 36, no. 1 (1999): 9–21.

15. Michael Warner, "Publics and Counterpublics," *Quarterly Journal of Speech* 88, no. 4 (2002): 413–25.

16. "About," Emerging Terrain, http://emergingterrain.org/about; Casey Logan, "Banners' Creators Are Gone, and Soon Grain Elevators' Art Will Be, Too," *Omaha World Herald*, June 6, 2014, http://www.omaha.com/news/metro/banners-creators-are-gone-and-soon-grain-elevators-art-will/article_678b4995-45dc-526b-b231-3ed5a6d7ecd3.html.

17. "Elevate," Emerging Terrain, http://emergingterrain.org/archives/projects/elevate.

18. This is generally consistent with the overall demographic of Omaha, in which 73 percent of people are white according to the 2010 U.S. Census.

19. Middleton, Senda-Cook, and Endres, "Articulating Rhetorical Field Methods," 293.

20. Endres and Senda-Cook, "Location Matters."

21. "Elevate," Emerging Terrain, http://emergingterrain.org/archives/projects/elevate.

22. Pezzullo, *Toxic Tourism*, 52.

23. Phaedra C. Pezzullo, "Resisting 'National Breast Cancer Awareness Month': The Rhetoric of Counterpublics and Their Cultural Performances," *Quarterly Journal of Speech* 89, no. 4 (2003): 345–65; Endres and Senda-Cook, "Location Matters."

24. Shome, "Space Matters," 40.

25. Endres and Senda-Cook, "Location Matters."

26. Ibid.

27. Clay Masters, "Rural or Urban, Food Deserts Are a Tough Fix," *Harvest Public Media*, July 21, 2011, http://harvestpublicmedia.org/article/657/rural-or-urban-food-deserts-are-tough-fix/5.

28. Some illustrative examples of research that address the variety of perspectives on material rhetoric include Ronald Walter Greene, "Another Materialist Rhetoric," *Critical Studies in Mass Communication* 15, no. 1 (1998): 21–41; Barbara A. Biesecker and John Louis Lucaites, *Rhetoric, Materiality, and Politics* (New York: Peter Lang, 2009); Dana L. Cloud, "The Materiality of Discourse as Oxymoron: A Challenge to Critical Rhetoric," *Western Journal of Communication* 58, no. 3 (1994): 141–63; Blair, "Contemporary U.S. Memorial Sites as Exemplars of Rhetoric's Materiality."

29. Endres and Senda-Cook, "Location Matters."

30. Logan, "Banners' Creators Are Gone, and Soon Grain Elevators' Art Will Be, Too."

31. Michael Middleton, "'SafeGround Sacramento' and Rhetorics of Substantive Citizenship," *Western Journal of Communication* 78, no. 2 (2014): 119–33.

Chapter 2

1. Our experience of marching underlined the improvisational structure of the Occupations. Individuals brought their own signs and initiated their own chants without a central orchestrating committee (all signs and chants featured in the dramatization of part 1 are taken from ethnographic notes from the October 15th, 22nd, and 29th marches). Although largely impromptu, the legal requirements for protesting did require some advance planning by a small organizing committee to acquire the legal permits to march. This minimal legalism aside, the marches themselves were filled with the kind of carnivalesque behavior now *de rigueur* for social protest: clever chants, rhythmic drumming, wide-ranging conversations, and occasionally people dressed in devil masks (Field Note 24). Perhaps in part because of the improvisational nature of the protests, a wide variety of people were there, including those with explicit religious associations. During our time at the protests we noticed a plethora of religious iconography and metaphor, an adaptation to a highly religious part of the country. For instance, a small child carried a sign declaring "Jesus was one of the 99%" (Field Note 19). [This note is reproduced from the original essay; field notes are available at http://damiensmithpfister.net/occupy-lincoln/.]

2. Joshua P. Ewalt, Jessy J. Ohl, and Damien Smith Pfister, "Activism, Deliberation, and Networked Public Screens: Rhetorical Scenes from the Occupy Moment in Lincoln, Nebraska (Part 1)," *Cultural Studies ⟷ Critical Methodologies* 13, no. 3 (2013): 173–83. These scenes were modeled with the conventions of theatrical performance foregrounded; although the dialogue is written, we do not foreclose the possibility that other rhetorical scenes might be composed with different media.

3. Scholars working with rhetorical field methods have similarly located the *rhetorical* in rhetorical field methods. Aaron Hess, for instance, considers "fieldwork as a site of rhetorical production," focusing critical attention toward localized acts of invention, *kairos*, and *phronesis*. See Hess, "Critical-Rhetorical Ethnography: Rethinking the Place and Process of Rhetoric," *Communication Studies* 62, no. 2 (2011): 133. Middleton, Senda-Cook, and Endres identify the rhetorical in both "rhetorical intervention into rhetorical spaces and action" and the "processual forms of rhetorical action that are accessible only through participatory methods." See Michael K. Middleton, Samantha Senda-Cook, and Danielle Endres, "Articulating Rhetorical Field Methods: Challenges and Tensions," *Western Journal of Communication* 75, no. 4 (2011): 387. Our focus is specifically on maintaining the rhetoricity of the field in the process of writing research.

4. The pivot in rhetorical studies toward vernacular discourse attends to the everyday instances of public address that were elided in the discipline's earlier focus on institutional rhetorics of the presidency and election campaigns. See, for instance, Gerard A. Hauser, *Vernacular Voices: The Rhetoric of Publics and Public Spheres* (Columbia: University of South Carolina Press, 1999); and Kent Ono and John Sloop, "The Critique of Vernacular Discourse," *Communication Monographs* 62, no. 1 (1995): 19–46. Karma R. Chávez argues that one pronounced limitation involved with the overemphasis on traditional public address methods when applied to social movements research is the rarely recorded rhetorical work of coalition-building that occurs "behind the scenes." See Chávez, "Counter-Public Enclaves and Understanding the Function of

Rhetoric in Social Movement Coalition-Building," *Communication Quarterly* 59, no. 1 (2011): 2. Robert Glenn Howard, in "The Vernacular Web of Participatory Media," *Critical Studies in Media Communication* 25, no. 5 (2008): 490–513, underlines the importance of studying vernacular communication in the context of the contemporary, internetworked media ecology which increases public participation (and the publicity of that participation). Regardless of whether vernacular discourse occurs in private coffeehouse discussions or on public online forums, rhetorical field methods provide an avenue to register spontaneous, inventive, and unconventional forms of communicative activity that often elude some of the traditional, text-centric approaches of rhetorical scholarship.

5. Michael Calvin McGee, "Text, Context, and the Fragmentation of Contemporary Culture," *Western Journal of Communication* 54, no. 3 (1990): 274–89.

6. Iris Marion Young, "Activist Challenges to Deliberative Democracy," in *Debating Deliberative Democracy*, ed. James Fishkin and Peter Laslett (Malden, MA: Blackwell, 2003), 102–20.

7. Rosi Braidotti, *The Posthuman* (Cambridge, UK: Polity Press, 2013).

8. Jenny Edbauer, "Unframing Models of Public Distribution: From Rhetorical Situation to Rhetorical Ecologies," *Rhetoric Society Quarterly* 35, no. 4 (2005): 5–24.

9. Lee Gutkind's *You Can't Make This Stuff Up: The Complete Guide to Writing Creative Nonfiction—From Memoir to Literary Journalism and Everything in Between* (Philadelphia: Da Capo Press, 2012) provides both a rationale for writing creative nonfiction and a method for engaging in this kind of reconstructive writing.

10. The phrase "rhetorical scenes" is used by Peter Simonson to describe key episodes in his ethnographic journey as a rhetorically trained participant observer embedded in South Texas during the 2008 presidential primary. See Simonson, "The Streets of Laredo: Mercurian Rhetoric and the Obama Campaign," *Western Journal of Communication* 74, no. 1 (2010): 94–126. Simonson usefully underlines the importance of embodied participation and performative criticism in rhetorical scholarship. We push his notion of rhetorical scenes further by moving beyond prose exposition to the actual production of scenes designed for dramatic reenactment. Such an approach takes seriously Richard Leo Enos's call for "the sort of adventurous fieldwork that pushes back the frontiers of our discipline." See Enos, "The Archaeology of Women in Rhetoric: Rhetorical Sequencing as a Research Method for Historical Scholarship," *Rhetoric Society Quarterly* 32, no. 1 (2002): 68. For an example of a decidedly performative take on the study of cultural rhetoric, see Malea Powell, Daisy Levy, Andrea Riley-Mukavetz, Marilee Brooks-Gillies, Maria Novotny, and Jennifer Fisch-Ferguson, "Our Story Begins Here: Constellating Cultural Rhetorics," *Enculturation* (October 2014): 1–25.

11. Kenneth Burke, *A Grammar of Motives* (Berkeley: University of California Press, 1945), 3.

12. Della Pollock, "Marking New Directions in Performance Ethnography," *Text and Performance Quarterly* 26, no. 4 (2006): 325.

13. John Muckelbauer, *The Future of Invention: Rhetoric, Postmodernism, and the Problem of Change* (Albany: State University of New York Press, 2008).

14. Ibid., 56.

15. Plato, *The Republic*, trans. Allan Bloom (New York: Basic Books, 1991).

16. Edward Erdmann, "Imitation Pedagogy and Ethical Indoctrination," *Rhetoric Society Quarterly* 23, no. 1 (1993): 1–11.

17. Robert Hariman, "Civic Education, Classical Imitation, and Democratic Polity," in *Isocrates and Civic Education*, ed. Takis Poulakos and David Depew (Austin: University of Texas Press, 2004), 217–35.

18. Cicero, *De Oratore*, trans. J. S. Watson (Carbondale: Southern Illinois University Press, 1970), 2.22.

19. Elaine Fantham, "Imitation and Evolution: The Discussion of Rhetorical Imitation in Cicero *De Oratore* 2.87–97 and Some Related Problems of Ciceronian Theory," *Classical Philology* 73, no. 1 (1978): 14.

20. D. Soyini Madison, "Performing Theory/Embodied Writing," *Text and Performance Quarterly* 19, no. 2 (1999): 109.

21. Linda Alcoff, "The Problem of Speaking for Others," *Cultural Critique* 20 (Winter 1991): 5–32.

22. Dwight Conquergood, "Rethinking Ethnography: Towards a Critical Cultural Politics," *Communication Monographs* 58, no. 2 (1991): 193.

23. See also Middleton, Senda-Cook, and Endres, "Articulating Rhetorical Field Methods."

24. Jacques Derrida, "Signature, Event, and Context," in *Limited Inc* (Evanston, IL: Northwestern University Press, 1998), 9.

25. Ibid.

26. Quintilian, *On the Teaching and Speaking of Writing: Translations from Books One, Two, and Ten of the Institutio Oratoria*, trans. J. Murphy (Carbondale: Southern Illinois University Press, 1987), 130.

27. Quintilian, *Institutio Oratoria*, X, ii, 26.

28. Rob Pope, *Textual Intervention: Critical and Creative Strategies for Literary Studies* (New York: Routledge, 1995), 1.

29. Hess, "Critical-Rhetorical Ethnography," 139.

30. Subsequent informal conversations with Occupiers who were disenchanted by the process supported our point. On the one hand, some more deliberative members did not appreciate the activists who showed up late after other camps had been closed because "they were too radical" and did not cooperate with the police. On the other, we have talked to activists who thought the consensus process ruined the movement.

31. We believe the deconstructive-analytic sensibility that undergirds many efforts to capture vernacular interaction is absolutely crucial in generating vocabularies supple enough to theorize everyday communication, but that the reconstructive-performative vein we are mining opens up new avenues for inquiry. The reconstructive-performative and deconstructive-analytic are not competitive modes, as evidenced by how our initial production of rhetorical scenes was paired with a more traditional essay grounded in the scholarly literature. See Joshua P. Ewalt, Jessy J. Ohl, and Damien Smith Pfister, "Activism, Deliberation, and Networked Public Screens (Part 2)," *Cultural Studies ↔ Critical Methodologies* 13, no. 3 (2013): 184–90.

32. Muckelbauer, *Future of Invention*, 74.

33. Ibid., 75.

34. Ibid., 74–75.

35. Ibid., 76.

36. Quintilian, *The Orator's Education*, ed. and trans. Donald A. Russell (Cambridge, MA: Harvard University Press, 2001), II, xxi.

37. Terrill, "Mimesis, Duality, and Rhetorical Education," *Rhetoric Society Quarterly* 41, no. 4 (2011): 306.

38. Quintilian, *Orator's Education*, II, xxi.

39. David Fleming, "Rhetoric as a Course of Study," *College English* 61, no. 2 (1998): 178–79.

40. Elaine Fantham, "Imitation and Decline: Rhetorical Theory and Practice in the First Century after Christ," *Classical Philology* 73, no. 2 (1978): 109.

41. Quintilian, *Institutio Oratoria*, X, v, 4–8.

42. Madison, "Performing Theory," 109.

43. John Sloop, "Learning to Perform," *Text and Performance Quarterly* 34, no. 1 (2014): 108–10.

44. Stephen Ramsay, *Reading Machines: Toward an Algorithmic Criticism* (Urbana: University of Illinois Press, 2011), 31.

45. Alcoff, "Problem of Speaking for Others." See, particularly, Hess, "Critical-Rhetorical Ethnography."

46. Celeste Condit, "How Should Our Rhetoric Make Us Feel," in *Purpose, Practice, and Pedagogy in Rhetorical Criticism*, ed. Jim A. Kuypers (Lanham, MD: Lexington Books, 2014), 50–51. For an example of Isocratean criticism cited by Condit, see Leah Ceccarelli, "Manufactured Scientific Controversy: Science, Rhetoric, and Public Debate," *Rhetoric and Public Affairs* 14, no. 2 (2011): 195–228. For a similar argument about the social change potential of *imitatio*, see Charles E. Morris III, "Sunder the Children: Abraham Lincoln's Queer Rhetorical Pedagogy," *Quarterly Journal of Speech* 99, no. 4 (2013): 395–422.

Chapter 3

1. I avoid imposed Spanish and U.S. colonial terminology, and take ownership of otherwise borrowed names for the island and indigenous population. See Julian Aguon, *Just Left of the Setting Sun* (Tokyo: Blue Ocean Press, 2006), 12–15.

2. Jon M. Van Dyke, Carmen Di Amore-Siah, and Gerald W. Berkley-Coats, "Self-Determination for Nonself-governing Peoples and for Indigenous Peoples: The Cases of Guam and Hawai'i," *University of Hawai'i Law Review* 18, no. 2 (1996): 623–44.

3. Joseph Gerson, "Offensive Military Bases and a Troubled Alliance in Japan," *Peace Review: A Journal of Social Justice* 22, no. 2 (2010): 128–35.

4. David Hanlon, "The 'Sea of Little Lands': Examining Micronesia's Place in 'Our Sea of Islands,'" *The Contemporary Pacific* 21, no. 1 (2009): 91–110. See also Keith L. Camacho, "Transoceanic Flows: Pacific Islander Interventions across the American Empire," *Amerasia Journal* 37, no. 3 (2011): ix–xxxiv.

5. Tiara R. Na'puti, "Speaking the Language of Peace: Chamoru Resistance and Rhetoric in Guåhan's Self-Determination Movement," *Anthropologica* 56, no. 2 (2014): 301–13.

6. Hanlon, "Sea of Little Lands," 100. See Vicente M. Diaz, "No Island Is an Island," in *Native Studies Keywords*, ed. Stephanie Nohelani Teves, Andrea Smith, and Michelle H. Raheja (Tucson: University of Arizona Press, 2015), 90–91.

7. Raka Shome, "Postcolonial Interventions in the Rhetorical Canon: An 'Other' View," *Communication Theory* 6, no. 1 (1996): 40–59; Raka Shome and Radha Hegde, "Culture, Communication, and the Challenge of Globalization," *Critical Studies in Media Communication* 19, no. 2 (2010): 172–89; Darrel A. Wanzer, "Delinking Rhetoric, or Revisiting McGee's Fragmentation Thesis through Decoloniality," *Rhetoric and Public Affairs* 15, no. 4 (2012): 647–57.

8. Shome, "Postcolonial Interventions," 41.

9. Kuan-Hsing Chen, introduction to *Trajectories: Inter-Asia Cultural Studies*, ed. Kuan-Hsing Chen (New York: Routledge, 1998), 2.

10. Shome and Hegde, "Culture, Communication," 187.

11. Wanzer, "Delinking Rhetoric," 648.

12. Candace Fujikane, "Asian American Critique and Moana Nui, 2011: Securing a Future beyond Empires, Militarized Capitalism, and APEC," *Inter-Asia Cultural Studies* 13, no. 2 (2012): 189–210.

13. This approach follows arguments for extending the study of Asia as a method to reorient an Asian American critique and shift toward post-imperial futures. See ibid., 192.

14. Penelope Bordallo Hofschneider, *A Campaign for Political Rights on the Island of Guam, 1899–1950* (Saipan: CNMI Division of Historic Preservation), 18.

15. LisaLinda Natividad and Gwyn Kirk, "Fortress Guam: Resistance to U.S. Military Mega-Buildup," *Asia-Pacific Journal* (May 2010): http://www.japanfocus.org/-Gwyn-Kirk/3356.

16. Frank Quimby, "Fortress Guåhan: Chamorro Nationalism, Regional Economic Integration, and U.S. Defence Interests Shape Guam's Recent History," *Journal of Pacific History* 46, no. 3 (2011): 357–80.

17. Tiara R. Na'puti and Allison Hahn, "Plebiscite Deliberations: Self-Determination and Deliberative Democracy in Guam," *Journal of Public Deliberation* 9, no. 2 (2014): http://www.publicdeliberation.net/jpd/vol9/iss2/art11/.

18. Michael P. Perez, "Chamorro Resistance and the Prospects for Sovereignty in Guam," in *Sovereignty Matters: Locations of Contestation and Possibility in Indigenous Struggles for Self-Determination*, ed. Joanne Barker (Lincoln: University of Nebraska Press, 2005), 172.

19. Ronald Stade, *Pacific Passages: World Culture and Local Politics in Guam* (Stockholm: Department of Social Anthropology, Stockholm University, 1998), 47.

20. Keith L. Camacho and Laurel A. Monnig, "Uncomfortable Fatigues: Chamorro Soldiers, Gendered Identities, and the Question of Decolonization in Guam," in *Militarized Currents: Toward a Decolonized Future in Asia and the Pacific*, ed. Setsu Shigematsu and Keith L. Camacho (Minneapolis: University of Minnesota Press, 2010), 150. See also Ronni Alexander, "Militarization and Identity on Guåhan/Guam: Exploring Intersections of Indigeneity, Gender, and Security," *Journal of International Cooperation Studies* 21, no. 7 (2013): 11–22.

21. Catherine Lutz, "U.S. Military Bases on Guam in Global Perspective," *Asia-Pacific Journal* (July 2010): http://www.japanfocus.org/-catherine-lutz/3389.

22. Leevin Camacho and Daniel Broudy, "'Sweetening' the Pentagon's Deal in the Marianas: From Guam to Pagan," *Asia-Pacific Journal* (July 2013): http://www.japanfocus.org/-Leevin-Camacho/3963.

23. Patrick Wolfe, *Settler Colonialism and the Transformation of Anthropology: The Politics and Poetics of an Ethnographic Event* (London: Cassell, 1999), 26–27.

24. Ibid., 1.

25. Linda Tuhiwai Smith, *Decolonizing Methodologies: Research and Indigenous Peoples* (New York: Zed Books, 2012), 204; see also Jodi A. Byrd, *The Transit of Empire: Indigenous Critiques of Colonialism* (Minneapolis: University of Minnesota Press, 2011), xix.

26. Kevin Bruyneel, *The Third Space of Sovereignty: The Postcolonial Politics of U.S.-Indigenous Relations* (Minneapolis: University of Minnesota Press, 2007), 220.

27. Natividad and Kirk, "Fortress Guam"; Camacho and Broudy, "Sweetening."

28. Lutz, "U.S. Military Bases."

29. Epeli Hau'ofa, "Our Sea of Islands," in *A New Oceania: Rediscovering Our Sea of Islands*, ed. Eric Waddell, Vijay Naidu, and Epeli Hau'ofa (Suva: University of the South Pacific, 1993), 6–8.

30. Vicente M. Diaz, "Sniffing Oceania's Behind," *The Contemporary Pacific* 24, no. 2 (2012): 324–44.

31. Ilana Gershon, "Viewing Diasporas from the Pacific: What Pacific Ethnographies Offer Pacific Diaspora Studies," *The Contemporary Pacific* 19, no. 2 (2007): 474–502.

32. Wolfe, *Settler Colonialism*, 5.

33. Patricia Hill Collins, "Learning from the Outsider Within: The Sociological Significance of Black Feminist Thought," *Social Problems* 33, no. 6 (1986): S14–S15.

34. Victor Turner, *Blazing the Trail: Way Marks in the Exploration of Symbols* (Tucson: University of Arizona Press, 1992), 49–50.

35. Gloria Anzaldúa, *Borderlands / La Frontera: The New Mestiza* (San Francisco: Aunt Lute Books, 1999), 78–86.

36. Homi K. Bhabha, *The Location of Culture* (London: Routledge, 1994), 53–54.

37. Collins, "Learning," S14; Patricia Hill Collins, *Fighting Words: Black Women and the Search for Justice* (Minneapolis: University of Minnesota Press, 1998), 5–6.

38. Turner, *Blazing the Trail*, 49–50.

39. Bhabha, *Location of Culture*, 1; Homi K. Bhabha, "Culture's In Between," in *Questions of Cultural Identity*, ed. Stuart Hall and Paul DuGay (London: Sage, 1996), 57–58.

40. Byrd, *Transit of Empire*, xv.

41. Bo Wang, "Comparative Rhetoric, Postcolonial Studies, and Transnational Feminisms: A Geopolitical Approach," *Rhetoric Society Quarterly* 43, no. 2 (2013): 226–42.

42. Dwight Conquergood, "Ethnography, Rhetoric, and Performance," *Quarterly Journal of Speech* 78, no. 1 (1992): 80–97; Gerald Hauser, "Attending the Vernacular: A Plea for Ethnographical Rhetoric," in *The Rhetorical Emergence of Culture, 1780–1834*, ed. Christian Meyer and Felix Girke (New York: Berghahn Books), 163–64.

43. Michael K. Middleton, Samantha Senda-Cook, and Danielle Endres, "Articulating Rhetorical Field Methods: Challenges and Tensions," *Western Journal of Communication* 75, no. 4 (2011): 389.

44. Karma R. Chávez, "Remapping *Latinidad*: A Performance Cartography of Latina/o Identity in Rural Nebraska," *Text and Performance Quarterly* 29, no. 2 (2009): 165–82; Middleton, Senda-Cook, and Andres, "Articulating Rhetorical Field Methods," 388.

45. Lisa Flores, "Creating Discursive Space through a Rhetoric of Difference: Chicana Feminists Craft a Homeland," *Quarterly Journal of Speech* 82, no. 2 (1996): 142–56.

46. Ibid., 143–45.

47. Paul D'Arcy, *The People of the Sea: Environment, Identity, and History* (Honolulu: University of Hawai'i Press, 2006), 8.

48. Jodi A. Byrd and Michael Rothberg, "Between Subalternity and Indigeneity: Critical Categories for Postcolonial Studies," *Interventions* 13, no. 1 (2011): 3–4; Vicente M. Diaz and J. Kehaulani Kauanui, "Native Pacific Cultural Studies on the Edge," *The Contemporary Pacific* 13, no. 2 (2001): 315–42.

49. Camacho, "Transoceanic Flows," xiii.

50. Mishuana Goeman, "From Place to Territories and Back Again: Centering Storied Land in the Discussion of Indigenous Nation-Building," *International Journal of Critical Indigenous Studies* 1, no. 1 (2008): 23–34.

51. Diaz, "No Island Is an Island," 90–92.

52. Hau'ofa, "Our Sea of Islands," 13–15.

53. Goeman, "From Place to Territories," 24.

54. Hau'ofa, "Our Sea of Islands," 13–15.

55. Chela Sandoval, *Methodology of the Oppressed* (Minneapolis: University of Minnesota, 2000), 44.4–44.5.

56. Aimee Carrillo Rowe, "Be Longing: Toward a Feminist Politics of Relation," *NWSA Journal* 17, no. 2 (2005): 15–46.

57. Karma R. Chávez, "Border (In)Securities: Normative and Differential Belonging in LGBTQ and Immigrant Rights Discourse," *Communication and Critical/Cultural Studies* 7, no. 2 (2010): 136–55.

58. Bernadette M. Calafell, "Identities: Considering Accountability, Reflexivity, and Intersectionality in the I and the We," *Liminalities: A Journal of Performance Studies* 9, no. 2 (2013): 6–13.

59. Rowe, "Be Longing," 15.

60. Stacey Sowards, "Rhetorical Agency as *Haciendo Caras* and Differential Consciousness through Lens of Gender, Race, Ethnicity, and Class: An Examination of Dolores Huerta's Rhetoric," *Communication Theory* 20, no. 2 (2010): 223–47.

61. Lanita Jacobs-Huey, "The Natives Are Gazing and Talking Back: Reviewing the Problematics of Positionality, Voice, and Accountability among 'Native' Anthropologists," *American Anthropologist* 104, no. 3 (2002): 791–804.

62. Vicente M. Diaz, *Repositioning the Missionary: Rewriting the Histories of Colonialism, Native Catholicism, and Indigeneity in Guam* (Honolulu: University of Hawai'i Press, 2010), 1–7.

63. Jacobs-Huey, "The Natives," 791.

64. Darrel Enck-Wanzer, "Trashing the System: Social Movement, Intersectional Rhetoric, and Collective Agency in the Young Lords Organization's Garbage Offensive," *Quarterly Journal of Speech* 92, no. 2 (2006): 176–77; Sowards, "Rhetorical Agency," 226–27.

65. Epeli Hau'ofa, "Pasts to Remember," in *Remembrances of Pacific Pasts: An Invitation to Remake History*, ed. Robert Borofsky (Honolulu: University of Hawai'i Press, 2000), 458–59.

66. Smith, *Decolonizing Methodologies*, 39.

67. Jolanta A. Drzewiecka and Rona Tamiko Halualani, "The Structural-Cultural Dialectic of Diasporic Politics," *Communication Theory* 12, no. 3 (2002): 340–66. See also Michael L. Bevacqua, "The Exceptional Life and Death of a Chamorro Soldier: Tracing the Militarization of Desire in Guam," in *Militarized Currents: Toward a Decolonized Future in Asia and the Pacific*, ed. Setsu Shigematsu and Keith L. Camacho (Minneapolis: University of Minnesota Press, 2010), 42; Smith, *Decolonizing Methodologies*, 24.

68. Vicente M. Diaz, "Voyaging for Anti-colonial Recovery: Austronesian Seafaring, Archipelagic Rethinking, and the Re-mapping of Indigeneity," *Pacific Asia Inquiry* 2, no. 1 (2011): 21–32.

69. Barry Brummett, *Rhetoric in Popular Culture* (New York: St Martin's Press, 1994), 80.

70. Bernard J. Armada, "Memorial Agon: An Interpretive Tour of the National Civil Rights Museum," *Southern Communication Journal* 63, no. 3 (1998): 235–43.

71. Greg Dickinson, Brian L. Ott, and Erik Aoki, "Spaces of Remembering and Forgetting: The Reverent Eye/I at the Plains Indian Museum," *Communication and Critical/Cultural Studies* 3, no. 1 (2006): 227–47.

72. Middleton, Senda-Cook, and Endres, "Articulating Rhetorical Field Methods," 387–94.

73. Wang, "Comparative Rhetoric," 228.

74. Kent A. Ono and John M. Sloop, "Commitment to *Telos*: A Sustained Critical Rhetoric," *Communication Monographs* 59, no. 1 (1992): 48–60; Hauser, "Attending the Vernacular," 165.

75. Wanzer, "Delinking Rhetoric," 652.

76. Smith, *Decolonizing Methodologies*, 39.

77. Richard Wilkins and Karen Wolf, "The Role of Ethnography in Rhetorical Analysis: The New Rhetorical Turn," *Empedocles: European Journal for the Philosophy of Communication* 3, no. 1 (2011): 7–23.

78. Camacho and Broudy, "Sweetening."

79. Bevacqua, "Exceptional Life," 33.

80. Michael P. Perez, "Contested Sites: Pacific Resistance in Guam to U.S. Empire," *Amerasia Journal* 27, no. 1 (2001): 97–114.

81. J. Kehaulani Kauanui, "Diasporic Deracination and 'Off-Island' Hawaiians," *The Contemporary Pacific* 19, no. 1 (2007): 138–60.

82.   Stade, *Pacific Passages*, 48.

83.   Perez, "Contested Sites," 97.

84.   "'Heritage Hikes: Tungo' I Estoria-Ta' throughout the Month of November," *Marianas Variety*, November 4, 2010, mvguam.com.

85.   Interview 1, interview by Tiara Na'puti, Hagåtña, Guam, August 4, 2011. All interviews were conducted in confidentiality. For the Manenggon Walk see KUAM News, "Manenggon Walk Honors Chamorro Lives Lost in WWII," *YouTube* video, 9:34, posted by "kuamnews," July 9, 2011, http://www.youtube.com/watch?v=9h8ccJDkBk4.

86.   Interview 1, August 4, 2011. For further discussion of inafa' maolek and Heritage Hikes, see Tiara R. Na'puti and Michael Lujan Bevacqua, "Militarization and Resistance from Guåhan: Protecting and Defending Pågat," *American Quarterly* 67, no. 3 (2015): 847–52.

87.   Ibid.

88.   Leevin Camacho, "Resisting the Proposed Military Buildup on Guam," in *Under Occupation: Resistance and Struggle in a Militarised Asia-Pacific*, ed. Daniel Broudy, Peter Simpson, and Makoto Arakaki (Newcastle upon Tyne, UK: Cambridge Scholars Publishing, 2013), 189.

89.   Epeli Hau'ofa, "The Ocean in Us," *The Contemporary Pacific* 10, no. 2 (1998): 391–410.

90.   Michael P. Perez, "Pacific Identities beyond U.S. Racial Formations: The Case of Chamorro Ambivalence and Flux," *Social Identities* 8, no. 3 (2002): 457–79.

91.   Rowe, "Be Longing," 15.

92.   Julian Aguon, "On Loving the Maps Our Hands Cannot Hold: Self-Determination of Colonized and Indigenous Peoples in International Law," *UCLA Asian Pacific American Law Journal* 16, no. 1 (2010–11): 47–73.

93.   Bevacqua, "Exceptional Life," 42.

94.   Mindy Aguon, "Guam Gets 90 Days to Review EIS," KUAM News, October 28, 2009, http://www.kuam.com/global/story.asp?s=11402872.

95.   LisaLinda S. Natividad and Victoria-Lola Leon Guerrero, "The Explosive Growth of U.S. Military Power on Guam Confronts People Power: Experiences of an Island People under Spanish, Japanese, and American Colonial Rule," *Asia-Pacific Journal* (December 2010): http://www.japanfocus.org/-Victoria_Lola_Leon-Guerrero/3454.

96.   Ibid.

97.   Ibid.

98.   Camacho and Broudy, "Sweetening."

99.   Ibid.

Chapter 4

1.   Michael Osborn, "'I've Been to the Mountaintop': The Critic as Participant," in *Texts in Context: Critical Dialogues on Significant Episodes in American Political Rhetoric*, ed. Michael C. Leff and Fred J. Kauffeld (Davis, CA: Hermagoras Press, 1989), 149.

2.   For a critique of how ideological rhetorical criticism subsumes or subordinates affect or emotion with ideology and logos, see Celeste M. Condit, "Pathos in Criticism: Edwin Black's Communism-as-Cancer Metaphor" *Quarterly Journal of Speech* 99, no. 2 (2013): 1–26.

3.   Michael Calvin McGee, "A Materialist's Conception of Rhetoric," in *Explorations in Rhetoric: Studies in Honor of Douglas Ehninger*, ed. Raymie E. McKerrow (Glenview, IL: Scott Foresman and Company, 1982), 23–48; Michael Calvin McGee, "Text, Context, and the Fragmentation of Contemporary Culture," *Western Journal of Speech Communication* 54, no. 3 (1990): 274–89; Philip Wander, "The Ideological Turn in Modern Criticism," *Central States Speech Journal* 34, no. 1 (1983): 1–18; Philip Wander, "The Third Persona: An Ideological Turn in Rhetorical Theory," *Communication Studies* 35, no. 4 (1984): 197–216; Raymie McKerrow, "Critical Rhetoric: Theory and Praxis," *Communication Monographs* 56, no. 2 (1989): 91–111.

4.   Sharon Crowley, "Reflections on an Argument That Won't Go Away: or, A Turn of the Ideological Screw," *Quarterly Journal of Speech* 78, no. 4 (1992): 450–65.

5.   McGee, "Text, Context," 275.

6.   Ibid., 282.

7.   An extended version of McGee's article, "Text, Context, and the Fragmentation of American Culture," was documented online, at http://mcgeefragments.net/OLD/text.htm, though it is no longer available.

8. Wander, "Ideological Turn," 18.

9. McKerrow, "Critical Rhetoric," 108.

10. John M. Sloop, *Disciplining Gender: Rhetorics of Sex Identity in Contemporary U.S. Culture* (Amherst: University of Massachusetts Press, 2004), 18.

11. Ibid., 143–44.

12. Charles E. Morris III, "(Self-)Portrait of Prof. R.C.: A Retrospective," *Western Journal of Communication* 74, no. 1 (2010): 9.

13. Phaedra C. Pezzullo, *Toxic Tourism: Rhetorics of Pollution, Travel, and Environmental Justice* (Tuscaloosa: University of Alabama Press, 2009), 18.

14. Debra Hawhee, "Rhetoric's Sensorium," *Quarterly Journal of Speech* 101, no. 1 (2015): 2–17.

15. Thomas Benson, "Another Shooting in Cowtown," *Quarterly Journal of Speech* 67, no. 1 (1981): 387.

16. Peter Simonson, "The Streets of Laredo: Mercurian Rhetoric and the Obama Campaign," *Western Journal of Communication* 74, no. 1 (2010): 97.

17. Thomas Benson, "A Scandal in Academia: Sextext and CRTNET," *Western Journal of Communication* 76, no. 1 (2012): 11.

18. Thomas K. Nakayama and Robert L. Krizek, "Whiteness: A Strategic Rhetoric," *Quarterly Journal of Speech* 81, no. 3 (1995): 231–309.

19. Michaela D. E. Meyer, "Women Speak(ing): Forty Years of Feminist Contributions to Rhetoric and an Agenda for Feminist Rhetorical Studies," *Communication Quarterly* 55, no. 1 (2007): 9.

20. Joshua Gunn, "On Speech and Public Release," *Rhetoric and Public Affairs* 13, no. 2 (2010): 1–41.

21. Ibid., 3–4.

22. Ibid., 22.

23. Gunn presented an early version of this essay in 2008 at the Eleventh Biennial Public Address Conference and the audience "went with it," since people "laughed and had a good time," according to Gunn in an e-mail to me. The scheduled conference response was also titled "In Praise of the Yawp," which affirms the feeling critic. However, Gunn said that the reviewers of his submission to *Rhetoric and Public Affairs* were, "as is the case with academic writing, more reserved." I mention this discrepancy to demonstrate the "disciplinary" conventions of *writing* and *publishing* feeling rhetorical criticism in particular.

24. Joshua Gunn and Jenny E. Rice, "About Face/Stuttering Discipline," *Communication and Critical/Cultural Studies* 6, no. 2 (2009): 215–19.

25. Ibid., 217.

26. Joshua Gunn, "Speech Is Dead; Long Live Speech," *Quarterly Journal of Speech* 94, no. 3 (2008): 360.

27. In 1991 Dwight Conquergood diagnosed this problem in most academic disciplines (including communication) when noting, "Patriarchal constructions that align women with the body, and men with mental faculties, help keep the mind-body, reason-emotion, objective-subjective, as well as masculine-feminine hierarchies stable." See "Rethinking Ethnography: Towards a Critical Cultural Politics," *Communication Monographs* 58, no. 2 (1991): 180.

28. Amanda Lotz points out this criticism of reflexivity in "Assessing Qualitative Television Audience Research: Incorporating Feminist and Anthropological Theoretical Innovation," *Communication Theory* 10, no. 4 (2000): 455.

29. Wen Shu Lee, "In the Names of Chinese Women," *Quarterly Journal of Speech* 84, no. 3 (1998): 297–98.

30. Ibid., 297.

31. Carole Blair, Julie R. Brown, and Leslie A. Baxter, "Disciplining the Feminine," *Quarterly Journal of Speech* 80, no. 4 (1994): 383–409.

32. Gunn, "On Speech and Public Release," 35n63.

33. Brian Massumi, *Parables for the Virtual: Movement, Affect, Sensation* (Durham, NC: Duke University Press, 2002), 27.

34. Ibid., 35.

35. Ibid., 28.

36. Deborah B. Gould, *Moving Politics: Emotion and ACT UP's Fight against AIDS* (Chicago: University of Chicago Press, 2009), 22.

37. Hawhee, "Rhetoric's Sensorium," 12.

38. See phenomenological philosophy by Edmund Husserl, Jean Paul Sartre, Martin Heidegger, and Maurice Merleau-Ponty.

39. Sara Ahmed, *The Cultural Politics of Emotion* (New York: Routledge, 2004), 14.

40. Conquergood, "Rethinking Ethnography;" Carolyn Ellis, "Evocative Autoethnography: Writing Emotionally about Our Lives," in *Representation and the Text: Reframing the Narrative Voice*, ed. William Tierney and Yvonna Lincoln (Albany: State University of New York Press, 1997), 115–39; Carolyn Ellis, "Heartful Autoethnography," *Qualitative Health Research* 9, no. 5 (1999): 669–83; Laura L. Ellingson, "Embodied Knowledge: Writing Researchers' Bodies into Qualitative Health Research," *Qualitative Health Research* 16, no. 2 (2006): 298–310; Laura. L. Ellingson and Carolyn Ellis, "Autoethnography as Constructionist Project," in *Handbook of Constructionist Research*, ed. James A. Holstein and Jaber F. Gubrium (New York: Guilford Press, 2008), 445–66.

41. Gunn, "On Speech and Public Release," 21.

42. Ibid., 23.

43. Emily Winderman, "S(anger) Goes Postal in *The Woman Rebel*: Angry Rhetoric as Collectivizing Moral Emotion," *Rhetoric and Public Affairs* 17, no. 3 (2014): 381–420.

44. Ahmed, *Cultural Politics of Emotion*, 12.

45. Gould, *Moving Politics*, 233.

46. Thomas R. Lindlof and Bryan C. Taylor, *Qualitative Communication Research Methods* (Thousand Oaks, CA: Sage, 2002), 159.

47. Ibid., 159.

48. Ibid., 158–69.

49. Massumi, *Parables for the Virtual*, 35–36.

50. Gunn, "On Speech and Public Release," 5.

51. Ibid., 15.

52. Ibid., 11.

53. Gould, *Moving Politics*, 23.

54. Ibid., 30.

55. Ibid., 329–31.

56. Samuel McCormick and Mary Stuckey, "Presidential Disfluency: Literacy, Legibility, and Vocal Political Aesthetics in the Rhetorical Presidency," *Review of Communication* 13, no. 1 (2013): 4.

57. Along with Gunn and McCormick and Stuckey, see Greg Goodale, "The Presidential Sound: From Orotund to Instructional Speech, 1892–1912," *Quarterly Journal of Speech* 96, no. 2 (2010): 164–84; Greg Goodale, *Sonic Persuasion: Reading Sound in the Recorded Age* (Urbana: University of Illinois Press, 2011).

58. Carole Blair, "Contemporary U.S. Memorial Sites as Exemplars of Rhetoric's Materiality," in *Rhetorical Bodies*, ed. Jack Selzer and Sharon Crowley (Madison: University of Wisconsin Press, 1999), 16–57; Carole Blair and Neil Michel, "Commemorating in the Theme Park Zone: Reading the Astronauts Memorial," in *At the Intersection: Cultural Studies and Rhetorical Studies*, ed. Thomas Rosteck (New York: Guilford Press, 1999), 29–83; Greg Dickinson, Carole Blair, and Brian L. Ott, eds., *Places of Public Memory: The Rhetoric of Museums and Memorials* (Tuscaloosa: University of Alabama Press, 2010).

59. Condit, "Pathos in Criticism," 20.

60. Lindlof and Taylor, *Qualitative Communication Research Methods*, 16.

61. Nakayama and Krizek, "Whiteness," 303.

62. Ellingson, "Embodied Knowledge," 304.

63. Stephen King, *On Writing: A Memoir of the Craft* (New York: Scribner, 2000), 103–6.

64. Sabina Magliocco, "Beyond Belief: Context, Rationality, and Participatory Consciousness," *Western Folklore* 71, no. 1 (2012): 10–11.

65. Peter Elbow, *Writing without Teachers* (New York: Oxford University Press, 1998), 9.

66. Ibid., 4–8.

67. In addition to literature discussed in this chapter, a number of books outside of and within the field of communication are devoted exclusively to alternative writing formats. See, for example, John Van Maanen, *Tales of the Field: On Writing Ethnography* (Chicago: University of Chicago Press, 1988); Carolyn Ellis and Arthur P. Bochner, eds., *Composing Ethnography: Alternative Forms of Qualitative Writing* (Lanham, MD: AltaMira Press, 1996).

68. "About Premier Exhibitions," Premier Exhibitions, http://www.premierexhibitions.com/corporate/all/about-premier-exhibitions-inc.

69. "Premier Exhibitions Reports Full Year and Fourth Quarter 2013 Results," Premier Exhibitions, http://www.premierexhibitions.com/corporate/all/news/premier-exhibitions-reports-full-year-and-fourth-quarter-2013-results.

70. See "South Street Seaport" discussion on page 3 in Premier Exhibitions' annual report filed for the fiscal year ending in February 2014: http://www.premierexhibitions.com/sites/default/files/10K-05-27_0.pdf.

71. Reported statistical data from the "Bodies" website, accessed in October 2014: http://www.bodiestheexhibition.com/about-the-exhibition.html and http://www.bodiestheexhibition.com/ticket-pricing.html.

72. Rosalind Petchesky, "Fetal Images: The Power of Visual Culture in the Politics of Reproduction," in *Reproductive Technologies: Gender, Motherhood, and Medicine*, ed. Michelle Stanworth (Minneapolis: University of Minnesota Press, 1987), 57–79; Celeste M. Condit, *Decoding Abortion Rhetoric: Communicating Social Change* (Urbana: University of Illinois Press, 1990); Carole A. Stabile, *Feminism and the Technological Fix* (Manchester, UK: Manchester University Press, 1994); Susan M. Squier, *Babies in Bottles: Twentieth-Century Visions of Reproductive Technologies* (New Brunswick, NJ: Rutgers University Press, 1994).

73. For an astute sociological study of public museums that attends to the bodies of visitors, see Tony Bennett, "The Exhibitionary Complex," in *Thinking about Exhibitions*, ed. Reece Greenberg, Bruce W. Ferguson, and Sandy Nairne (London: Routledge, 1996), 81–112. Analyzing the bodies of visitors is also central to Blair's co-authored reading with Michel of people visiting the Kennedy Space Center and Walt Disney World in Florida, "Commemorating in the Theme Park Zone."

74. Laura L. Ellingson, "'Then You Know How I Feel': Empathy, Identification, and Reflexivity in Fieldwork," *Qualitative Health Inquiry* 4, no. 4 (1998): 510.

75. Carole Blair, "Reflections on Criticism and Bodies: Parables from Public Places," *Western Journal of Communication* 65, no. 3 (2001): 273.

Chapter 5

1. Robin Patric Clair, "Reflexivity and Rhetorical Ethnography: From Family Farm to Orphanage and Back Again," *Cultural Studies ↔ Critical Methodologies* 11, no. 2 (2011): 117–28; Gerard A. Hauser, "Attending the Vernacular: A Plea for an Ethnographic Rhetoric," in *The Rhetorical Emergence of Culture*, ed. Christian Meyer and Felix Girke (New York: Berghahn Books, 2011), 157–72; Aaron Hess, "Rhetorical Ethnography: Engaging the Politics of Advocacy" (PhD diss., Arizona State University, 2008); Don Waisanen, "Bordering Populism in Immigration Activism: Outlaw-Civic Discourse in a (Counter)Public," *Communication Monographs* 79, no. 2 (2012): 232–55.

2. Aaron Hess, "Critical-Rhetorical Ethnography: Rethinking the Place and Process of Rhetoric," *Communication Studies* 62, no. 2 (2011): 127–52.

3. Art Herbig and Aaron Hess, "Convergent Critical Rhetoric at the 'Rally to Restore Sanity': Exploring the Intersection of Rhetoric, Ethnography, and Documentary Production," *Communication Studies* 63, no. 3 (2012): 270.

4. Karma R. Chávez, "Counter-Public Enclaves and Understanding the Function of Rhetoric in Social Movement Coalition-Building," *Communication Quarterly* 59, no. 1 (2011): 1–18; Michael K. Middleton, Samantha Senda-Cook, and Danielle Endres, "Articulating Rhetorical Field Methods: Challenges and Tensions," *Western Journal of Communication* 75, no. 4 (2011): 386–406. For a discussion about the intersection of participant observation, rhetoric, and performance, see also Phaedra C. Pezzullo, "Resisting 'National Breast Cancer Awareness Month': The Rhetoric of Counterpublics and Their Cultural Performances," *Quarterly Journal of Speech* 89, no. 4 (2003): 345–65.

5. Hess, "Critical-Rhetorical Ethnography"; Hess, "Rhetorical Ethnography"; Clair, "Reflexivity and Rhetorical Ethnography"; Michael Middleton, Aaron Hess, Danielle Endres, and Samantha Senda-Cook, *Participatory Critical Rhetoric: Theoretical and Methodological Foundations for Studying Rhetoric in Situ* (Lanham, MD: Lexington Press, 2015).

6. Hess, "Critical-Rhetorical Ethnography."

7. Ibid.

8. Waisanen, "Bordering Populism."

9. Hess, "Critical-Rhetorical Ethnography."

10. Barry Brummett, "Some Implications of 'Process' or 'Intersubjectivity': Postmodern Rhetoric," *Philosophy and Rhetoric* 9, no. 1 (1976): 31.

11. See also Kent A. Ono and John M. Sloop, "The Critique of Vernacular Discourse," *Communication Monographs* 62, no. 1 (1995): 19; John M. Sloop and Kent A. Ono, "Out-Law Discourse: The Critical Politics of Material Judgment," *Philosophy and Rhetoric* 30, no. 1 (1997): 50–69; Kent A. Ono and John M. Sloop, "Critical Rhetorics of Controversy," *Western Journal of Communication* 63, no. 4 (1999): 526–38; Robert Glenn Howard, "The Vernacular Web of Participatory Media," *Critical Studies in Media Communication* 25, no. 5 (2008): 490–513; Gerard A. Hauser, *Vernacular Voices: The Rhetoric of Publics and Public Spheres* (Columbia: University of South Carolina Press, 1999).

12. Ono and Sloop, "Critique of Vernacular Discourse," 27.

13. Aaron Hess, "In Digital Remembrance: Vernacular Memory and the Rhetorical Construction of Web Memorials," *Media, Culture, and Society* 29, no. 5 (2007): 812–30; Aaron Hess, "Resistance up in Smoke: Analyzing the Limitations of Deliberation on YouTube," *Critical Studies in Media Communication* 26, no. 5 (2009): 411–34.

14. Bernadette Marie Calafell and Fernando P. Delgado, "Reading Latina/o Images: Interrogating Americanos," *Critical Studies in Media Communication* 21, no. 1 (2004): 1–24.

15. Raymie E. McKerrow, "Critical Rhetoric: Theory and Praxis," *Communications Monographs* 56, no. 2 (1989): 91–111.

16. Sloop and Ono, "Out-Law Discourse," 51.

17. Ibid., 52.

18. Hess, "Critical-Rhetorical Ethnography."

19. Benjamin R. Barber, *Strong Democracy: Participatory Politics for a New Age* (Berkeley: University of California Press, 2003).

20. Herbig and Hess, "Convergent Critical Rhetoric."

21. Hess, "Critical-Rhetorical Ethnography."

22. Edwin Black has a robust reading of Aristotle's take on judgment and rhetoric. See Black, *Rhetorical Criticism: A Study in Method* (Madison: University of Wisconsin Press, 1965), 93.

23. Ibid.; Wayne C. Booth, *The Company We Keep: An Ethics of Fiction* (Berkeley: University of California Press, 1988).

24. Black, *Rhetorical Criticism*, 135.

25. McKerrow, "Critical Rhetoric"; Michael Calvin McGee, "Text, Context, and the Fragmentation of Contemporary Culture," *Western Journal of Speech Communication* 54, no. 3 (1990): 274–89; Philip Wander, "The Third Persona: An Ideological Turn in Rhetorical Theory," *Central States Speech Journal* 35, no. 4 (1984): 197–216.

26. James Jasinski, "The Status of Theory and Method in Rhetorical Criticism," *Western Journal of Communication* 65, no. 3 (2001): 249–70.

27. Black, *Rhetorical Criticism*.

28. McKerrow, "Critical Rhetoric."

29. James P. McDaniel and John M. Sloop, "Hope's Finitude: An Introduction," in *Judgment Calls: Rhetoric, Politics, and Indeterminacy*, ed. John M. Sloop and James McDaniel (Boulder, CO: Westview Press, 1998), 3.

30. Sloop and Ono, "Out-Law Discourse."

31. Ono and Sloop, "Critical Rhetorics of Controversy," 535.

32. Jasinski, "Status of Theory and Method," 262.

33. Ibid., 260.

34. Hess, "Critical-Rhetorical Ethnography"; Aaron Hess, "On the Dance of Rhetoric: Ethnography, Embodiment, and Effect," in *The Effects of Rhetoric and the Rhetoric of Effects: Past, Present, Future*, ed. Amos Kiewe and Davis W. Houck (Columbia: University of South Carolina Press, 2015), 239–66.

35. Sloop and Ono, "Out-Law Discourse," 58.

36. Ronald Beiner, *Political Judgment* (London: Methuen Press, 1983), 7.

37. Sarah J. Tracy, *Qualitative Research Methods: Collecting Evidence, Crafting Analysis, Communicating Impact* (Malden, MA: Wiley-Blackwell, 2013); Bent Flyvbjerg, Todd Landman, and

Sanford Schram, *Real Social Science: Applied Phronesis* (Cambridge, UK: Cambridge University Press, 2012).

38. Beiner, *Political Judgment*, 72.

39. Lois S. Self, "Rhetoric and *Phronesis*: The Aristotelian Ideal," *Philosophy and Rhetoric* 12, no. 2 (1979): 130–45.

40. Takis Poulakos, *Speaking for the Polis: Isocrates' Rhetorical Education* (Columbia: University of South Carolina Press, 1997), 89.

41. Carrie Birmingham, "*Phronesis*: A Model for Pedagogical Reflection," *Journal of Teacher Education* 55, no. 4 (2004): 313–24.

42. Jim A. Kuypers, "*Doxa* and a Critical Rhetoric: Accounting for the Rhetorical Agent through Prudence," *Communication Quarterly* 44, no. 4 (1996): 452–62; Robert Hariman, "Prudence/Performance," *Rhetoric Society Quarterly* 21, no. 2 (1991): 26–35.

43. Self, "Rhetoric and *Phronesis*," 135.

44. Aristotle, *Nicomachean Ethics*, trans. F. H. Peters (New York: Barnes & Noble, 2004), 1141b; Barbara Warnick, "Judgment, Probability, and Aristotle's Rhetoric," *Quarterly Journal of Speech* 73, no. 3 (1989): 299–311; Christopher Lyle Johnstone, *Listening to the Logos: Speech and the Coming of Wisdom in Ancient Greece* (Columbia: South Carolina Press, 2009).

45. Steve Schwarze, "Performing *Phronesis*: The Case of Isocrates' *Helen*," *Philosophy and Rhetoric* 32, no. 1 (1999): 82.

46. Daniel L. Smith, "Intensifying *Phronesis*: Heidegger, Aristotle, and Rhetorical Culture," *Philosophy and Rhetoric* 36, no. 1 (2003): 88. For an additional discussion, see Michael Calvin McGee, "*Phronesis* in the Gadamer versus Habermas Debates," in *Judgment Calls: Rhetoric, Politics, and Indeterminacy*, ed. James. P. McDaniel and John. M. Sloop (Boulder, CO: Westview Press, 1998), 13–41.

47. Johnstone, *Listening to the Logos*, 207.

48. Scott Welsh, "Coming to Terms with the Antagonism between Rhetorical Reflection and Political Agency," *Philosophy and Rhetoric* 45, no. 1 (2012): 1–23.

49. Beiner, *Political Judgment*.

50. Hariman, "Prudence/Performance," 27.

51. Johnstone, *Listening to the Logos*, 210.

52. Thomas B. Farrell, *Norms of Rhetorical Culture* (New Haven, CT: Yale University Press, 1993), 98.

53. Sanford Schram, "Phronetic Social Science: An Idea Whose Time Has Come," in *Real Social Science: Applied Phronesis*, ed. Bent Flyvbjerg, Todd Landman, and Sanford Schram (Cambridge, UK: Cambridge University Press, 2012), 15–26.

54. Smith, "Intensifying *Phronesis*," 100.

55. Maurice Charland, "Finding a Horizon and *Telos*: The Challenge to Critical Rhetoric," *Quarterly Journal of Speech* 77, no. 1 (1991): 73. See also Maurice Charland, "Property and Propriety: Rhetoric, Justice, and Lyotard's *Differend*," in *Judgment Calls: Rhetoric, Politics, and Indeterminacy*, ed. John M. Sloop and James P. McDaniel (Boulder, CO: Westview Press, 1998), 220–36.

56. Charland, "Finding a Horizon," 74.

57. Smith, "Intensifying *Phronesis*," 101.

58. McGee, "*Phronesis* in the Gadamer versus Habermas Debates," 23.

59. Herbig and Hess, "Convergent Critical Rhetoric."

60. Schwarze, "Performing *Phronesis*," 83.

61. Art Herbig, Aaron Hess, and Alix Watson, *Never Forget: Public Memory and 9/11* (motion picture) (Living Text Productions, 2014).

62. Christopher P. Long, "The Ontological Reappropriation of *Phronēsis*," *Continental Philosophy Review* 35, no. 1 (2002): 45.

63. McGee, "*Phronesis* in the Gadamer versus Habermas Debates," 23.

64. For a more elaborate discussion about the successes and failures of advocacy, see Hess, "On the Dance of Rhetoric."

65. Birmingham, "*Phronesis*," 317.

66. Aaron Hess, "Health, Risk and Authority in a Dysfunctional World: Online Ecstasy User Discourse," *Ohio Communication Journal* 50 (2012): 6.

67. D. Soyini Madison, *Critical Ethnography: Method, Ethics, and Performance* (Thousand Oaks, CA: Sage, 2011).

68. Norman K. Denzin, *Interpretive Ethnography: Ethnographic Practices for the 21st Century* (Thousand Oaks, CA: Sage, 1997).

69. Bryant Keith Alexander, *Performing Black Masculinity: Race, Culture, and Queer Identity* (Lanham, MD: AltaMira Press, 2006), 105.

70. Ruth Behar, *The Vulnerable Observer: Anthropology That Breaks Your Heart* (Boston: Beacon Press, 1996); Art Bochner, "Narrative's Virtues," *Qualitative Inquiry* 7, no. 2 (2001): 131–57.

71. William Paul Simmons, "Making the Teaching of Social Justice Matter," in *Real Social Science: Applied Phronesis*, ed. Bent Flyvbjerg, Todd Landman, and Sanford Schram (Cambridge, UK: Cambridge University Press, 2012), 246.

72. Beiner, *Political Judgment*, 74.

73. See Jenny Edbauer Rice, "The New 'New': Making a Case for Critical Affect Studies," *Quarterly Journal of Speech* 94, no. 2 (2008): 200–212.

74. Ibid.

75. Bent Flyvbjerg, *Making Social Science Matter: Why Social Inquiry Fails and How It Can Succeed Again* (Cambridge, UK: Cambridge University Press, 2001), 21. See also Frederik Thuesen, "Navigating between Dialogue and Confrontation: *Phronesis* and Emotions in Interviewing Elites on Ethnic Discrimination," *Qualitative Inquiry* 17, no. 7 (2011): 614.

Chapter 6

1. "Boricu@" is a synonym for "Puerto Rican." Locals often deploy the identifier to describe their heritage and nationality. The term is derived from "Borikén," a name given to the Big Island by the Taíno indigenous community. Nouns expressing nationality are not capitalized in Spanish; I follow this language norm in the pages that follow. Also, I use the "@" sign to avoid "bigender normativity." Darrel Wanzer-Serrano, *The New York Young Lords and the Struggle for Liberation* (Philadelphia: Temple University Press, 2015), 23.

2. Bonnie Urciuoli, *Exposing Prejudice: Puerto Rican Experiences of Language, Race, and Class* (Long Grove, IL: Waveland Press, 1996), 42.

3. Michael K. Middleton, Samantha Senda-Cook, and Danielle Endres, "Articulating Rhetorical Field Methods: Challenges and Tensions," *Western Journal of Communication* 75, no. 4 (2011): 386–406.

4. Ibid., 389.

5. Gerard A. Hauser, "Attending the Vernacular: A Plea for an Ethnographical Rhetoric," in *The Rhetorical Emergence of Culture*, ed. Christian Meyer and Felix Girke (New York: Berghahn Books, 2011), 170. Studying this ongoing struggle is also important given that vernacular discourse sometimes supports dominant ideological commitments, rather than challenging them. See Robert G. Howard, "The Vernacular Web of Participatory Media," *Critical Studies in Media Communication* 25, no. 5 (2008): 490–513; Kent A. Ono and John M. Sloop, "The Critique of Vernacular Discourse," *Communication Monographs* 62, no. 1 (1995): 19–46.

6. Below, I explore the consequences of constituting Puerto Rico as an archipelago versus a singular island.

7. Often during interviews I employed a snowball approach by requesting the names of "personas entendidas," or "informed people," who might be interested in speaking with me. I also conducted five interviews via phone to accommodate schedules and geographic separation.

8. My positionality required me to make several decisions while in the field to gain acceptance. When writing e-mails, soliciting interviews over the phone, and in face-to-face encounters, I used the Spanish translation of my first name, Catalina. I also chose to mention my interest in studying the archipelago where my grandmother, Esther María Irizarry Rubio, was born. She endured the colonial discursive apparatus on two fronts: as a U.S. colonial "subject" and as the partner of a Spaniard who viewed her Puerto Ricanness as a weakness. My grandfather sometimes told her, "When the Spaniards came to Puerto Rico, your people were still hanging from trees."

9. Dwight Conquergood, "Ethnography, Rhetoric, and Performance," *Quarterly Journal of Speech* 78, no. 1 (1992): 80–97; Middleton, Senda-Cook, and Endres, "Articulating Rhetorical Field Methods"; Phaedra C. Pezzullo, "Resisting 'National Breast Cancer Awareness Month': The Rhetoric of Counterpublics and Their Cultural Performances," *Quarterly Journal of Speech*

89, no. 4 (2003): 345–65; Phaedra C. Pezzullo, *Toxic Tourism: Rhetorics of Pollution, Travel, and Environmental Justice* (Tuscaloosa: University of Alabama Press, 2007); Samantha Senda-Cook, "Rugged Practices: Embodying Authenticity in Outdoor Recreation," *Quarterly Journal of Speech* 98, no. 2 (2012): 131.

10. Pezzullo, *Toxic Tourism*.

11. Karma R. Chávez, *Queer Migration Politics: Activist Rhetoric and Coalitional Possibilities* (Urbana: University of Illinois Press, 2013), 8; María Lugones, *Pilgrimages/Peregrinajes: Theorizing Coalition against Multiple Oppressions* (Latham, MD: Rowman and Littlefield, 2003).

12. Chávez, *Queer Migration Politics*, 8.

13. Dwight Conquergood, "Between Rigor and Relevance: Rethinking Applied Communication," in *Applied Communication for the 21st Century*, ed. Kenneth N. Cissna (Mahwah, NJ: Erlbaum, 1995); Ana Celia Zentella, "'Dime con quién hablas, y te diré quién eres': Linguistic (In)security and Latina/o Unity," in *A Companion to Latina/o Studies*, ed. Juan Flores and Renato Rosaldo (Malden, MA: Blackwell, 2007), 25–39.

14. Pezzullo, "Resisting 'National Breast Cancer Awareness Month'"; Pezzullo, *Toxic Tourism*.

15. Middleton, Senda-Cook, and Endres, "Articulating Rhetorical Field Methods"; Pezzullo, *Toxic Tourism*; Senda-Cook, "Rugged Practices."

16. Chaïm Perelman and L. Olbrechts-Tyteca, *The New Rhetoric: A Treatise on Argumentation*, trans. John Wilkinson and Purcell Weaver (Notre Dame, IN: University of Notre Dame Press, 1969).

17. Pezzullo, "Resisting 'National Breast Cancer Awareness Month'"; Pezzullo, *Toxic Tourism*, 9.

18. Pezzullo, *Toxic Tourism*, 9.

19. Ibid., 198.

20. Middleton, Senda-Cook, and Endres, "Articulating Rhetorical Field Methods," 394.

21. See Carole Blair, "Contemporary U.S. Memorial Sites as Exemplars of Rhetoric's Materiality," in *Rhetorical Bodies*, ed. Jack Selzer and Sharon Crowley (Madison: University of Wisconsin Press, 1999), 16–57.

22. *Oxford English Dictionary*, 2nd ed., s.v. "co-."

23. Kirsten Weld, *Paper Cadavers: The Archives of Dictatorship in Guatemala* (Durham, NC: Duke University Press, 2014), 23.

24. My coalitional investment is with subaltern groups. Other scholars might extend the term to include additional communities and interlocutors with whom they share a collective commitment to social change and justice.

25. I realize that not all critics will identify with the Spanish term "compañer@s," given the varied communities within which we conduct research and our own positionalities. However, I hope this term assists in more reflexively considering how we position ourselves to our research and those we encounter in the field. It may be that the translated terms of "partner," "companion," and "colleague" speak to scholars committed to rhetorical field methods and/or these terms may open up possibilities for alternative ways of conceptualizing critic-community member relations. See Weld, *Paper Cadavers*, for another ethnographic study that uses "compañer@s."

26. Conquergood, "Ethnography, Rhetoric, and Performance." Linda Tuhiwai Smith encourages readers to reconsider who counts as a researcher and the violences inflicted on indigenous populations by Western modes of inquiry. See Linda Tuhiwai Smith, *Decolonizing Methodologies: Research and Indigenous Peoples*, 2nd ed. (London: Zed Books, 2012).

27. Alexis S. Dietrich, *The Drug Company Next Door: Pollution, Jobs, and Community Health in Puerto Rico* (New York: New York University Press, 2013), 5.

28. Katherine McCaffrey, "The Struggle for Environmental Justice in Vieques, Puerto Rico," in *Environmental Justice in Latin America: Problems, Promise, and Practice*, ed. David V. Carruthers (Cambridge, MA: MIT Press, 2008), 263–86.

29. Darrel Enck-Wanzer, "Race, Coloniality, and Geo-body Politics: The Garden as Latin@ Vernacular Discourse," *Environmental Communication: A Journal of Nature and Culture* 5, no. 3 (2011): 363–71; Danielle Endres, "The Rhetoric of Nuclear Colonialism: Rhetorical Exclusion of American Indian Arguments in the Yucca Mountain Nuclear Waste Siting Decision," *Communication and Critical/Cultural Studies* 6, no. 1 (2009): 44.

30. Pezzullo, *Toxic Tourism*, 5.

31. Katherine McCaffrey, *Military Power and Popular Protest: The U.S. Navy in Vieques, Puerto Rico* (New Brunswick, NJ: Rutgers University Press, 2002), 3.

32. McCaffrey, "Struggle for Environmental Justice," 264.

33. John Wargo, *Green Intelligence: Creating Environments That Protect Human Health* (New Haven, CT: Yale University Press, 2009).

34. McCaffrey, *Military Power and Popular Protest*.

35. One person was killed by the navy's activities, David Rodríguez Sanes, and his death sparked a transnational social movement. The worst bombing and toxic chemical releases occurred in eastern Vieques, where the zone was used as a live impact area. More than eighteen thousand acres remain littered with thousands of tons of unexploded, hard-to-locate ordnance. Furthermore, depleted uranium has penetrated deep beneath the soil and poses substantial radiation risks. To evade responsibility for remediating this site, in 2003 the U.S. Congress named almost half of the island a wildlife refuge, the majority of which is inaccessible to the public. This classification mischaracterizes the land and waters as "pristine." Thus, the area is perceived as a noncrisis, because human contact is assumed to be minimal. The U.S. Navy and Department of Fish and Wildlife currently oversee the area, although the former controls any (in)action conducted on the grounds. McCaffrey, "Struggle for Environmental Justice"; McCaffrey, *Military Power and Popular Protest*.

36. Wargo, *Green Intelligence*, 93.

37. Phaedra C. Pezzullo and Stephen P. Depoe, "Everyday Life and Death in a Nuclear World: Stories from Fernald," in *Public Modalities: Rhetoric, Culture, Media, and the Shape of Public Life*, ed. Daniel C. Brouwer and Robert Asen (Tuscaloosa: University of Alabama Press, 2010), 89.

38. María Lugones, "Radical Multiculturalism and Women of Color Feminisms," *Journal for Cultural and Religious Theory* 13, no. 1 (2014): 68–80.

39. I thank Phaedra C. Pezzullo for sharing EJOLT.org with me and for suggesting that I make a contribution for Puerto Rico; given the severity of the environmental justice struggles in Vieques, I felt a particular need to share this brutal story because of my co-presence experiences. The entry is available at http://ejatlas.org/conflict/vieques-puerto-rico.

40. See Kathleen M. de Onís, "'Looking Both Ways': Metaphor and the Rhetorical Alignment of Intersectional Climate Justice and Reproductive Justice Concerns," *Environmental Communication: A Journal of Nature and Culture* 6, no. 3 (2012): 308–27; Stacey K. Sowards, "Introduction: Environmental Justice in International Contexts: Understanding Intersections for Social Justice in the Twenty-First Century," *Environmental Communication: A Journal of Nature and Culture* 6, no. 3 (2012): 285–89.

41. Kathleen M. de Onís, "Lost in Translation: Challenging (White Monolingual Feminism's) <Choice> with *Justicia Reproductiva*," *Women's Studies in Communication* 38, no. 1 (2015): 1–19.

42. Déborah Berman Santana, *Kicking off the Bootstraps: Environment, Development, and Community Power in Puerto Rico* (Tucson: University of Arizona Press, 1996).

43. Robert Cox, *Environmental Communication and the Public Sphere*, 3rd ed. (Thousand Oaks, CA: Sage, 2013).

44. Ibid.

45. Shannon Speed, "At the Crossroads of Human Rights and Anthropology: Toward a Critically Engaged Activist Research," *American Anthropologist* 108, no. 1 (2006): 66.

46. Lawrence R. Frey and Kevin M. Carragee, *Communication Activism: Communication for Social Change*, vol. 1 (Cresskill, NJ: Hampton Press, 2007), 10.

47. Speed, "At the Crossroads," 75.

48. Senda-Cook, "Rugged Practices," 135.

49. Middleton, Senda-Cook, and Endres, "Articulating Rhetorical Field Methods," 402.

50. D. Soyini Madison, *Critical Ethnography: Method, Ethics, and Performance* (Thousand Oaks, CA: Sage, 2005), 5.

Chapter 7

1. Nicole Ghio, "From India to Appalachia, Coal Is a Human Rights Issue," *Sierra Club Compass*, May 8, 2012, http://sierraclub.typepad.com/compass/2012/05/from-india-to-appalachia-coal-is-a-human-rights-issue.html.

2. U.S. Energy Information Administration, "Quarterly Coal Report, October–December 2011," April 2012, http://www.eia.gov/coal/production/quarterly/.

3. U.S. Environmental Protection Agency, "Inventory of U.S. Greenhouse Gas Emissions and Sinks: 1990–2012," February 2012, http://epa.gov/climatechange/emissions/usinventoryreport.html.

4. The Environmental Integrity Project, "Getting Warmer: U.S. CO_2 Emissions from Power Plants: Emissions Rise 5.6% in 2010," February 18, 2011, http://environmentalintegrity.org/documents/CO2Report_2011RJD21811final.pdf.

5. See Karma R. Chávez, *Queer Migration Politics: Activist Rhetoric and Coalitional Possibilities* (Urbana: University of Illinois Press, 2013); Lynn Stephen, Jan Lanier, Ramon Ramirez, and Marty Westerling, *Building Alliances: An Ethnography of Collaboration between Rural Organizing Project (ROP) and CAUSA in Oregon* (New York: New York University and Leadership for a Changing World, 2005).

6. Robert Asen, "Seeking the 'Counter' in Counterpublics," *Communication Theory* 10, no. 4 (2000): 424–46.

7. Michael Warner, *Publics and Counterpublics* (New York: Zone Books, 2002).

8. Rita Felski, *Beyond Feminist Aesthetics: Feminist Literature and Social Change* (Cambridge, MA: Harvard University Press, 1989).

9. Nancy Fraser, "Rethinking the Public Sphere: A Contribution to the Critique of Actually Existing Democracy," in *Habermas and the Public Sphere*, ed. Craig J. Calhoun (Cambridge, MA: MIT Press, 1992); Warner, *Publics and Counterpublics*.

10. Kevin DeLuca and Jennifer Peeples, "From Public Sphere to Public Screen: Democracy, Activism, and the 'Violence' of Seattle," *Critical Studies in Media Communication* 19, no. 2 (2002): 125–51; Michel Foucault, "Sex, Power and the Politics of Identity," *Ethics: Subjectivity and Truth*, vol. 1, ed. Paul Rabinow (New York: New Press, 1997); Rita Felski, *Beyond Feminist Aesthetics: Feminist Literature and Social Change* (Cambridge, MA: Harvard University Press, 1989).

11. Asen, "Seeking the 'Counter' in Counterpublics"; DeLuca and Peeples, "From Public Sphere to Public Screen."

12. Daniel C. Brouwer, "ACT-ing UP in Congressional Hearings," in *Counterpublics and the State*, ed. Robert Asen and Daniel C. Brouwer (Albany: State University of New York Press, 2001), 89.

13. Warner, *Publics and Counterpublics*, 120–21.

14. G. Thomas Goodnight and David Hingstman, "Studies in the Public Sphere," *Quarterly Journal of Speech* 83, no. 3 (1997): 357.

15. Eric Doxtader, "In the Name of Reconciliation: The Faith and Works of Counterpublicity," in *Counterpublics and the State*, ed. Robert Asen and Daniel C. Brouwer (Albany: State University of New York Press), 66.

16. Allison Sliva of Bay City's No Coal Coalition loaned to me a large binder of local newspaper articles and letters to the editor about the White Stallion coal plant dispute.

17. Clifford Geertz, "Thick Description: Toward an Interpretive Theory of Culture," in *The Interpretation of Cultures: Selected Essays* (New York: Basic Books, 1973), 3–30.

18. Barry Brummett, *Rhetorical Dimensions of Popular Culture* (Tuscaloosa: University of Alabama Press, 2005), 9.

19. Robert Cervenka interview, June 6, 2012.

20. David Danbom, *Born in the Country: A History of Rural America* (Baltimore: Johns Hopkins University Press, 2006), 4.

21. Mario Diani, "Social Movement Networks Virtual and Real," *Information, Communication, and Society* 3, no. 3 (2000): 8.

22. In 2011 the campaign received a $50 million grant from the Bloomberg Foundation to fund a five-year national anti-coal campaign. See Kate Sheppard, "Bloomberg, Sierra Club Align against Coal," *Mother Jones*, July 21, 2011, http://www.motherjones.com/blue-marble/2011/07/bloomberg-sierra-club-align-against-coal.

23. Greenpeace International, "Quit Coal, Save the Climate! 2008 Campaign Highlights," December 22, 2008, http://www.greenpeace.org/international/en/news/features/quit-coal-save-the-climate-2/.

24. Ryan Rittenhouse interview, October 18, 2012.

25. Robert Asen, "A Discourse Theory of Citizenship," *Quarterly Journal of Speech* 90, no. 2 (2004): 202.

26. Eva Malina interview, June 14, 2012.

27. Rittenhouse worked for Public Citizen until 2011, when he began working for Greenpeace.

28. Malina interview.

29. Robert Lee interview, June 15, 2012.

30. Chávez, *Queer Migration Politics*, 136.

31. Ibid., 131.

32. Ibid., 130.

33. Flavia de la Fuente interview, December 4, 2012.

34. Niklas Luhmann, "Familiarity, Confidence, Trust: Problems and Alternatives," in *Trust: Making and Breaking Cooperative Relations*, ed. Diego Gambetta (New York: Basil Blackwell, 1988), 98.

35. Kenneth Newton, "Trust, Social Capital, Civil Society, and Democracy," *International Political Science Review* 22, no. 2 (2001): 206.

36. Gerard Hauser and Chantal Benoit-Barne, "Reflections on Rhetoric, Deliberative Democracy, Civil Society, and Trust," *Rhetoric and Public Affairs* 5, no. 2 (2002): 271.

37. Diego Gambetta, "Can We Trust Trust?" in *Trust: Making and Breaking Cooperative Relations*, ed. Diego Gambetta (New York: Basil Blackwell, 1988), 218.

38. De la Fuente interview.

39. Karen Hadden interview, September 17, 2012.

40. Ibid.

41. Charles English interview, May 24, 2012.

42. De la Fuente interview.

43. Kenneth Burke, *A Grammar of Motives* (Berkeley: University of California Press, 1969), 513.

44. Cervenka referred to EPA guidelines to regulate greenhouse gas (GHG) emissions from coal-fired power plants; the energy industry anticipated a March 2013 ruling and rushed to get proposed plants permitted beforehand so that they would be exempt from even stricter GHG regulations required for unpermitted new coal plants. The EPA submitted the new regulations in June 2013. See Claire Healy, "EPA Submits Its Regulation on Coal Power Plants," *American Spectator*, July 2, 2013, http://spectator.org/blog/2013/07/02/epa-submits-climate-rule-to-wh; see also Ashley Killough, "Obama Wants Limits on Coal Plants, Says Keystone Can't Boost Pollution," *CNN*, June 26, 2013, http://www.cnn.com/2013/06/25/politics/obama-climate-change.

45. TPGA is now Texans for Responsible Energy and Water.

46. Malina interview.

47. Valerie Thatcher, "Collaboration in the Face of Fast-Track Permitting in Texas," in *Environmental Leadership: A Reference Handbook*, ed. D. Rigling Gallagher (Thousand Oaks, CA: Sage, 2012), 295–303.

48. Rancher Cervenka fulfilled the legitimizing role during the 2004–2007 coal wars era.

49. Malina interview.

50. Ibid.

51. T. C. Calvert interview, July 20, 2012.

52. In 2011, the 2016 retirement of the Deely plant was announced. See Donna Hoffman, "San Antonio Expected to Close Coal Plant," Texas Green Report, Sierra Club Lone Star Chapter, June 20, 2011, http://texasgreenreport.wordpress.com/2011/06/20/san-antonio-expected-to-close-coal-plant/.

53. Ibid.

54. Hauser and Benoit-Barne, "Reflections on Rhetoric," 269.

55. Barbara Gray, "Strong Opposition: Frame-Based Resistance to Collaboration," *Journal of Community and Applied Social Psychology* 14, no. 3 (2004): 168.

56. Hauser and Benoit-Barne, "Reflections on Rhetoric," 270–71.

57. Hadden interview.

58. Calvert interview.

59. Saul Alinsky published *Rules for Radicals* (New York: Random House, 1971) to "make the difference between being a realistic radical and being a rhetorical one who uses the tired old words and slogans" (xviii).

60. Calvert interview.

61. Ibid.

62. Ibid.

63. Chávez, *Queer Migration Politics*, 141.

64. Ibid., 136.

65. Ibid., 131.

66. Asen, "A Discourse Theory," 195.

67. Calvert interview.

68. Daniel Faber, "A More 'Productive' Environmental Justice Politics: Movement Alliances in Massachusetts for Clean Production and Regional Equity," in *Environmental Justice and Environmentalism*, ed. Ronald Sandler and Phaedra C. Pezzullo (Cambridge, MA: MIT Press, 2007), 158.

Chapter 8

1. Carole Blair, "Reflections on Criticism and Bodies: Parables from Public Places," *Western Journal of Communication* 65, no. 3 (2001): 275.

2. For an overview of the two main ways of approaching audiences in rhetorical criticism, see Douglas B. Park, "The Meanings of 'Audience,'" *College English* 44, no. 3 (1982): 247–57; Lisa Ede and Andrea Lunsford, "Audience Addressed / Audience Invoked: The Role of Audience in Composition Theory and Pedagogy," *College Composition and Communication* 35, no. 2 (1984): 155–71; James Jasinski, "Audience," in *Sourcebook on Rhetoric: Key Concepts in Contemporary Rhetorical Studies* (Thousand Oaks, CA: Sage, 2001), 68–74.

3. Cristina M. Morus, "The SANU Memorandum: Intellectual Authority and the Constitution of an Exclusive Serbian People," *Communication and Critical/Cultural Studies* 2, no. 4 (2007): 142–65; Alina Haliliuc, "*Manele* Music and the Discourse of Balkanism in Romania," *Communication, Culture, and Critique* 8, no. 2 (2015): 290–308.

4. Timothy Barney, "When We Was Red: *Good Bye Lenin!* and Nostalgia for the 'Everyday GDR,'" *Communication and Critical/Cultural Studies* 6, no. 2 (2009): 132–51.

5. Lane M. Bruner, "Taming 'Wild' Capitalism," *Discourse and Society* 13, no. 2 (2002): 167–81.

6. Zala Volcic, "The Notion of 'the West' in Serbian National Imaginary," *European Journal of Cultural Studies* 8, no. 2 (2005): 155–75.

7. Serguei Oushakine, "In the State of Post-Soviet Aphasia: Symbolic Development in Contemporary Russia," *Europe-Asia Studies* 52, no. 6 (2000): 993–94.

8. Ibid. Oushakine illustrates how public discourse in post-socialist Russia does not offer young post-Soviet subjects resources for imagining subjectivities different from Soviet ones, thus prolonging a state of symbolic crisis he calls "post-Soviet aphasia."

9. Maurice Charland, "Constitutive Rhetoric: The Case of the 'Peuple Québécois,'" *Quarterly Journal of Speech* 73, no. 2 (1987): 133–50.

10. Maria Bucur, "Fascism and the New Radical Movements in Romania," in *Fascism and Neofascism: Critical Writings on the Radical Right in Europe*, ed. Angelica Fenner and Eric D. Weitz (New York: Palgrave Macmillan, 2004), 171.

11. Vlad Mixich, "Dan Puric's Conversion," *HotNews*, February 8, 2010, http://www.hotnews.ro/stiri-esential-6886607-convertirea-lui-dan-puric.htm.

12. In 2014 the Constitutional Court ruled as unconstitutional the existing mandatory religion courses in public schools. Religious education subsequently became an optional course in the students' curriculum. In an effort to convince students and their legal guardians to enroll in such courses, the Association of Parents for Religious Courses (APRC), an organization promoting religious education, started a promotional campaign in which Dan Puric was centrally featured. The APRC campaign is available on the organization's website, http://www.oradereligie.ro/category/sustinatori.

13. Dan Puric, *Who We Are* (Bucharest: Platytera, 2008); *The Beautiful Man* (Bucharest: Dan Puric Company, 2009); *Be Dignified!* (Bucharest: Dan Puric Company, 2011); *Romanian Soul* (Bucharest: Dan Puric Company, 2014).

14. Simona Chitan, "Dan Puric: 'It's Been Tragic Parting with Father Iustin Parvu,'" *The Truth*, January 3, 2013, http://adevarul.ro/cultura/spiritualitate/interviu-video-dan-puric-Il-visez-des-parintele-iustin-1_52c6ade2c7b855ff562ee78e/index.html.

15. Gerard A. Hauser, "Attending the Vernacular: A Plea for an Ethnographical Rhetoric," in *The Rhetorical Emergence of Culture*, ed. Christian Meyer and Felix Girke (New York: Berghahn Books, 2011), 164.

16. Phaedra C. Pezzullo, *Toxic Tourism: Rhetorics of Pollution, Travel, and Environmental Justice* (Tuscaloosa: University of Alabama Press, 2007); Phaedra C. Pezzullo, "Resisting 'National Breast Cancer Awareness Month': The Rhetoric of Counterpublics and Their Cultural Performances," *Quarterly Journal of Speech* 89, no. 4 (2003): 347.

17. Samantha Senda-Cook, "Rugged Practices: Embodying Authenticity in Outdoor Recreation," *Quarterly Journal of Speech* 98, no. 2 (2012): 129.

18. Hauser, "Attending the Vernacular," 169.

19. Sara L. McKinnon, "Essentialism, Intersectionality, and Recognition: A Feminist Rhetorical Approach to the Audience," in *Standing in the Intersection: Feminist Voices, Feminist Practices in Communication Studies*, ed. Karma R. Chávez and Cindy L. Griffin (Albany: State University of New York Press, 2012), 192.

20. See, for example, James Clifford and George E. Marcus, *Writing Culture: The Poetics and Politics of Ethnography* (Berkeley: University of California Press, 1986); George E. Marcus and Michael M. J. Fischer, *Anthropology as Cultural Critique: An Experimental Moment in the Human Sciences* (Chicago: University of Chicago Press, 1986); Clifford Geertz, *Works and Lives: The Anthropologist as Author* (Stanford, CA: Stanford University Press, 1988).

21. Amanda Coffey, "Ethnography and Self: Reflections and Representations," in *Qualitative Research in Action*, ed. Tim May (London: Sage, 2002), 322.

22. See, for example, Margery Wolf, *A Thrice-Told Tale: Feminism, Postmodernism, and Ethnographic Responsibility* (Stanford, CA: Stanford University Press, 1992); Jim Mienczakowski, "The Theater of Ethnography: The Reconstruction of Ethnography in Theater with Emancipatory Potential," *Qualitative Inquiry* 1, no. 3 (1995): 360–75; Carolyn Ellis, *Final Negotiations: A Story of Love, Loss, and Chronic Illness* (Philadelphia: Temple University Press, 1995).

23. Tindale, "Rhetorical Argumentation and the Nature of Audience: Toward an Understanding of Audience—Issues in Argumentation," *Philosophy and Rhetoric* 46, no. 4 (2013): 512.

24. Karlyn Kohrs Campbell, "Agency: Promiscuous and Protean," *Communication and Critical/Cultural Studies* 2, no. 1 (2005): 1–19.

25. Dilip P. Gaonkar, "Object and Method in Rhetorical Criticism: From Wichelns to Leff and McGee," *Western Journal of Speech Communication* 54 (Summer 1990): 291.

26. Ibid., 299.

27. Lauren Berlant, "Slow Death (Sovereignty, Obesity, Lateral Agency)," *Critical Inquiry* 33, no. 4 (2007): 754–80.

28. Ibid., 759.

29. Ibid., 761–62.

30. Ibid., 780.

31. Ibid., 779.

32. Ibid., 778.

33. Berlant's word is "attrition," a synonym.

34. Michael Shafir, "The Mind of Romania's Radical Right," in *The Radical Right in Central and Eastern Europe since 1989*, ed. Sabrina P. Ramet (University Park: Penn State University Press, 1999), 213–32.

35. Bucur, "Fascism and the New Radical Movements," 162.

36. Ibid., 164–65.

37. Gail Kligman, *The Politics of Duplicity: Controlling Reproduction in Ceaușescu's Romania* (Berkeley: University of California Press, 1998), 124–33.

38. Walter Benjamin, "The Storyteller: Reflections on the Works of Nikolai Leskov," in *The Novel: An Anthology of Criticism and Theory, 1900–2000*, ed. Dorothy J. Hale (Malden, MA: Blackwell, 2006), 367.

39. Gyorgy Enyedi, "Urbanization under Socialism," in *Cities after Socialism: Urban and Regional Change and Conflict in Post-Socialist Societies*, ed. Gregory Andrusz, Michael Harloe, and Ivan Szelenyi (Cambridge, MA: Blackwell, 1996), 115–18.

40. Robert Glenn Howard, "Vernacular Authority: Critically Engaging 'Tradition,'" in *Tradition in the 21st Century: Locating the Role of the Past in the Present*, ed. Trevor J. Blank and Robert Glenn Howard (Logan: Utah State University Press, 2013), 73.

41. Charland, "Constitutive Rhetoric," 139.

42. Dan V. Caprar, "Foreign Locals: A Cautionary Tale on the Culture of MNC Local Employees," *Journal of International Business Studies* 42, no. 5 (2011): 609.

43. Victor Turner, *From Ritual to Theatre: The Human Seriousness of Play* (New York: Performing Arts Journal Publications, 2001), 48.

44. Aimee Carrillo Rowe, "Be Longing: Toward a Feminist Politics of Relation," *NWSA Journal* 17, no. 2 (2005): 18.

45. Ibid., 16.

46. In addition to his four books and numerous video material available on YouTube, Puric also released a DVD containing selections from his lectures and an original television production. See *Lectures at the Romanian Athenaeum*, performed by Dan Puric (Bucharest: Foundation Art Production and Romanian Television Corporation, 2009), DVD.

Chapter 9

1. Raka Shome and Radha Hegde, "Culture, Communication, and the Challenge of Globalization," *Critical Studies in Media Communication* 19, no. 2 (2002): 175.

2. For further discussion see Renée L. Bergland, *The National Uncanny: Indian Ghosts and American Subjects* (Hanover, NH: University Press of New England, 2000).

3. Leah Dilworth, *Imagining Indians in the Southwest: Persistent Visions of a Primitive Past* (Washington, DC: Smithsonian Institution Press, 1997).

4. D. H. Lawrence as quoted in Marta Weigle, "From Desert to Disney World: The Santa Fe Railway and the Fred Harvey Company Display the Indian Southwest," *Journal of Anthropological Research* 45, no. 1 (1989): 132.

5. Richard A. Rogers, "Deciphering Kokopelli: Masculinity in Commodified Appropriations of Native American Imagery," *Communication and Critical/Cultural Studies* 4, no. 3 (2007): 244.

6. Yvonna S. Lincoln and Egon G. Guba, *Naturalistic Inquiry* (Newbury Park, CA: Sage, 1985), 56, 59.

7. Trinh T. Minh-ha, *Woman Native Other: Writing Postcoloniality and Feminism* (Bloomington: Indiana University Press, 1989), 54.

8. Darrel Allan Wanzer, "Delinking Rhetoric, or Revisiting McGee's Fragmentation Thesis through Decoloniality," *Rhetoric and Public Affairs* 15, no. 4 (2012): 648.

9. Ibid., 648.

10. I borrow this language from Sarah Amira de la Garza's problematization and subsequent reframing of the "guiding ideals" of ethnographic inquiry, a discussion that has influenced my thinking about the epistemological and ontological assumptions we inadvertently reproduce even as we attempt to engage in the work of decolonizing. See Sarah Amira de la Garza, writing as María Cristina González, "The Four Seasons of Ethnography: A Creation-Centered Ontology for Ethnography," *International Journal of Intercultural Relations* 24, no. 5 (2000): 623–50.

11. I am grateful to Marie-Louise Paulesc for helping me to conceptualize the intertwining of symbolic, material, and social dimensions within public memory places.

12. Carole Blair, Greg Dickinson, and Brian L. Ott, "Introduction: Rhetoric/Memory/Place," in *Places of Public Memory: The Rhetoric of Museums and Memorials*, ed. Greg Dickinson, Carole Blair, and Brian L. Ott (Alabama: University of Alabama Press, 2010), 28.

13. Roger C. Aden, Min Wha Han, Stephanie Norander, Michael E. Pfahl, Timothy P. Pollack, Jr., and Stephanie L. Young, "Re-collection: A Proposal for Refining the Study of Collective Memory and Its Places," *Communication Theory* 19, no. 3 (2009): 311.

14. See, for example, Carole Blair, "Contemporary U.S. Memorial Sites as Exemplars of Rhetoric's Materiality," in *Rhetorical Bodies*, ed. Jack Selzer and Sharon Crowley (Madison: University of Wisconsin Press, 1999), 16–57; and Blair, Dickinson, and Ott, "Introduction."

15. Many of the scholars cited in this essay have taken up this question in their work. As just one example, Carole Blair's provocative discussion of the relationship between the material presence of the critic and validity in the rhetorical study of public places includes the following reflection: "How much credence would we be willing to grant a critic's treatment of Rushmore if we knew s/he had not been to the Black Hills . . . ? Very little, I suspect." See

"Reflections on Criticism and Bodies: Parables from Public Places," *Western Journal of Communication* 65, no. 3 (2001): 276.

16. Michael K. Middleton, Danielle Endres, and Samantha Senda-Cook, "Articulating Rhetorical Field Methods: Challenges and Tensions," *Western Journal of Communication* 75, no. 4 (2011): 388.

17. Blair, "Contemporary U.S. Memorial Sites"; Greg Dickinson, Brian L. Ott, and Eric Aoki, "Spaces of Remembering and Forgetting: The Reverent Eye/I at the Plains Indian Museum," *Communication and Critical/Cultural Studies* 3, no. 1 (2006): 27–47; Richard Marback, "Unclenching the Fist: Embodying Rhetoric and Giving Objects Their Due," *Rhetoric Society Quarterly* 38, no. 1 (2008): 46–65; Kenneth S. Zagacki and Victoria Gallagher, "Rhetoric and Materiality in the Museum Park at the North Carolina Museum of Art," *Quarterly Journal of Speech* 95, no. 2 (2009): 171–91.

18. Blair, Dickinson, and Ott, "Introduction," 29.

19. Dickinson, Ott, and Aoki, "Spaces of Remembering," 29.

20. Marouf Hasian, Jr., "Remembering and Forgetting the 'Final Solution': A Rhetorical Pilgrimage through the U.S. Holocaust Memorial Museum," *Critical Studies in Media Communication* 21, no. 1 (2004): 64–92.

21. Bernard J. Armada, "Memorial Agon: An Interpretive Tour of the National Civil Rights Museum," *Southern Communication Journal* 63, no. 3 (2009): 235–43.

22. Aden at al., "Re-collection," 312.

23. Richard Handler and Eric Gable, *The New History in an Old Museum: Creating the Past at Colonial Williamsburg* (Durham, NC: Duke University Press, 1997), 9.

24. John Bodnar, *Remaking America: Public Memory, Commemoration, and Patriotism in the Twentieth Century* (Princeton, NJ: Princeton University Press, 1991), 16.

25. Aden et al., "Re-collection," 321.

26. For further discussion see Lincoln and Guba, *Naturalistic Inquiry*.

27. Daniel C. Brouwer and Robert Asen, "Introduction: Public Modalities, or the Metaphors We Theorize By," in *Public Modalities: Rhetoric, Culture, Media, and the Shape of Public Life*, ed. Daniel C. Brouwer and Robert Asen (Tuscaloosa: University of Alabama Press, 2010), 2.

28. Irene J. Dabrowski, "David Bohm's Theory of the Implicate Order: Implications for Holistic Thought Processes," *Issues in Integrative Studies* 13 (1995): 3.

29. Mary Ellen Pitts, "The Holographic Paradigm: A New Model for the Study of Literature and Science," *Modern Language Studies* 20, no. 4 (1990): 83.

30. Roberta Chevrette and Aaron Hess, "Unearthing the Native Past: Citizen Archaeology and Modern (Non)Belonging at the Pueblo Grande Museum," *Communication and Critical/Cultural Studies* 12, no. 2 (2015): 146.

31. Marie-Louise Paulesc, "Living Relationships with the Past: Remembering Communism in Romania" (PhD diss., Arizona State University, 2014).

32. Erna Fergusson as quoted in Dilworth, *Imagining Indians*, 58.

33. Johannes Fabian, *Time and the Other: How Anthropology Makes Its Object* (New York: Columbia University Press, 1983).

34. Blair, "Contemporary U.S. Memorial Sites," 46.

35. Dickinson, Ott, and Aoki, "Spaces of Remembering," 29.

36. Dean MacCannell, "Staged Authenticity: Arrangements of Social Space in Tourist Settings," *American Journal of Sociology* 79, no. 3 (1973): 589–603.

37. Renato Rosaldo, "Imperialist Nostalgia," *Representations* 26 (1989): 108.

38. Bergland, *National Uncanny*, 2.

39. See Shari M. Huhndorf, *Going Native: Indians in the American Cultural Imagination* (Ithaca, NY: Cornell University Press, 2001).

40. See Philip Joseph Deloria, *Playing Indian* (New Haven, CT: Yale University Press, 1998).

41. Other scholars make similar arguments regarding how visitors' performative encounters with the site may differ from rhetorical readings of the fixed elements of display. See, for example, Carole Blair and Neil Michel, "Commemorating in the Theme Park Zone: Reading the Astronauts Memorial," in *At the Intersection: Cultural Studies and Rhetorical Studies*, ed. Thomas Rosteck (New York: Guilford Press, 1999), 29–83. I offer the holographic analytic as another means by which to think through these methodological intersections.

42. Pitts, "Holographic Paradigm," 86.

43. Karen Barad, "Posthumanist Performativity: Toward an Understanding of How Matter Comes to Matter," *Gender and Science* 28, no. 3 (2003): 822.

44. Aaron Hess and Aden et al., among others, also draw our attention to rhetorical processes rather than rhetorical products. See Aden et al., "Re- collection"; and Aaron Hess, "Critical-Rhetorical Ethnography: Rethinking the Place and Process of Rhetoric," *Communication Studies* 62, no. 2 (2011): 127–52.

45. Scott Lauria Morgensen, *Spaces between Us: Queer Settler Colonialism and Indigenous Decolonization* (Minneapolis: University of Minnesota Press, 2011), 18.

46. Pitts, "Holographic Paradigm," 85.

47. See Sara McKinnon, Robert Asen, Karma Chávez, and Robert Glenn Howard, "Introduction: Articulating Text and Field in the Nodes of Rhetorical Scholarship," this volume.

48. Brian L. Ott, Eric Aoki, and Greg Dickinson, "Ways of (Not) Seeing Guns: Presence and Absence at the Cody Firearms Museum," *Communication and Critical/Cultural Studies* 8, no. 3 (2011): 215–39.

49. See de la Garza, writing as González, "Four Seasons of Ethnography," 629.

50. Mishuana Goeman, "(Re)Mapping Indigenous Presence on the Land in Women's Literature," *American Quarterly* 60, no. 2 (2008): 296.

51. Hannah Kihalani as quoted in Manulani Aluli-Meyer, "Indigenous and Authentic: Hawaiian Epistemology and the Triangulation of Meaning," in *The Global Intercultural Communication Reader*, ed. Molefi Kete Asante, Yoshitaka Miike, and Jing Yin, 2nd ed. (New York: Routledge), 136.

52. Mishuana R. Goeman, "Toward a Native Feminism's Spatial Practice," *Wicazo Sa Review* 24, no. 2 (2009): 169–70.

53. Roberto A. Jackson, "Community Members Spread Art and Culture at Valley Museums," *Gila River Indian News* (Sacaton, AZ), March 2011, 17.

54. Ibid.

55. Laura L. Mielke, "Introduction," in *Native Acts: Indian Performance, 1603–1832*, ed. Joshua David Bellin and Laura L. Mielke (Lincoln: University of Nebraska Press, 2011), 3.

56. Goeman, "(Re)Mapping Indigenous Presence," 296.

57. "Indigenous Tours Project 06: Huhugam Homeland to Phoenix and Back Again," *Vimeo* video, 7:47, posted by "Steven Yazzie & Digital Preserve," http://vimeo.com/95179964.

58. Ibid.

59. Kathleen Wilson, "Therapeutic Landscapes and First Nation Peoples: An Exploration of Culture, Health, and Place," *Health and Place* 9, no. 2 (2003): 83.

60. Manulani Aluli Meyer, "Our Own Liberation: Reflections on Hawaiian Epistemology," *The Contemporary Pacific* 13, no. 1 (2001): 128.

61. "Indigenous Tours Project 06."

62. Ibid.

63. See Chevrette and Hess, "Unearthing the Native Past," for further discussion.

64. Goeman, "Toward a Native Feminism's Spatial Practice," 170.

65. Jenny Edbauer, "Unframing Models of Public Distribution: From Rhetorical Situation to Rhetorical Ecologies," *Rhetoric Society Quarterly* 35, no. 4 (2005): 5–24.

66. Doreen Massey, *Space, Place, and Gender* (Minneapolis: University of Minnesota Press, 1994).

67. Barbara A. Biesecker, "Remembering World War II," *Quarterly Journal of Speech* 88, no. 4 (2002): 406.

68. Wanzer, "Delinking Rhetoric," 650.

Chapter 10

1. Seoyeon Hong, Edson Tandoc, Jr., Eunjin Anna Kim, Bokyung Kim, and Kevin Wise, "The Real You? The Role of Visual Cues and Comment Congruence in Perceptions of Social Attractiveness from Facebook Profiles," *Cyberpsychology, Behavior, and Social Networking* 15, no. 7 (2012): 339–44.

2. I first saw the phrase "digital intimacy" in a title to a *New York Times* article, which went on to use the alternate phrase "ambient intimacy" to describe the phatic, personal,

play-by-play style of communication ushered in by technologies like Facebook and Twitter. See Clive Thompson, "Brave New World of Digital Intimacy," *New York Times*, September 5, 2008, http://www.nytimes.com/2008/09/07/magazine/07awareness-t.html?pagewanted=all.

3. Toke Haunstrup Christensen, "'Connected Presence' in Distributed Family Life," *New Media and Society* 11, no. 3 (2009): 433–51.

4. Yet, even with all this emphasis on context, it is important that "texts" remain the primary object for rhetorical critics whose chief investment is in the constitutive role of language and discourse. For rhetorical critics the text anchors the critique.

5. Stefana Broadbent, "The Democratization of Intimacy," *Observing the Evolution of Technology Usage Blog*, March 23, 2012, accessed December 9, 2012, http://stefanabroadbent.com /2012/03/23/the-democratisation-of-intimacy/.

6. David Russell Brake, "Who Do They Think They're Talking To? Framings of the Audience by Social Media Users," *International Journal of Communication* 6, no. 1 (2012): 1058, 1069.

7. Paying close attention to textual indicators of audience should be a familiar exercise to rhetorical critics who read the second- and third-persona essays of the 1970s and '80s: Edwin Black, "The Second Persona," *Quarterly Journal of Speech* 56, no. 2 (1970): 109–19; Phillip Wander, "The Third Persona: An Ideological Turn in Rhetorical Theory," *Central States Speech Journal* 35, no. 4 (1984): 197–216.

8. Mirca Madianou and Daniel Miller, "Polymedia: Towards a New Theory of Digital Media in Interpersonal Communication," *International Journal of Cultural Studies* 16, no. 2 (2013): 169–87.

9. Gerard Hauser, "Attending the Vernacular: A Plea for Ethnographical Rhetoric," in *The Rhetorical Emergence of Culture*, ed. Christian Meyer and Felix Girke (New York: Berghahn Books, 2011), 163.

10. E. Gabriella Coleman, "Ethnographic Approaches to Digital Media," *Annual Review of Anthropology* 39 (2010): 487–505.

11. Robert Glenn Howard, *Digital Jesus: The Making of a New Christian Fundamentalist Community on the Internet* (New York: New York University Press, 2011).

12. Daniel C. Brouwer and Aaron Hess, "Making Sense of 'God Hates Fags' and 'Thank God for 9/11': A Thematic Analysis of Milbloggers' Responses to Reverend Fred Phelps and the Westboro Baptist Church," *Western Journal of Communication* 71, no. 1 (2007): 69–90; Aaron Hess, "Resistance up in Smoke: Analyzing the Limitations of Deliberation on YouTube," *Critical Studies in Media Communication* 26, no. 5 (2009): 411–34; Lisa Silvestri, "Surprise Homecomings and Vicarious Sacrifices," *Media, War, and Conflict* 6, no. 2 (2013): 101–15.

13. Alice E. Marwick and danah boyd, "I Tweet Honestly, I Tweet Passionately: Twitter Users, Context Collapse, and the Imagined Audience," *New Media and Society* 13, no. 1 (2011): 114–33.

14. Lisa Silvestri, *Friended at the Front: Social Media in the American War Zone* (Lawrence: University Press of Kansas, 2015).

15. Lisa Silvestri, "A Rhetorical Forecast," *Review of Communication* 13, no. 2 (2013): 131.

16. Christine Hine, "How Can Qualitative Internet Researchers Define the Boundaries of Their Projects?" in *Internet Inquiry: Conversations about Method*, ed. Annette N. Markham and Nancy K. Baym (Los Angeles: Sage, 2009), 12. See also Howard Becker, *Tricks of the Trade: How to Think about Your Research While You're Doing It* (Chicago: University of Chicago Press, 1998).

17. Clifford Geertz, "Deep Play: Notes on the Balinese Cock Fight," in *Rethinking Popular Culture: Contemporary Perspectives in Cultural Studies*, ed. Chandra Mukerji and Michael Schudson (Berkeley: University of California Press, 1991), 239.

18. Lawrence Grossberg, *Cultural Studies in the Future Tense* (Durham, NC: Duke University Press, 2010), 13.

19. I use *doxa* as described in Pierre Bourdieu, *Outline of a Theory of Practice* (Cambridge, UK: Cambridge University Press, 1977), 159–77; also as it appears in John M. Sloop, "Disciplining the Transgendered: Brandon Teena, Public Representation, and Normativity," *Western Journal of Communication* 64, no. 2 (2000): 165–89.

20. For instance, Hugo Liu explored "taste statements," or the way taste is performed through friendship networks and Facebook profiles in "Social Network Profiles as Taste Performances," *Journal of Computer-Mediated Communication* 13, no. 1 (2007): 252–75.

21. IRB ID #201109764.

22.	Richard Bauman and Charles Briggs stress the performative nature of culture in "Poetics and Performance as Critical Perspectives on Language and Social Life," *Annual Review of Anthropology* 19, no. 1 (1990): 59–88.

23.	Deven Friedman, ed., *This Is Our War: Servicemen's Photographs of Life in Iraq* (New York: Artisan, 2006); Liam Kennedy, "Soldier Photography: Visualizing the War in Iraq," *Review of International Studies* 35, no. 4 (2009): 817–33; Janina Struk, *Private Pictures: Soldiers' Inside View of War* (London: I.B.Tauris, 2011).

24.	The portable satellite units developed the nickname "Cheetahs," for their mobility and speed. See Elaine Wilson, "'Cheetahs' Offer Swift Connection Home for Deployed Troops," *U.S. Department of Defense*, February 4, 2011, http://archive.defense.gov/news/newsarticle.aspx ?id=62707.

25.	Harvard student Mark Zuckerberg launched Facebook February 4, 2004, with restricted access. Only university-affiliated individuals with .edu e-mail addresses could become members. Facebook opened to the general public in 2005.

26.	Quotations appearing without attribution are from the author's interview research. The University of Iowa's Institutional Review Board (IRB) approved the use of on-base interviews for the purposes of this research. IRB ID #201101755.

27.	AKO provides web-based services through a single, more secure portal.

28.	James Katz and Mark Aakhus, eds., *Perpetual Contact: Mobile Communication, Private Talk, Public Performance* (New York: Cambridge University Press, 2002).

29.	Naomi Baron, *Always On: Language in an Online and Mobile World* (New York: Oxford University Press, 2008); Naomi Baron and Rich Ling, "Emerging Patterns of American Mobile Phone Use: Electronically Mediated Communication in Transition," in *Mobile Media, 2007: Proceedings of an International Conference on Social and Cultural Aspects of Mobile Phones, Media and Wireless Technologies, June 2–4,* ed. G. Goggin and L. Hjorth (Sydney: University of Sydney, 2007), 1–25; Jeffrey A. Hall and Nancy K. Baym, "Calling and Texting (Too Much): Mobile Maintenance Expectations, (Over)dependence, Entrapment, and Friendship Satisfaction," *New Media and Society* 14, no. 2 (2011): 316–31.

30.	Hall and Baym, "Calling and Texting," 317.

31.	"The Marine Corps, A Young and Vigorous Force, Demographics Update," June 2012, http://www.ala-national.org/asset.aspx?AssetId=12654.

32.	Facebook introduced its real-time chat feature in 2008. See Josh Wiseman, "Facebook Chat: Now We're Talking," *The Facebook Blog,* April 6, 2008, https://www.facebook.com/notes /facebook/facebook-chat-now-were-talking/12811122130/.

33.	Lisa Silvestri, "Shiny Happy People Holding Guns: 21st Century Images of War," *Visual Communication Quarterly* 20, no. 2 (2014): 106–18.

34.	The wire is the defensive perimeter surrounding the forward operating base. A reference to going outside the wire means you are exposed and open to direct contact with the enemy.

35.	Sherry Turkle, "Always-on/Always-on-you: The Tethered Self," in *Handbook of Mobile Communication Studies*, ed. James E. Katz (Cambridge, MA: MIT Press, 2008), 121–37; Sherry Turkle, "The Tethered Self: Technology Reinvents Intimacy and Solitude," *Continuing Higher Education Review* 75, no. 1 (2011): 28–31; Christian Licoppe, "Connected Presence: The Emergence of a New Repertoire for Managing Social Relationships in a Changing Communication Technoscape," *Society and Space* 22, no. 1 (2004): 135–56.

36.	James E. Katz and Mark A. Aakhus, "Introduction: Framing the Issues," 1–13, and Rich Ling and B. Ytrri, "Hyper-coordination via Mobile Phones in Norway," 139–69, both in *Perpetual Contact: Mobile Communication, Private Talk, Public Performance*, ed. James Katz and Mark Aakhus (New York: Cambridge University Press, 2002), 139–69.

37.	The social dimension of information-sharing has become a major concern for public affairs officers, who worry that sensitive information such as death or injury can pass to families and friends via Facebook before the military has the opportunity to inform them according to procedure.

38.	Dave Axe, "How to Prevent Drone Pilot PTSD: Blame the 'Bot," *Wired*, June 7, 2012, http://www.wired.com/2012/06/drone-pilot-ptsd/; Elisabeth Bumiller, "A Day Job Waiting for a Kill Shot a World Away," *New York Times*, July 29, 2012, http://www.nytimes.com/2012/07/30 /us/drone-pilots-waiting-for-a-kill-shot-7000-miles-away.html?pagewanted=all&_r=1&.

39. I want to emphasize that we should talk "with" rather than "for." Building on Gayatri Chakravorty Spivak's seminal essay, "Can the Subaltern Speak?" Linda Alcoff argues that researchers should "strive to create wherever possible the conditions for dialogue and the practice of *speaking with and to* rather than speaking for others." Anyone who speaks for others "should only do so out of a concrete analysis of the particular power relations and discursive effects involved." See Alcoff, "The Problem of Speaking for Others," *Cultural Critique* 20, no. 1 (1992): 23, 24; emphasis added.

Afterword

1. In this essay I use "critical ethnographic practices" as a broad umbrella to signify qualitative fieldwork as a praxis involving theory and method at multiple stages of research, including research practices, data collection, interviews, interpretation, and writing. In the introduction to this book, the editors list a wider cluster of terms authors use to name their own approaches; therefore I feel no need to reiterate them here. For an accessible and compelling introduction to "critical ethnography" see D. Soyini Madison, *Critical Ethnography: Method, Ethics, and Performance* (Thousand Oaks, CA: Sage, 2011).

2. There are notable exceptions, of course. One exemplar that reprints essays drawing on critical ethnographic practices throughout the book's organization is Brian Ott and Greg Dickinson, eds., *The Routledge Reader in Rhetorical Criticism* (London: Routledge, 2012).

3. Raka Shome, "Postcolonial Interventions in the Rhetorical Canon: An 'Other' View," *Communication Theory* 6, no. 1 (1996): 41; Raka Shome, "Space Matters: The Power and Practice of Space," *Communication Theory* 13, no. 1 (2003): 39–56.

4. Lisa A. Flores, "Creating Discursive Space through a Rhetoric of Difference: Chicana Feminists Craft a Homeland," *Quarterly Journal of Speech* 82, no. 2 (1996): 142–56.

5. Kirt Wilson, *Reconstruction's Desegregation Debate: The Politics of Equality and the Rhetoric of Place, 1870–1875* (East Lansing: Michigan State University Press, 2002), esp. pp. 8, 12.

6. Phaedra C. Pezzullo, *Toxic Tourism: Rhetorics of Travel, Pollution, and Environmental Justice* (Tuscaloosa: University of Alabama Press, 2007).

7. This is a point reiterated in chapter 1 of this volume by Samantha Senda-Cook, Michael Middleton, and Danielle Endres, as well as elsewhere beyond this book. Two of the authors of chapter 1 also published a related piece on art advocacy and rhetorics of place: Danielle Endres, Samantha Senda-Cook, and Brian Cozen, "Not Just a Place to Park Your Car: Park(ing) as a Spatial Argument," *Argumentation and Advocacy* 50, no. 3 (2014): 121–40. As I note in the conclusion of *Toxic Tourism*, space is inextricably intertwined with power and time, particularly given that, as Doreen Massey writes, time-space "inherently implies the existence of the lived world of a simultaneous multiplicity of spaces: cross-cutting, intersecting, aligning one another, or existing in relations of paradox or antagonism." See *Space, Place, and Gender* (Minneapolis: University of Minnesota Press, 1994), 3. See also Yi-Fu Tuan, *Space and Place: The Perspective of Experience*, 5th ed. (Minneapolis: University of Minnesota Press, 2001).

8. As I wrote previously, "As a critical tool, participant observation compels critics to travel to public spaces to feel, to observe, and to participate in cultural performances firsthand. It also helps critics to consider the rhetorical force of counterpublics and of cultural performances, and to consider that the ways in which we interact with and engage specific publics can influence our judgments. It reminds us that publics are not phenomena that exist 'out there,' involving other people and affecting bodies other than our own." Phaedra C. Pezzullo, "Resisting 'National Breast Cancer Awareness Month': The Rhetoric of Counterpublics and Their Cultural Performances," *Quarterly Journal of Speech* 89, no. 4 (2003): 361.

9. Another exemplar of this type of fieldwork is based on interviews with Mexicans about the word "sustainability" and the ways this language does and does not translate in meaningful ways: M. Nils Peterson, Markus J. Peterson, and Tarla Rai Peterson, "Moving toward Sustainability: Integrating Social Practice and Material Process," in *Environmental Justice and Environmentalism: The Social Justice Challenge to the Environmental Movement*, ed. Ronald Sandler and Phaedra C. Pezzullo (Cambridge, MA: MIT Press, 2007), 189–222.

10. Important to those who worry that all of this work is merely ideological, the authors do not romanticize this community but point out, "While temporarily challenging norms of

transportation and food systems in place, Elevate [the name of the event in question] also served to reinforce economic privilege and the majority white participants."

11.   Of course there are textual archives that do exist of subaltern people and elements. My use of this term "undocumented" aims to be suggestive of the broader logic of compulsory documentation, which assumes that possessing a document or "being documented" is the only valid way to establish existence or significance. See, for example, contemporary debates over voter ID laws, requirements for noncitizens in the United States to possess legal documentation at all times, or the ways transgender people are policed (and resist) documentation in everyday life. As these debates illustrate, a lack of documents is an indicator of a fraught relationship with the state or private institutions. Rhetoricians should be reflexive about not reinforcing such power relations requiring state or corporate documentation as the sole grounds to establish standing or value.

12.   For more on the logics of transparency, see Rachel C. Hall, *The Transparent Traveler: The Performance and Culture of Airport Security* (Durham, NC: Duke University Press, 2015).

13.   Conquergood's arguments about why ethnographic practices are worthwhile inside and outside of rhetorical studies have been formative to my own work, as well as that of many of my teachers and students. My citation of him is minimized here so that I might keep my remarks closer to the content of essays in this volume. The most noteworthy essays include Dwight Conquergood, "Ethnography, Rhetoric, and Performance," *Quarterly Journal of Speech* 78, no. 1 (1992): 80–97; "Rethinking Ethnography: Towards a Critical Cultural Politics," *Communication Monographs* 58, no. 2 (1991): 179–94; and, as cited here, "Performance Studies: Interventions and Radical Research," *TDR: The Drama Review*, 46, no. 2 (2002): 150. Notably, as my conversations with Michael and Ruth Bowman, D. Soyini Madison, Della Pollock, Mary Strine, and others have confirmed, Conquergood's own academic training speaks to the intertwined relationship between rhetoric and performance—one worthy of an essay unto itself. Suffice it to say here that he began his undergraduate work at Indiana State University in oral interpretation, including reading Kenneth Burke; his master's work at the University of Utah focused on a rhetorical analysis of William Faulkner's *Light in August*; and then his dissertation at Northwestern continued this blurring between rhetoric and performance by focusing on Old English / Anglo-Saxon literature. He also enrolled in seminars with not only his director, Wallace Bacon, but also rhetorical scholars.

14.   For a more elaborated analysis of the relationship between performance studies and rhetorical studies, including critical ethnographic practices, as well as reprints of exemplary scholarship that bridges these fields, see Stephen Olbrys Gencarella and Phaedra C. Pezzullo, eds., *Readings on Rhetoric and Performance* (State College, PA: Strata Publishing, 2010).

15.   Phaedra C. Pezzullo, "Performing Critical Interruptions: Rhetorical Invention and Narratives of the Environmental Justice Movement," *Western Journal of Communication* 64, no. 1 (2001): 1–25.

16.   Phaedra C. Pezzullo, "Touring 'Cancer Alley,' Louisiana: Performances of Community and Memory for Environmental Justice," *Text and Performance Quarterly* 23, no. 3 (2003): 226–52. See also the appendix in Pezzullo, *Toxic Tourism*.

17.   Although not exhaustive, seminal pieces cited in this volume provide evidence of the consistent call for and/or use of critical ethnographic practices and attitudes in rhetorical criticism and communication studies more broadly over at least the past three decades, including: Thomas Benson, "Another Shooting in Cowtown," *Quarterly Journal of Speech* 67, no. 4 (1981): 387; Michael Osborn, "'I've Been to the Mountaintop': The Critic as Participant," in *Texts in Context: Critical Dialogues on Significant Episodes in American Political Rhetoric*, ed. Michael C. Leff and Fred J. Kauffeld (Davis, CA: Hermagoras Press, 1989), 149; Raymie McKerrow, "Critical Rhetoric: Theory and Praxis," *Communication Monographs* 56, no. 2 (1989): 91–111; Kent Ono and John Sloop, "The Critique of Vernacular Discourse," *Communication Monographs* 62, no. 1 (1995): 19–46; Frederick C. Corey and Thomas K. Nakayama, "Sextext," *Text and Performance Quarterly* 17, no. 1 (1997): 56–68; Gerard A. Hauser, *Vernacular Voices: The Rhetoric of Publics and Public Spheres* (Columbia: University of South Carolina Press, 1999); Carole Blair, "Contemporary U.S. Memorial Sites as Exemplars of Rhetoric's Materiality," in *Rhetorical Bodies*, ed. Jack Selzer and Sharon Crowley (Madison: University of Wisconsin Press, 1999), 16–57; Pezzullo, "Resisting 'National Breast Cancer Awareness Month,'" 345–65; Daniel C. Brouwer and Aaron Hess, "Making Sense of 'God Hates Fags' and 'Thank God for 9/11': A Thematic Analysis of

Milbloggers' Responses to Reverend Fred Phelps and the Westboro Baptist Church," *Western Journal of Communication* 71, no. 1 (2007): 69–90; Jeffrey A. Bennett, *Banning Queer Blood: Rhetorics of Citizenship, Contagion, and Resistance* (Tuscaloosa: University of Alabama Press, 2009); Charles E. Morris III, "(Self-)Portrait of Prof. R.C.: A Retrospective," *Western Journal of Communication* 74, no. 1 (2010): 12; Greg Dickinson, Carol Blair, and Brian L. Ott, eds., *Places of Public Memory: The Rhetoric of Museums and Memorials* (Tuscaloosa: University of Alabama Press, 2010); Isaac West, "PISSAR's Critically Queer and Disabled Politics," *Communication and Critical/Cultural Studies* 7, no. 2 (2010): 156–75; Gerard A. Hauser, "Attending the Vernacular: A Plea for an Ethnographic Rhetoric," in *Readings on Rhetoric and Performance*, ed. Christian Meyer and Felix Girke (New York: Berghahn Books, 2011), 157–72; Karma R. Chávez, "Counter-Public Enclaves and Understanding the Function of Rhetoric in Social Movement Coalition-Building," *Communication Quarterly* 59, no. 1 (2011): 1–18; Sara L. McKinnon, "Approach to the Audience," in *Standing in the Intersection: Feminist Voices, Feminist Practices in Communication Studies*, ed. Karma R. Chávez and Cindy L. Griffin (Albany: State University of New York Press, 2012), 189–210; Robert Asen, *Democracy, Deliberation, and Education* (University Park: Penn State University Press, 2015).

18. This question is a variation of Butler's: "At what cost do I establish the familiar as the criterion by which a human life is grievable?" See *Precarious Life: The Powers of Mourning and Violence* (New York: Verso, 2004), 38. For another valuable piece worth reading on the performative way that certain comments and practices in academia diminish the voices and experiences of women and people of color, in particular, through norms of conduct and behavioral bonds, see Sara Ahmed, "White Men," *Feminist Killjoys*, November 4, 2014, http://feministkilljoys.com /2014/11/04/white-men/.

19. For compelling exemplars with which to discuss this question, see Daniel C. Brouwer, "Counterpublicity and Corporeality in HIV/AIDS Zines," *Critical Studies in Media Communication* 22, no. 5 (2005): 351–71; Gencarella and Pezzullo, *Readings*; Morris, "Self-Portrait"; Jules Odendahl, "Embodied Views to the Visual through Interdisciplinary and Reflexive Methodologies," *Text and Performance Quarterly* 23, no. 1 (2003): 87–104.

INDEX

and performance, 8, 102, 156. *See also*
    performance, embodied
and persuasion, 136–37
and place, 10, 24, 32, 37–38
and practice, 26, 32, 65, 89
and presence, 10, 146–47, 161
and proxemics, 184
racialized, 156
and rhetoric, 3, 43, 71–73, 179
and situation, 181
and writing, 81
Emerging Terrain, 22–23, 26–29
emotion, 73–85, 145, 174–75. *See also* affect
    and feelings
emotion words, 78–79, 81
energy plants, 117–32
English monolingualism, 111–13, 187
environment, the, 58–59, 103–4, 106–7
environmental justice, 108, 118–32
ephemerality, 30, 182
epistemology
    indigenous 61–62, 70, 153
    Native American, 152–62
    Oceanic, 57–59, 66–68
    participatory, 86–100
Erasmus, 45
erosion, 140
ethics, 17–20, 51–53, 93–94, 103, 106, 186
ethnicity, 102, 134, 146
ethnocentrism, 184
ethnography
    auto, 74, 77, 80, 182
    critical, 18, 134, 137, 146–47, 178–88,
        223 n. 1
    critical rhetorical, 15–16, 52, 86, 136,
        224 n. 17
    performance, 44, 47
    postmodern, 137
    reflective, 146
    rhetorical, 86, 92, 114, 120
European Union, 135, 141
evaluation, 38
everyday life, 26, 174
evidence, 29, 34–35, 178
experience, 10, 29–30, 58, 65, 167
    lived, 26, 39, 63, 69–70, 76
experiential seascapes, 67–69
expertise, 95–96

Facebook, 163–76, 222 n. 25
failure, 98–99
fascism, 142
feedback, 115–16
feeling rhetorical criticism, 73, 76–82, 85
feelings, 34–35, 72–85, 100, 104–5
feminine, the, 75

feminist studies, 59, 74–75
fetal development, 84
fetal personhood, 82–84
fetus, 82–84
"the field"
    boundaries of, 179
    qualitative approach to, 4–7, 176
    reimagining, 23–39, 105, 151
    and rhetoric, 180
    scholarship on, 178
field notes, 52, 72, 79, 82–84, 103, 167
field-text, 104, 114
focus groups, 4
food culture, 27–28, 32–33
foreign locals, 144–45
freewriting, 81
futurity, 48

Geertz, Clifford, 2
gender, 179
generational norms, 172
genocide, 108–10
global, the 65, 150, 165, 171, 180
"going Native," 156
grain elevators, 29–39
grassroots organizing, 112–13, 117–18
greenhouse gas emissions, 117–32, 215 n. 44
Greenpeace, 122
grounded-theory, 157
Guåhan, 56–71
Guam. *See* Guåhan

Hawai'i, 65
health care, 110–11
Heritage Hikes, 65
hiking, 65–66
Hohokam, the, 152–53
hologram, 21, 150–62
holographic rhetoric, 150–62
home, 171–72
human instrument, 16. *See also* critic as
        instrument
human subjects review boards, 18
hybridity, 59

identity
    and activism, 118–20
    colonial, 59–63, 149
    of critic, 86–87
    diasporic, 66–68
    diversity of, 184
    liminal, 143. *See also* liminality
    online, 164–76
    plurality, 59
    transformation, 129–30
imaginative geographies, 157, 160–62